American Churches and the First World War

 McMaster Divinity College Press
McMaster General Series 7

American Churches and the First World War

edited by
GORDON L. HEATH

☙PICKWICK *Publications* · Eugene, Oregon

AMERICAN CHURCHES AND THE FIRST WORLD WAR

McMaster Divinity College General Series 7

Copyright © 2016 Gordon L. Heath. All rights reserved. Except for brief quotations in critical publications or reviews, no part of this book may be reproduced in any manner without prior written permission from the publisher. Write: Permissions, Wipf and Stock Publishers, 199 W. 8th Ave., Suite 3, Eugene, OR 97401.

Pickwick Publications
An Imprint of Wipf and Stock Publishers
199 W. 8th Ave., Suite 3
Eugene, OR 97401

McMaster Divinity College Press
1280 Main Street West
Hamilton, ON, Canada L8S 4K1

www.wipfandstock.com

PAPERBACK ISBN: 978-1-5326-0114-9
HARDCOVER ISBN: 978-1-5326-0116-3
EBOOK ISBN: 978-1-5326-0115-6

Cataloguing-in-Publication data:

Names: Heath, Gordon L.

Title: American churches and the first world war / Gordon L. Heath.

Description: Eugene, OR: Pickwick Publications, 2016 | McMaster Divinity College General Series 7 | Includes bibliographical references and index.

Identifiers: ISBN 978-1-5326-0114-9 (paperback) | ISBN 978-1-5326-0116-3 (hardcover) | ISBN 978-1-5326-0115-6 (ebook)

Subjects: LSCH: World War, 1914–1918—Religious aspects—Christianity. | World War, 1914–1918—Roman Catholics. | World War, 1914–1918—American Lutherans. | World War, 1914–1918—Pentecostals. | World War, 1914–1918—Mennonites. | World War, 1914–1918—Quakers. | World War, 1914–1918—Mormons. | World War, 1914–1918—Jehovah's Witnesses. | Armenian massacres, 1915–1923—Foreign public opinion, American.

Classification: CALL NUMBER 2016 (print) | CALL NUMBER (ebook)

Manufactured in the U.S.A.   10/17/16

Chapter 5, "As Citizens of Heaven: Peace, War, and Patriotism among Pentecostals in the United States during the First World War" by Zachary Michael Tackett is reprinted and adapted from "As Citizens of Heaven: Peace, War, and Patriotism among Pentecostals in the United States During World War I," *Canadian Journal of Pentecostal-Charismatic Christianity* 4, no. 1 (2013) 27–43. Used by permission.

Contents

List of Contributors | vii

1. American Churches and the First World War: An Introduction
—*Gordon L. Heath* | 1

2. Together for the Gospel of Americanism: Evangelicals and the First World War—*Richard M. Gamble* | 15

3. The First World War and Catholics in the United States
—*Patrick Carey* | 32

4. American Lutherans and the First World War
—*Mark Granquist* | 53

5. As Citizens of Heaven: Peace, War, and Patriotism among Pentecostals in the United States during the First World War
—*Zachary Michael Tackett* | 71

6. Mennonites and the Great War
—*Perry Bush* | 87

7. Quakers and World War One: Negotiating Individual Conscience and the Peace Testimony—*Robynne Rogers Healey* | 107

8. "We do not love war, but . . .": Mormons, the Great War, and the Crucible of Nationalism—*J. David Pulsipher* | 129

Contents

9 The Bible Students / Jehovah's Witnesses in the United States during the First World War—*M. James Penton* | 149

10 Military Chaplains in the First World War—*Timothy J. Demy* | 167

11 "The accursed partnership of Turk and Teuton": American Churches and the Armenian Genocide—*Gordon L. Heath* | 181

Index of Subjects | 205

Index of Persons | 211

Contributors

EDITOR AND CONTRIBUTOR

Gordon L. Heath (PhD, St. Michael's College) is Associate Professor of Christian History as well as Centenary Chair in World Christianity at McMaster Divinity College, Hamilton, Ontario, Canada. He also serves as Director of the Canadian Baptist Archives. His research interests rest primarily in the area of Christians and war, or the intersection of church and state. His publications include *A War with a Silver Lining: Canadian Protestant Churches and the South African War, 1899–1902* (McGill-Queen's University Press, 2009) and *Doing Church History: A User-Friendly Introduction to Researching the History of Christianity* (Clements, 2008). He has also edited a number of volumes, one of which is a companion to this present work: *Canadian Churches and the First World War* (Pickwick, 2014).

CONTRIBUTORS

Perry Bush (PhD, Carnegie Mellon University) is Professor of History at Bluffton University, Bluffton, Ohio, where he has been teaching since 1994. He has written widely on peace and religious history in twentieth-century America in both popular and scholarly journals, and is the author of four books, including *Two Kingdoms, Two Loyalties: Mennonite Pacifism in Modern America* (Johns Hopkins University Press, 1998), *Rust Belt Resistance: How a Small Community Took on Big Oil and Won* (Kent State University Press, 2012) and, more recently, *Peace, Progress and the Professor: The Mennonite History of C. Henry Smith* (Herald, 2015). In 2012 he taught US history as a Fulbright Scholar in Ukraine.

Contributors

Patrick W. Carey (PhD, Fordham University) is Emeritus Professor of Historical Theology at Marquette University. He is a former chair of Marquette's Theology Department and former president of the American Catholic Historical Society. He specializes in the history of American Protestant and Catholic life and thought, and has published in a number of historical and theological journals. He has also written or edited twenty books, including his latest, *Avery Cardinal Dulles, SJ: A Model Theologian* (2010). He is currently working on a cultural and theological history of the confessional in the United States.

Timothy J. Demy (PhD, Salve Regina University; ThD, Dallas Theological Seminary) is professor of military ethics US Naval War College, Newport, Rhode Island. He is the author and editor of numerous books on ethics, theology, and current issues, and also contributor to many journals and encyclopedias. He is co-author of *War, Peace, and Christianity: Questions and Answers from a Just-War Perspective* and co-editor of the three-volume *War and Religion: An Encyclopedia of Faith and Conflict*. He serves as the American managing editor of the international *Journal of Military Ethics*.

Richard M. Gamble (PhD, University of South Carolina) is Professor of History and holds the Anna Margaret Ross Alexander Chair in History and Politics at Hillsdale College, Hillsdale, Michigan. His publications include *The War for Righteousness: Progressive Christianity, the Great War, and the Rise of the Messianic Nation* (ISI Books, 2003), the chapter on World War I for the *Cambridge History of Religions in America* (Cambridge UP, 2012), *In Search of the City on a Hill: The Making and Unmaking of an American Myth* (Continuum, 2012), and a history of the "Battle Hymn of the Republic" forthcoming from Cornell University Press. He is currently at work on the first intellectual and religious biography of Julia Ward Howe. His courses, essays, and reviews focus on the history of American civil religion and the long argument over American identity.

Mark Granquist (PhD, University of Chicago Divinity School) is Associate Professor of the History of Christianity at Luther Seminary, St. Paul, Minnesota, with a specialty in the history of Lutherans in North America. He serves as the editor of the *Journal of the Lutheran Historical Conference* and also of the journal *Word & World,* and is on the board of the journal *Lutheran Quarterly*. He has written widely on Lutherans in North America, especially his *Lutherans in America: A New History* (Fortress, 2015), and is the managing editor of the *Dictionary of Luther and the Lutheran Traditions* (Baker, 2016).

Robynne Rogers Healey (PhD, University of Alberta) is Professor of History as well as co-director of the Gender Studies Institute and the Centre for Equity and Global Engagement at Trinity Western University, Langley, British Columbia. Her publications include *From Quaker to Upper Canadian: Faith and Community among Yonge Street Friends, 1801–1850* (McGill-Queen's University Press, 2006) and a number of articles on Quakers and Quakerism, including a recent chapter on Canadian Quakers and Mennonites and the Great War in Gordon Heath's edited collection *Canadian Churches and the First World War*. Her research interests include gender and Quakerism, the transatlantic world in the eighteenth and nineteenth centuries, the twentieth-century peace testimony, and Canadian Quakerism.

M. James Penton (PhD, University of Iowa) is Professor Emeritus of the University of Lethbridge. His interests relate largely to North American and Latin American sectarian religions and questions involving church-state relations. His major publications deal with the history of Jehovah's Witnesses. They are: *Jehovah's Witnesses in Canada: Champions of Freedom of Speech and Worship* (Macmillan, 1976); *Apocalypse Delayed: The Story of Jehovah's Witnesses* (University of Toronto Press, 1985, 1997, 2015); *Jehovah's Witnesses and the Third Reich: Sectarian Politics under Persecution* (University of Toronto Press, 2004). He is presently working on a history of violations of religious freedom in Canada since Confederation.

J. David Pulsipher (PhD, University of Minnesota) is a Professor of History at Brigham Young University–Idaho. In 2007–8 he was a visiting professor and Fulbright scholar at Jamia Millia Islamia in New Delhi, India. His research focuses on the intersections of Mormon history/theology with just war, peace, and nonviolence traditions. Recent publications include "Buried Swords: Excavating the Shifting Interpretive Ground of a Book of Mormon Narrative" (2015) and "Prepared to Abide the Penalty: Latter-day Saints and Civil Disobedience" (2013), and with Patrick Q. Mason and Richard L. Bushman he co-edited *War and Peace in Our Time: Mormon Perspectives* (2012).

Contributors

Zachary Michael Tackett (PhD, Southern Baptist Theological Seminary) is Associate Professor of Historical Theology as well as chair of undergraduate studies in the College of Christian Ministries and Religion at Southeastern University in Lakeland, Florida. His also serves as Secretary/Treasurer of the Society for Pentecostal Studies. His research interests primarily focus on American Pentecostalism.

1

American Churches and the First World War

An Introduction

GORDON L. HEATH

UNLIKE CITIZENS IN EUROPE who were stunned by the sudden onset of war in the summer of 1914, Americans experienced an altogether different situation. Their nation seemed to be drifting slowly but inexorably towards participating in what had become a vortex of unparalleled death and destruction. President Woodrow Wilson had promptly declared US neutrality at the outbreak of war, a political impartiality due in no small measure to the fact that American public opinion was initially divided over the war, often on ethnic lines. However, German activities such as alleged battlefield atrocities, meddling in the Mexican–American relationship, and especially the resumption of unrestricted submarine warfare, eventually led to the US declaration of war on 6 April 1917 against the German Empire. In doing so it joined with the Entente Powers of Britain, France, Italy, Russia, and smaller nations against Germany. America declared war against Austria-Hungary later that same year, but not against other Central Powers Turkey and Bulgaria. The war was global, with battles in Europe, Africa, and Asia, as well as in the Atlantic, Pacific, and Indian Oceans, however the theatre of operations of the American Expeditionary Force (AEF) led by General John J. Pershing was in France and the Western Front.

The AEF arrival in France was "absolutely decisive," for it provided vital reinforcements to bolster the exhausted and depleted British and French forces.[1] By 1918, the AEF was strong enough to participate in the summer Aisne Offensive, as well as in fall offensives such as Saint-Mihiel and Meuse-Argonne. The Meuse-Argonne Offensive was one of the bloodiest battles in US history, with over 120,000 casualties. Total American casualties for the war were approximately 235,000 injured and 115,000 killed.

After an exhaustive struggle, the Central Powers were defeated in late 1918. The total cost of human life for combatants among all nations was astonishing: over eight million dead and twenty-one million wounded, out of the sixty-five million mobilized.[2] The rate of deaths for the entire war was an average of 6,000 soldiers a day.[3] The death toll did not end there, however. The postwar outbreak and spread of the Spanish Influenza (fifty to one hundred million deaths) can be blamed on the war. The "war to end all wars" also directly contributed to the Second World War (sixty to eighty million deaths). Those horrors that followed in the wake of the Great War have led historians to portray the First World War as the "opening of an age of catastrophe"[4] and the beginning of the "bloodiest century in modern history."[5]

From the vantage point of the twenty-first century, American involvement in the Great War can be understood as just another step towards American military engagement (or entanglement in the eyes of its detractors) beyond its borders, reinforcing and advancing pre-existing trajectories such as those seen in the Spanish–American War (1898) and Philippine-American War (1899–1902).[6] The postwar isolationism that resulted in America refraining from joining the League of Nations was a return to a form of traditional American isolationism, but it was merely a temporary retreat from a *telos* towards American global engagement and the *Pax Americana*. Those tensions and trajectories remain to this day and continue to shape American domestic debates over projecting US power abroad.

1. Mosier, *Myth of the Great War*.
2. Bourne, "Total War I." Figures of casualties vary considerably.
3. Clodfelter, *Warfare and Armed Conflicts*, 479.
4. Stevenson, *1914–1918*, 503.
5. Ferguson, *War of the World*, xxxiv.
6. Miller, *Benevolent Assimilation*; May, *Imperial Democracy*; E. Thomas, *War Lovers*; Brands, *Reckless Decade*; Musicant, *Empire by Default*.

But what of religion and the war? Popular early-twentieth-century notions of America being a Christian nation were bolstered by census data. America was a nation of 103 million in 1916, and just over half of the population were adherents of a church.[7] Protestantism still dominated the religious landscape of early twentieth-century America. However, recent influxes of Catholic immigrants meant that roughly 38 percent of church members were Catholics.[8] Religion played a critical role in the wartime discourse of all combatants.[9] Not only did it provide spiritual comfort and solace for soldiers in trenches and families on the home-front, it constructed a meta-narrative of good versus evil that motivated and justified fighting an ungodly (even demonic) enemy. As for American soldiers, they were deeply religious and religion "informed their sense of duty, gave them language, narratives, ideas, and symbols to frame the conflict and to understand their part in it."[10] For Christians opposed to the war, the teaching and example of Jesus provided a compelling motivation to abstain from violence and claim conscientious objector status.

The US government could not automatically assume churches would baptize their decisions, and it needed to tread carefully in order to avoid stirring up religious opposition.[11] Just as in previous wars, such as the one against Spain only a few years earlier, religion had stimulated resistance to the war in the form of Christian pacifism, or condemnation of aspects of it such as the rise of jingoistic militarism.[12] Clergy expectations of righteousness had dictated that US foreign policy be exemplary, and for some the cause and means of the war against Spain and the Philippines did not pass muster.

---

7. Finke and Stark, *Churching of America*, 23.

8. McKeown, *War and Welfare*, 35.

9. Jenkins, *Great and Holy War*.

10. Ebel, *Faith in the Fight*, 193. For religion and the British soldier, see Snape, *God and the British Soldier*.

11. Since the earliest days of the founding of the Thirteen Colonies, religious leaders had much to say about foreign policy and their efforts had a powerful influence in the formation of popular sentiment as well as American foreign policy. See Preston, *Sword of the Spirit*.

12. For instance, see Welch, "Organized Religion"; Smylie, "Protestant Clergymen"; Hudson, "Protestant Clergy"; Quinn, "Mormon Church"; Nugent, "Mormons"; Herbst, "Methodism and Aggressive Christianity"; Reed, "American Foreign Policy"; MacKenzie, *The Robe and the Sword*; I. B. Thomas, "Baptist Anti-Imperialist Voice"; Heath, "Self Perception."

Likewise, during the First World War there were those opposed to the drift to war, who were distressed when the declaration of war was announced. Individual ministers found the courage to speak out against the war with Germany, but those who did usually found themselves pariahs among their colleagues and congregants if their denomination had formally supported the war. Those opposed to the war who declared conscientious objector status experienced violence in the streets, and were often required to do labor in harsh and often dehumanizing camps. Peace societies had tried their best to keep America out of the war, but when those efforts failed, a number relented under the pressure to support the war. However, some organizations such as the Fellowship of Reconciliation (FOR) continued to provide a voice and community for those on the margins who opposed the war.[13] The anti-war position of the historic peace churches such as the Quakers and Mennonites was shaped by centuries of commitment to Christian pacifism, and their response could have been anticipated by the government. Ethnic identities also contributed to denominations hesitating to support the war. The German identity of many Mennonites meant that they had further reason to be ambivalent about the war besides their commitment to living the Sermon on the Mount. A number of Irish Catholics were pleased to see England face a mortal foe, and German Lutherans were torn between loyalty to the Old Country and their identity as Americans. Further influencing antiwar attitudes was a commitment among some pastors to a form of socialism. In the case of Walter Rauschenbusch, the famous German-American Baptist theologian, a number of those factors coalesced: ethnic identity, socialist ideals, and a commitment to national righteousness all shaped his refusal to support the US in the war against Germany. For that he faced intense criticism; he was attacked on many fronts, even having people threaten to burn his cottage in Ontario (and he was warned to stay out of Canada).[14] As a result of such opposition, along with a concern for the outcome of the war and its effects on the social gospel movement, Rauschenbusch's life was filled with a "deep depression."[15] A few months before his death in 1918 he wrote: "I leave my love to those of my friends whose souls have never grown dark against me,

---

13. Dekar, *Dangerous People*.

14. Sharpe, *Walter Rauschenbusch*, 377.

15. Rauschenbusch, "Personal Correspondence," as quoted by Sharpe, *Walter Rauschenbusch*, 449.

I forgive the others and hate no man . . . Since 1914 the world is full of hate, and I cannot expect to be happy again in my lifetime."[16]

Despite examples of religiously motivated opposition to the war, the majority of clergy and denominations officially supported President Wilson's call to arms. Formal denominational resolutions, varieties of tracts and publications, and innumerable sermons trumpeted the righteousness of the cause. The discourse ranged from sober conviction to exuberant calls for a holy war against the demonic Hun. The flamboyant evangelist Billy Sunday's comment, "If you turn hell upside-down you will find 'Made In Germany,'" is an example of the fervent rhetoric of holy war proponents, as is his referring to the enemy as "pretzel-chewing, sauerkraut spawn of blood-thirsty Huns."[17] Passionate and fairly uniform Protestant, Catholic, and Jewish responses reveal a fusion of religious and national identity, a form of civil religion that would mature over the war years; the war was an important catalyst for the development of a "Tri-Faith America."[18] While the conflation of Christianity with national causes indicates how the dominant Protestant churches were ardently supportive of a form of Protestant Christendom, churches that historically had been on the margins such as Roman Catholics or German Lutherans hoped by their declarations of support to mitigate hostile nativism and demonstrate to critics that they too were patriotic Americans.[19] Church structures were established at the local, regional, and national level to support the war effort. Through such means funds were raised, congregants were recruited, and clergy transitioned to become chaplains. The Federal Council of the Churches of Christ in America provided a coordinated war effort for Protestants, and lobbying power when they had concerns. The National Catholic War Council performed a similar function for Roman Catholics.[20] The parachurch Protestant YMCA played a critical role in providing direct ministry to troops who were in

---

16. Rauschenbsuch, "Instructions in Case of My Death," as quoted by Sharpe, *Walter Rauschenbusch*, 448.

17. Rosen, *Preaching Eugenics*, 95.

18. The "fusion of Protestant-Catholic-Jew in American civil religion, now instantly familiar, was of course nothing new, but the Great War marked its period of maturation." Preston, *Sword of the Spirit*, 236. See also Mislin, "One Nation."

19. This was a pressing concern for American Catholics. In 1916, almost half of all Catholics attended a parish where English was a second language. See Finke and Stark, *Churching of America*, 134.

20. Williams, *American Catholics*.

training and overseas (the YWCA cared for women stationed with the AEF), as did the Catholic organization Knights of Columbus.[21]

Considering the American response in the larger context of America's relationship with Britain and Canada, it is apparent that there were important nuances and differences between the American experience and that of its English-speaking allies. Americans had been spectators of the war for almost three years, whereas Britain and Canada had been at war from the opening days of the German offensive in Belgium. American religious views on the war were fluid and evolved to respond to new political realities, so much so that by the time President Wilson declared war he could count on the majority of churches as supporters, something not at all possible even a year earlier. While that gradual movement from passive observer to passionate combatant was unique to the American experience, Americans, Canadians, and Britons all would have been familiar with the vivid metaphors and passionate language of "holy war," for their religious leaders often used similar language to frame the conflict as a battle against the "barbarous hordes of the German Kaiser."[22] The vast majority of religious leaders in Britain and Canada portrayed the war as a just war, and across the Anglo-Saxon world there was a hope that the war would usher in a new world devoid of conflict, and result in the realization of the kingdom of Christ in national and international relations. In this regard the progressives or "modernist" American clergy shared much in common with kindred spirit social gospel proponents in Britain and Canada; the war was eventually enthusiastically embraced as a way to refashion or reconstruct the social order (national as well as international) according to social gospel ideals.[23]

Americans also shared with Britons and Canadians a sense of national destiny. It was increasingly believed that the United States and the British Empire shared a common mission, perhaps best known by the title of Rudyard Kipling's poem to the United States in 1899: "The White Man's Burden." Edward Kohn notes that while this poem was written by a Briton to Americans, it was a burden "that belonged not only to the United States, but to all Anglo-Saxons, Canadians included."[24] That concept of national

21. Lancaster, *Serving*.

22. This quotation is from a Canadian religious publication, "Universal Service," *Presbyterian Witness*, 6 November 1915, 4. See also Wilkinson, *Church of England*; Heath, *Canadian Churches*.

23. Gamble, *War for Righteousness*; Allen, *Social Passion*.

24. Kohn, *This Kindred People*, 132.

destiny, or "manifest destiny" as some would call it, was distinctly racial, in particular a conviction that the "Americans stood shoulder-to-shoulder with the British people as upholders of Anglo-Saxon civilization."[25] Such ties of blood played an important role in sympathy for Britain's wartime plight. Central to Kipling's exhortation was the conviction that the rise of Anglo-Saxons to world prominence was ultimately due to God's providence, and that God had raised up the Anglo-Saxons to be a blessing to the world; in the case of the war against Germany, that meant to protect the weak, to defend civilization, to defeat the militaristic and autocratic Hun, and to promote democracy.

The promotion of democracy was central to American religious discourse on the war. In his address to a joint session of Congress on 2 April 1917 requesting a declaration of war, President Wilson declared that the United States would go to war to make the world "safe for democracy."

> The world must be made safe for democracy. Its peace must be planted upon the tested foundations of political liberty. We have no selfish ends to serve. We desire no conquest, no dominion. We seek no indemnities for ourselves, no material compensation for the sacrifices we shall freely make. We are but one of the champions of the rights of mankind. We shall be satisfied when those rights have been made as secure as the faith and the freedom of nations can make them.

The churches that supported the war effort enthusiastically echoed the President, and church commentary reflected the idealism implicit in Wilson's appeal: "The welfare of the nation is the uppermost thought of each one. . . . Men of all classes have willingly laid aside their own interests . . . [in order to] help 'make democracy safe.'"[26] Supportive American clergy extolled the idealism of America fighting solely for the good of others, unlike, it was claimed, European powers that may have joined in the war for hidden or selfish reasons.[27] That impulse to wage a righteous war to spread democracy—rather than fight for selfish personal, national, or imperial

---

25. Judd, *Empire*, 145. Kohn argues that race did not cause the hoped for reunion of Anglo-Saxons, but did give it a "device with which to adapt to the changing context of Canadian-American relations" and "helped foster . . . [closer relations] by giving North Americans a common lexicon, the rhetoric of Anglo-Saxon kinship and Canadian-American affinity." Kohn, *This Kindred People*, 4, 8.

26. "Today," *The Spirit of Missions*, June 1917, 373.

27. Americans generally distrusted the motives of all European empires—Britain's included.

gain—united a great many clergy from both ends of the theological spectrum, as well as Protestants and Catholics and Jews.

Despite the importance of religion among Americans in the early decades of the twentieth century, there is a paucity of research on religion and the war. That is problematic, for, as Richard Gamble argues, to ignore religion at the time is to "miss the key to understanding the way many Americans interpreted world events."[28] It also fails to recognize the powerful role of the churches in shaping public opinion. The most significant immediate postwar work to examine the responses of the wartime churches was Ray H. Abrams's *Preachers Present Arms*.[29] Despite the book's widespread circulation, Abrams's work suffers from his ardent personal opposition to the pro-war response of the churches, and in his one-sided vilification of the pro-war clergy he failed to see the nuances and ranges of reactions within American churches. More recent research has benefited from the passage of time, the cooling of emotions, and access to new archival material. The efforts of John Piper, Jr. and Elizabeth McKeown in the 1980s mark the beginning of a more modern analysis of the churches and the war.[30] A number of even more recent works have developed important themes. Richard Gamble and Andrew Preston identify among a wide spectrum of American clergy the fusion of religion, national identity, and waging war for righteousness.[31] Jonathan Ebel and Philip Jenkins draw attention to the importance of faith among soldiers and in the populace at large—a much needed reminder for those today who read back into the past the contemporary marginalization of religion from public life.[32] The chapters in this volume build upon these works and that of others to provide a fuller sense of American churches and the First World War.

In chapter two Richard Gamble takes a second look at "No False Peace" signed in 1917 by some sixty prominent American clergy from both ends of the theological spectrum. He argues that signatories such as progressive Harry Emerson Fosdick and conservative Billy Sunday put aside theological differences in order "to form a coalition for the sake of American intervention" and victory. He shows how such leaders "held a common evangelical

---

28. Gamble, *War for Righteousness*, 181.

29. An earlier work was Williams, *American Catholics*. However, for over the next half-century, Abrams's work became the standard text on the churches and the war.

30. Piper, *American Churches*; McKeown, *War and Welfare*.

31. Gamble, *War for Righteousness*; Preston, *Sword of the Spirit*.

32. Ebel, *Faith in the Fight*; Jenkins, *Great and Holy War*.

faith in a Christian America and its God-given destiny to be a global force for righteousness. For the war's duration, they adhered to a civil religion powerful enough to make sectarian differences trivial (or at least beside the point) in the midst of a national and international emergency." Gamble argues that Fosdick and Sunday, rather than being strange bedfellows, were "comfortably together in the bed they had all helped make. Whatever their differences, they had all emerged from the long pietist consensus in the nineteenth century that affirmed a Christian America and an American Christianity with a moral mission at home and abroad."

Patrick Carey details the Catholic responses to the war, tracing developments from initial hesitation, division, and ambivalence in 1914 to widespread support for the declaration in 1917. He shows how the new Catholic institutions created during the war had a long-lasting influence upon the development of Catholic life in the United States, and how the war brought the Catholic Church in the United States into a much more active engagement with American public life than had been common or even possible in the nineteenth century. He concludes that the "war brought Catholics out of their parishes and dioceses into the national arena where they could, for the first time, contribute as a group to the public welfare and develop national institutions that voiced Catholic concerns in the common life. The bishops in particular gained a national voice and even though they were not always united on specific issues, they established a platform in Washington, DC that has continued on into the twenty-first century."

Mark Granquist shows how Lutherans were "divided generationally, with the older generation trying to hold back the rising tide of change and assimilation, while a newer Lutheran generation of 'hyphenated Americans' sought to take full advantage of the new world of which they were now a part." He goes on to demonstrate how the First World War radically and rapidly worked to change those realities; one of the most dramatic changes being the shift away from European languages to English in schools and churches, a move that "meant that American Lutherans would become more fully engaged in the American religious world." Wartime pressures—especially nativist suspicions—also forced "American Lutherans to cooperate with each other, and to begin the long process of institutional re-arrangement and merger." The war, he concludes, led to changes and trajectories that shaped American Lutheranism for the century to come.

Perry Bush argues that "peacetime commonly induces pacifists to deemphasize principles that otherwise set them apart from their fellow citizens; it can anesthetize their convictions. Wartime, however, works opposite effects. While it can separate pacifists from the mass of their fellow citizens, even in uncomfortable and sometimes dangerous ways, it tends to sharpen their convictions." Bush contends that this was the experience of American Mennonites during the war. In fact, despite the fact that they had been slowly but surely becoming more American over the preceding generation, the war "reminded them that they could never fully fit in. Indeed, the trauma associated with the war—including the horrible violence directed at conscientious objectors—lingered for decades." In regards to identity, the pressures of the war helped to revitalize Mennonite principles and provide opportunities for Mennonites to demonstrate their patriotism.

Robynne Healey notes that while accurate and reliable statistics on Quaker enlistment in the war are not readily available, it is estimated that roughly half of eligible American Quakers enlisted. Her chapter explores tensions among Quakers over issues of conscience, conscription, and conscientious objection. She demonstrates how the reluctance of yearly meetings to alienate Friends who, on the basis of conscience, had enlisted is an indication of the multiple ways in which American Quakers negotiated the line between individual conscience and the peace testimony. Those tensions, she argues, "demanded sustained examination of the tradition of Quaker pacifism, the conditions that caused and might prevent war, and the individual and corporate responsibility for the witness to peace making." In this way, Healey concludes, "World War One acted as a catalyst for a renewed commitment to peace as well as reconciliation among American Friends themselves."

Zachary Tackett contends that the war tested Pentecostals and their commitment to peace and patriotism. While a number of key leaders voiced pacifist opposition to the war, and called upon church members to exercise the right to claim conscientious objector status, American Pentecostals were not consistent in their views. He argues that "pacifism was far from universal among America's Pentecostals," and identifies three types of responses among Pentecostals. Some directly prophetically opposed the war effort. Others "attempted to simultaneously embrace nationalism and oppose the war in Europe." Yet others "who upheld the *status quo* either failed to oppose the war or accepted that Pentecostals, like all Americans, should fulfill their patriotic duty by participating in the war effort."

J. David Pulsipher traces the trajectory of Mormonism from a marginalized and persecuted religion throughout the nineteenth century to one increasingly identified with the war effort and its concomitant patriotic notions in the early twentieth century. There was a cost to the shift, for "Latter-day Saints emerged on the other side of the war arguing more with each other as members of partisan factions than with the nation as a whole." But in terms of Mormons and American identity, support for the war effort meant that the "outsiders were now insiders, or at least more comfortably so than they had been before the war. Previously united as Zion-focused 'Saints' arrayed against nationalist 'Gentiles,' Mormons now engaged the great political issues of the day as Americans first, a transformation of corporate identity that has continued until today."

M. James Penton describes the position and plight of the Bible Student movement (commonly known today as Jehovah's Witnesses). During the first two years of warfare in Europe, it was believed that both the churches and governments of Christendom would shortly collapse under divine judgment. He also illustrates how war was deemed to be unchristian, and how most clergy were denounced for supporting the war effort. Like members of all "peace churches" in America, the Bible Students came under attack after April 1917. Their men of military age were often placed under brutal army control or imprisoned for refusing to be conscripted. His conclusion is that with the possible exception of the Hutterites, the Bible Students "suffered more than any other American religious community" for their wartime convictions. And, like other cases of "vigilantism directed at various anti-war groups during the years 1917 and 1918, those actions were the result of excessive crusading nationalism and are a stain on the history of the United States."

Timothy Demy notes how numerous American military chaplains served with distinction in the First World War, despite not having a central chaplain corps or chief of chaplains. He also claims that the military chaplaincy in the United States Army and United States Navy was simply not ready for war, and that "the rapid increase in the recruiting of soldiers, sailors, airmen, and marines to whom chaplains were called to minister exacerbated problems of administration, oversight, and ministry of chaplains." He goes on to demonstrate how the "lack of command organization to provide directives, oversight, assignment, coordination, and resources for chaplains created a ministry environment of confusion and uncertainty for individual chaplains." Some of the turmoil surrounding chaplains was due to unresolved questions over how to apply the separation of church and state to the issue of clergy in the military.

Gordon Heath asks why, despite the extraordinary outpouring of support for those facing genocide, there was no groundswell of church backing for military action to protect Armenians and punish Turkey. Church leaders were wary of adding to the suffering of the afflicted by encouraging America going to war with Turkey, and thus counseled against such action. What made that difficult decision easier to bear was the sense that America was—in a way—already at war with Turkey. Stated differently, there is ample evidence of what could best be called a proxy war between America and Turkey. While people may have known that technically America was not formally at war with Turkey, the heated wartime rhetoric often conflated America's war with Germany with opposition to the horrors transpiring in Turkey. The "accursed partnership of Turk and Teuton" had led to the global conflagration, and America's war against the Teuton was considered, for all intents and purposes, a war against Germany's ally Turkey.

While America was victorious in its first foray into Europe's continental conflicts, and its rapid mobilization demonstrated to the world the potential of America's military might, the postwar years were marked by disappointment, doubt, and division. Events on the ground failed to live up to the lofty rhetoric of the churches who supported the war as a war to end all wars. America's subsequent failure to join the League of Nations, as well as the nation's retreat into isolationism, also threatened the vision for the Christianization of international affairs and the advance of democracy. In regards to divisions, the conflict had united America's Protestants, Catholics, and Jews in a common patriotic cause, and some denominations had used the opportunity to demonstrate their readiness and suitability for public trust and engagement; it was their opportunity to move from the margins to mainstream. Yet denominational tensions remained. Those churches that had opposed the war effort remembered the discrimination at the hands of the pro-war churches, and those painful memories did not fade quickly. Some denominations on the margins were further alienated by their antiwar position or ethnic identity. Still others suffered because of internal divisions over a proper response to the war. The chapters of this book explore such issues, yet there is a great deal more to be done on the war, churches, and national identity. It is hoped that at the centenary of America's entrance into the war these chapters will inspire or provoke others to examine further this pivotal experience for the churches and the nation.

BIBLIOGRAPHY

Primary Sources

NEWSPAPERS

The Spirit of Missions, 1917.
Presbyterian Witness, 1915.

Secondary Sources

Ebel, Jonathan H. *Faith in the Fight: Religion and the American Soldier in the Great War.* Princeton: Princeton University Press, 2010.

Abrams, Ray H. *Preachers Present Arms.* New York: Round Table, 1933.

Allen, Richard. *The Social Passion: Religion and Social Reform in Canada.* Toronto: University of Toronto Press, 1971.

Bourne, John. "Total War I: The Great War." In *The Oxford History of Modern War*, edited by Charles Townshend, 117–37. Oxford: Oxford University Press, 2005.

Brands, H. W. *The Reckless Decade: America in the 1890's.* New York: St. Martins, 1995.

Clodfelter, Michael. *Warfare and Armed Conflicts: A Statistical Encyclopedia of Casualty and Other Figures, 1494–2007.* Jefferson, NC: McFarland, 2008.

Dekar, Paul. *Dangerous People: The Fellowship of Reconciliation Building a Nonviolent World of Freedom, Justice, and Peace.* Virginia Beach: Donning, 2016.

Ferguson, Niall. *The War of the World: History's Age of Hatred.* London: Penguin, 2007.

Finke, Roger, and Rodney Stark. *The Churching of America, 1776–2005: Winners and Losers in Our Religious Economy.* New Brunswick, NJ: Rutgers University Press, 2005.

Gamble, Richard M. *The War for Righteousness: Progressive Christianity, the Great War, and the Rise of the Messianic Nation.* Wilmington, KY: ISI, 2003.

Heath, Gordon L. "Canadian and American Baptist Self-Perceptions in the Age of Imperialism." In *Mirrors & Microscopes*, edited by Douglas Weaver, 87–109. Milton Keynes, UK: Paternoster, 2015.

———, ed. *Canadian Churches and the First World War.* Eugene, OR: Pickwick, 2014.

Herbst, Matthew T. "Methodism and Aggressive Christianity: The Detroit Annual Conference of the Methodist Episcopal Church and the US Occupation of the Philippines (1898–1903)." *Journal of Religion and Society* 7 (2005) 1–25.

Hudson, Winthrop S. "Protestant Clergy Debate the Nation's Vocation, 1898–1899." *Church History* 42 (1973) 110–18.

Jenkins, Philip. *The Great and Holy War: How World War I Became a Religious Crusade.* New York: HarperOne, 2014.

Judd, Denis. *Empire: The British Imperial Experience from 1765 to the Present.* London: Fontana, 1997.

Kohn, Edward P. *This Kindred People: Canadian-American Relations and the Anglo-Saxon Idea, 1895–1903.* Montreal and Kingston: McGill-Queen's University Press, 2004.

Lancaster, Richard C. *Serving the US Armed Forces, 1861–1986: The Story of the YMCA's Ministry to Military Personnel for 125 Years.* Schaumburg: Armed Services YMCA of the USA, 1987.

MacKenzie, Kenneth M. *The Robe and the Sword: The Methodist Church and the Rise of American Imperialism.* Washington, DC: Public Affairs, 1961.

May, Ernest R. *Imperial Democracy: The Emergence of America as a Great Power.* New York: Harper & Row, 1973.

McKeown, Elizabeth. *War and Welfare: American Catholics and World War I.* New York: Garland, 1988.

Miller, Stuart Creighton. *Benevolent Assimilation: The American Conquest of the Philippines, 1899–1903.* New Haven: Yale University Press, 1982.

Mislin, David. "One Nation, Three Faiths: World War I and the Shaping of 'Protestant-Catholic-Jewish' America." *Church History* 84 (December 2015) 828–62.

Mosier, John. *The Myth of the Great War: A New Military History of World War I.* New York: HarperCollins, 2001.

Musicant, Ivan. *Empire by Default: The Spanish–American War and the Dawn of the American Century.* New York: Henry Holt, 1998.

Nugent, Walter. "The Mormons and America's Empires." *Journal of Mormon History* 36 (Spring 2010) 1–27.

Piper, John F., Jr. *The American Churches in World War I.* Athens, OH: Ohio University Press, 1985.

Preston, Andrew. *Sword of the Spirit, Shield of Faith: Religion in American War and Diplomacy.* New York: Alfred A. Knopf, 2012.

Quinn, D. Michael. "The Mormon Church and the Spanish–American War: An End to Selective Pacifism." *Pacific Historical Review* 43 (1974) 342–66.

Reed, James Eldin. "American Foreign Policy, the Politics of Mission and Josiah Strong, 1890–1900." *Church History* 41 (June 1972) 230–45.

Rosen, Christine. *Preaching Eugenics: Religious Leaders and the American Eugenics Movement.* Oxford: Oxford University Press, 2004.

Sharpe, Dores Robinson. *Walter Rauschenbusch.* New York: Macmillan, 1984.

Smylie, John Edwin. "Protestant Clergymen and American Destiny: II. Prelude to Imperialism, 1865–1900." *Harvard Theological Review* 56 (October 1963) 297–311.

Snape, Michael. *God and the British Soldier: Religion and the British Army in the First and Second World Wars.* Abingdon: Routledge, 2009.

Stevenson, David. *1914–1918: The History of the First World War.* London: Allen Lane, 2004.

Thomas, Evan. *The War Lovers: Roosevelt, Lodge, Hearst, and the Rush to Empire, 1898.* New York: Little, Brown, 2010.

Thomas, Ivor B. "A Baptist Anti-Imperialist Voice: George Horr and *The Watchman.*" *Foundations* 18 (1975) 340–57.

Welch, Richard E., Jr. "Organized Religion and the Philippine-American War, 1899–1902." *Mid-America: An Historical Review* 55 (January 1973) 184–206.

Wilkinson, Alan. *The Church of England and the First World War.* Cambridge: Lutterworth, 2014.

Williams, Michael. *American Catholics in the War: National Catholic War Council, 1917–1921.* New York: Macmillan, 1921.

2

Together for the Gospel of Americanism

Evangelicals and the First World War

RICHARD M. GAMBLE

I

ON 10 JANUARY 1917, before Germany resumed unrestricted submarine warfare, before word of the Zimmerman telegram reached the press, and well before the United States Congress declared war, the *Outlook* magazine published a manifesto signed by some sixty prominent American clergy. Names included mainline Protestants, liberals, modernists, and more orthodox revivalists; pastors, college presidents, editors, missionaries, and evangelists; prominent Methodists, Episcopalians, Congregationalists, Presbyterians, Baptists, and one lone Roman Catholic, former Secretary of the Navy and Attorney-General Charles J. Bonaparte, a progressive Catholic who had advocated preparedness since August 1914. Entitled, "No False Peace," the statement in the sober-minded, high-toned, and progressive *Outlook* protested not just pacifists' efforts to prevent American intervention in the European war but any negotiations to end hostilities short of the war reaching its proper outcome. Any push for peace at this stage would be premature and betray the noble crusade for which so many had died since August 1914. "Peace is the triumph of righteousness and not the mere sheathing of the sword," the ministers agreed. War could not stop without securing justice for Belgians, Armenians, Serbs, and Poles; without an accounting for lives lost in 1915 on the *Lusitania*; and without answering the Kaiser's attempt to lure the Ottoman Empire into an Islamic "Holy War." Moving seamlessly from Christ's atonement to international justice in a way so common among Americans at the time, the clergy affirmed that "the just God, who withheld not his own Son from the cross, would not look with favor upon a people who put their fear of pain and death, their dread of suffering and loss, their concern for comfort and ease, above the holy claims of righteousness and justice and freedom and mercy and truth."[1]

Exactly how the machinery of modern total war would accomplish "spiritual values" and "great and divine ideals," the signers did not pause to explain. Perhaps they assumed their target audience already thought the connection between spiritual warfare and earthly warfare self-evident. Nor did they answer the possible objection from more old-fashioned realists that governments were established in large part precisely to secure their people from "pain and death" and "suffering and loss." Nevertheless, the manifesto demonstrated the public resolve of one vocal sector of the American clergy (and a few affiliated laity) to pursue total victory against Imperial Germany and its allies. Twenty-three names and affiliations appeared on the statement along with the assurance that "some forty others" had signed. The list included *Outlook* editor Lyman Abbott, liberal Congregationalist minister Newell Dwight Hillis, Oberlin College president Henry Churchill King, Princeton president John Grier Hibben, Union Seminary professor Harry Emerson Fosdick, social-gospel novelist Winston Churchill, revivalist Billy Sunday, and William Revell Moody, son of the famed evangelist. "No False Peace" brought together celebrity liberal and celebrity conservative evangelicals. Those like Fosdick who denied the inspiration of Scripture, the substitutionary atonement, the Virgin Birth, and the literal Second Coming of Christ joined forces with those like Moody who wore the mantel of his father Dwight L. Moody and managed the fundamentalist Northfield conferences in Massachusetts. The signatories put aside divisions over theology and worship to form a coalition for the sake of American intervention, Allied victory, and a vibrant creedal Americanism inherited from a long line of nineteenth-century preachers, politicians, philosophers, and poets. They held a common evangelical faith in a Christian America and

---

1. "No False Peace: A Warning by American Religious Leaders," *Outlook* 115, 10 January 1917, 63.

its God-given destiny to be a global force for righteousness. For the war's duration, they adhered to a civil religion powerful enough to make sectarian differences trivial (or at least beside the point) in the midst of a national and international emergency. A world safe for democracy was also a world safe for Christianity, international brotherhood, and a righteous peace. The exception would prove to be the University of Chicago Divinity School's treatment of premillennialists, but even in this case the accusation leveled against those who believed in Christ's imminent return was that they subverted the war effort by allegedly counseling cultural despair. Indeed, the premillennialists often responded by reaffirming their own fidelity to the American mission. Historian George Marsden put his finger on the paradox in which premillennialists entangled themselves in 1917 and 1918: "they had to say that there was no hope for culture, but at the same time they were traditional American evangelicals who urged a return to Christian principles as the only cultural hope."[2] This commitment to "Christian principles" found liberal and conservative evangelicals often fighting on the same side in the culture war and the World War.

If this claim is so broad that it risks obliterating important differences, and strikes some as falling too far to one side of the "lumper-splitter" divide in historical method, it is also true that resetting the paradigm allows other patterns to emerge. "Lumping" these clergy together under "Americanism" or a vaguer civil religion need not require historians to return to the lopsided analysis of Ray H. Abrams's 1933 *Preachers Present Arms*, which overlooked the untidy variety of Christian responses to the war. For the antiwar sociologist, the churches had by and large served merely as the tools of the United States' wartime efforts at social control through jingoist propaganda. The clergy were dupes of those who held the real power. Dissident voices Abrams confined to a handful of principled pacifists. To his credit, Abrams undertook massive research involving hundreds of sermons and newspaper and journal articles, but he presupposed that the nation's clergy had been divided into strict doctrinaire pacifists and bloodthirsty jingoists, into the good guys and bad guys of popular postwar revisionism. Unfortunately, Abrams's book has proven so handy and quotable over the past eighty years that his name shows up in footnotes far more often than the quality of his research and analysis warrants. Indeed, one corrective to Abrams's oversimplification of the story is to "lump" the clergy in a different way. Looking at American evangelicalism through the lens of civil religion,

---

2. Marsden, *Fundamentalism and American Culture*, 149.

at a moment when this broad-based Protestant movement still thought of itself as culturally dominant and just on the eve of its being sorted out into its warring fundamentalist and modernist camps, allows other options for historical investigation to emerge, options that Abrams failed to consider in the interwar period. Indeed, those Catholic priests and Jewish rabbis who were eager to prove their Americanism during the First World War often resorted to sounding as much like Protestant evangelicals as possible, a strategy that did not end with the war in 1918.

Abrams aside, if we read the "No False Peace" manifesto with expectations formed by the standard historiography of American Protestantism, we will be puzzled by fundamentalist Billy Sunday appearing on the same document as outspoken theological modernists Abbott and Fosdick. We might chalk up the apparently anomalous alliance to the white-hot forge of war enthusiasm. But it would be a mistake to dismiss the problem as a quirk of the moment that does not require further explanation. A decade ago, in *The War for Righteousness*, I fell into this error when I dismissed Sunday's name at the bottom of "No False Peace" as out of place for his theology but among his bedfellows for his jingoism. The list did not strike me as evidence of any deeper unity or coherence. That simplistic "explanation" should not have satisfied me at the time. I should have been more curious. A better account would see Abbott and Fosdick and Sunday, rather than strange bedfellows, as belonging comfortably together in the bed they had all helped make. Whatever their differences, they had all emerged from the long pietist consensus in the nineteenth century that affirmed a Christian America and an American Christianity with a moral mission at home and abroad.

Just how powerful and forgiving that moral message could be as an ecumenical force was demonstrated at the time by John Haynes Holmes. The prominent New York Unitarian preached a sermon at his Church of the Messiah about Billy Sunday's Paterson, New Jersey, revival in 1915. As reported in the *New York Times*, Holmes told his congregation that the evangelist's orthodoxy was only skin deep. As much as Sunday railed against Unitarians, he only seemed to be an enemy of liberalism. He was no descendent of George Whitefield. Surrounded by the forms but not the substance of the "old-time religion," Sunday preached "the new truth of modern liberalism—that religion finds its true expression in the moral life." "At the bottom of his work ... is not theology, not conversion, not faith in Christ as the Son of God, not acceptance of the Cross, but plain, matter of fact, everyday morality." "In spite of all his ignorance, shocking vulgarity, and wild denunciation of the advocates of liberalism," Holmes continued, "this man is himself a liberal and a standing proof of the fact that the old religion of faith is gone and the new religion of plain morality is come."[3] Holmes's purpose was not to welcome Sunday into a pro-war alliance. Indeed, Holmes was a fairly consistent pacifist and later an organizer of the ACLU and NAACP. Nevertheless, he may have been on to something in his sermon. He saw in Sunday an ally in the common cause of promoting a Christianity that was first and foremost a quest for public morality.

II

As a first step in rethinking American evangelicalism and the First World War, the category "evangelical" itself has to be challenged. It is even worth thinking about how historians might tell not just the story of the First World War but also the much larger stories of American religion, of war and religion, and of nationalism and religion, without resorting to this category at all. Sam Haselby, in *The Origins of American Religious Nationalism*, has argued that since nearly everybody identified himself or herself as evangelical in nineteenth-century America, "evangelical" as a category of analysis does not highlight the most meaningful differences and similarities in the contours of American life and thought.[4] Assuming we are probably stuck with word "evangelical," we need to keep it as broad in analysis as it was in practice. By doing so, we quickly see that the people we might otherwise scratch our heads over as "strange bedfellows" during the war were not strangers to each other at all. In 1917, evangelicalism was still the world it had been decades before, a world in which D. L. Moody's song leader Ira D. Sankey could work with social gospel radical Walter Rauschenbusch on editing German translations of his *Gospel Hymns* (*Neue Lieder* and the two volumes of *Evangeliums-Lieder*) and where Rauschenbusch and Harry Emerson Fosdick could work with the YMCA.[5]

Short of abandoning the term, employing "evangelicalism" in a way that is more sensitive to how Americans actually thought and worshipped in the late nineteenth and early twentieth century opens a fresh perspective

3. "Sunday's New Religion," *New York Times*, 19 April 1915, 16.
4. Haselby, *Origins of American Religious Nationalism*, 24.
5. Rauschenbusch delivered his address "The Kingdom of God" in 1913 to the Cleveland YMCA. The YMCA's Association Press published a number of Fosdick's books and sponsored his speaking tour of the front in France during the war.

on the First World War. This approach requires going back to the group of enthno-cultural historians (working mostly in the 1970s) who rejected the conventional liberal-conservative continuum as an unconvincing way to analyze culture and politics in favor of a continuum ranging from pietist to ritualist. Paul Kleppner, for instance, in his 1970 classic *The Cross of Culture*, argued that the best predictor of voting behavior was not class or even broadly speaking citizens' ethnicity or religious affiliation but more narrowly how they worshipped, whether they looked at the world and politics as pietists eager to transform American manners and morals or as confessionalists[6] determined to adhere to their denomination's creeds, liturgy, and sacraments, regardless of their impact on the wider culture or how often they were accused of being sectarian. Differences between the pietist Republicans and ritualist Democrats cut right across class lines but also right through German ethnicity, language, and Lutheranism. For example, pietist Lutherans aligned against confessionalist Lutherans in politics and culture. The Democratic Party remained the haven of culturally alienated ritualists until the pietist evangelical William Jennings Bryan transformed it in 1896 into a movement to moralize America, breaking down the secular-sacred distinction in church and politics that had been important to many Democrats.[7] Under Bryan, the Democrats sought to beat the Republicans by becoming more like them as crusading interventionists, first at home in movements like prohibition and then abroad under Woodrow Wilson in his "war of righteousness."[8]

Historian Frederick C. Luebke applied this analysis directly to the German-American experience in the First World War.[9] After 1914, denominations such as the Lutheran Church Missouri Synod became "the single most severely criticized body" in the United States. As confessionalists, they understood themselves as a distinct group worshipping outside the mainstream of American religion and culture. They faced a choice between embracing Americanism, as more pietist Lutherans opted to do, or retreating along with other minorities "into their ethnoreligious shells." They could assimilate or retain their distinctiveness at great cost. From the

---

6. By "confessionalist" I mean denominations that subscribe to (and take seriously) a confession of faith, often with a high regard for sacraments, liturgy etc.

7. Kleppner, *Cross of Culture*. On "Democratic pietism," see 338–39.

8. Gamble, *War for Righteousness*.

9. Luebke, *Bonds of Loyalty*, 238, 315, and passim. For Luebke's statement of the ritualist-pietist paradigm, see 34.

outbreak of war in 1914 until American intervention in 1917, these confessionalist Lutherans tried hard to keep a low profile, stay out of trouble with their neighbors, and retain their German language and culture in their schools and churches. After 1917, they contributed to the war effort as loyal American citizens but were repeatedly tested by the limited tolerance of the dominant religious nationalism (or dominant nationalist religion). They had to ask themselves whether they could submit to those in authority under the trying circumstances of intense mobilization for total war and still keep separate the two kingdoms of church and state and of church and culture. Could they embrace the creed of Americanism (as even many Catholics did during the war), become super-patriots like their evangelical neighbors, and still retain their doctrinal purity in faith and practice? Could they be religious sectarians and still good Americans? Would they display the American flag in their churches and on their altars? Would they promote the sale of Liberty Bonds from their pulpits? Would they preach on the war and directly promote loyalty and drum up enlistment while clothed with the authority of their ministerial office?

Historian Darryl G. Hart applied the cultural and political insights of the ethno-cultural historians such as Kleppner to the story of American Protestantism more generally than Luebke attempted.[10] He argued that American religious history is best understood not along a continuum of liberal to conservative that clouds our understanding by making it appear as though controversies within evangelicalism constitute the whole range of Protestantism in the United States, but rather along a pietist-confessionalist continuum that does a much better job of accounting for the words and behavior we actually find in the past. Historians would encounter fewer anomalies in the past and at the same time accommodate much greater diversity of religious faith and practice in their narratives if they were to adopt and apply this method to their analysis of American religion. Applying it to the story of American evangelicals and the First World War shows the potential inherent in such an approach and points to ways it might be applied to the investigation of America's other wars.

III

What does the story of wartime American evangelicalism look like if we take Kleppner's, Luebke's, and Hart's organizational scheme as a starting point? It suddenly looks like a story in which it makes perfect sense that

10. Hart, *Lost Soul of American Protestantism*.

more orthodox evangelicals like Billy Sunday and William R. Moody labored among the "superpatriots" who put their evangelistic crusades and publications at the disposal of war mobilization in 1917. They did so in part because they assumed, as it was still possible for them to do before the nasty culture wars of the 1920s taught them otherwise, that as evangelicals they constituted the dominate religious and cultural force in America, that America's wars were *Christian* America's wars, and that therefore the churches in America had something deeply (or transcendently) at stake in the outcome of these wars beyond the safety and wellbeing of their parishioners. On the whole, American evangelicals, whether liberal or conservative, had never had to choose between loyalty to their churches and loyalty to the government. Only ethnic, cultural, and religious minorities had had to do that, those semi-aliens who shared a version of what W. E. B. Du Bois described in 1903 as the "two souls" of African-Americans at the beginning of the twentieth century.[11] Simply put, dominant evangelicalism in 1917 didn't have two souls.

Certainly no signer of "No False Peace" in 1917 had any sensation of the "twoness" of being in a religious or cultural minority, and Americanism was not a problem. That was true for Lyman Abbott and for Billy Sunday. The two preachers' wartime alliance looks unaccountable in hindsight only if we start with the wrong presuppositions. Lyman Abbott operated as a considerable cultural force in late nineteenth- and early twentieth-century America. For many years he served as pastor of Brooklyn's Plymouth Church, a liberal Congregationalist landmark since the 1840s and for decades the pulpit of Henry Ward Beecher, son of Lyman Beecher and brother to Harriet Beecher Stowe. Abbott had made a name for himself not only as a leader in the emerging social gospel movement but also, and perhaps primarily, as an advocate of reconciling Christianity and evolution. Under his leadership, the *Outlook* combined liberal evangelicalism with social reform, adopted a bold posture on national defense, and promoted arts and letters.[12] He and his journal believed "in the immortality of the spirit and in change of forms, in the old religion and in a new theology, in the old patriotism and in the new politics, in the old philanthropy and in new institutions, in the old brotherhood and in a new social order."[13] Abbott sided with his former *Outlook* contributing editor Theodore Roosevelt on the

---

11. Du Bois, *Souls of Black Folk*, 12.
12. Mott, *History of American Magazines*, 432.
13. Abbott, quoted in ibid., 429.

question of war and intervention in 1917. He called for a strong American defense and a muscular international righteousness policed by the United States. He worked with the Army League and the Navy League, served on the National Security League and the League to Enforce Peace, and became a board member of the American Rights League.

The American Rights League mobilized the clergy to sign "No False Peace" and then publicized it in the *Outlook* and also as a separate "bulletin" in February 1917.[14] The League operated from Manhattan as the brainchild of George Haven Putnam. Putnam founded the organization in 1915 in response to Germany's sinking of the British passenger liner *Lusitania* and the death of 128 Americans aboard. Its purpose was to mobilize public opinion. Born in London in 1844 to the influential American publisher George Putnam, the younger Putnam was educated in America and Europe, and had returned to the United States in 1862 to fight in the Union army. In 1915, he was also one of the founders of the National Security League, a vocal preparedness organization, and the League to Enforce Peace.[15] The American Rights League's dozens of vice-presidents included Lyman Abbott, novelist Hamlin Garland, Johns Hopkins intellectual historian Arthur O. Lovejoy, Harvard literary scholar Barrett Wendell, Princeton classicist Paul Elmer More, Philadelphia essayist Agnes Repplier, and novelist Booth Tarkington in the Indianapolis office. A declaration by the American Rights League that Germany was already at war with the United States appeared in the *New York Times* on 12 January 1917. The organization survived the war and turned its efforts to promoting Americanism. In 1920, Putnam boasted that he had founded his organization "for the purpose of getting this country into the war at the earliest possible date" and said that the United States was "shamefully late in coming into the war."[16]

"No False Peace" put Abbott and Sunday literally on the same page, but the two preachers emphasized their common cause in other ways,

---

14. "No False Peace: A Warning by American Religious Leaders." *American Rights League Bulletin* 23, February 1917. The *Outlook* published the complete text. The bulletin carried the same list of names and the same assurance that "some forty others" had endorsed the manifesto. An earlier publication of the ARL, *Bulletin* 11, 1 September 1916, reprinted Bruce Barton's "A Personal Letter to the Kaiser," which first appeared in *Every Week*, 7 August 1916, and warned the Kaiser that the war would democratize Germany. Barton went on to write *The Man Nobody Knows*, the bestselling biography of Jesus seen through the eyes of the modern man of business.

15. "Putnam, George Haven."

16. *New York Legislative Documents*, 3169.

Abbott more so than Sunday. In May 1917, just weeks after US entry into the war, Abbott published a first-person account in the *Outlook* of his visit to Billy Sunday's New York revival.[17] The evangelistic campaign lasted from April to June, and Sunday preached a powerful mix of patriotism, prohibition, and the gospel. The former baseball player's gigantic "Tabernacle" held an audience of 20,000. On 1 May, a rainy day with lower attendance, Abbott sat in front of the section reserved for ministers. The service began with "The Star-Spangled Banner." Sunday preached on the Old Testament story of Ahab and Jehoshaphat to call for "militancy in religion and everyday life," according to the *New York Times* reporter present. When Sunday demanded President Wilson allow Theodore Roosevelt to raise a regiment and go to Europe to fight, as he was eager to do, Abbott reportedly "smiled and nodded his head" while the crowd cheered and waved flags.[18] Contrary to Abbott's expectations (or his prejudices, he admitted), the liberal editor found Sunday's message "a coherent, well-ordered, impressionistic" *tour de force* that pressed home the "forceful urgency of the duty of courage in the Christian life." Sunday may have slipped into occasional slang, but Abbott praised him for avoiding entirely the stock phrases of old-fashioned revivalists. He found the evangelist intolerant in the right way: "He is frankly intolerant of wickedness, hates it, and calls on his congregation to join him in hating it." To that end, he promoted the "campaign against vice and crime" in Manhattan. He sought to equip Christians for both social and spiritual battle.[19]

Abbott found it possible to give Sunday at least two cheers because he believed he and the evangelist promoted a common faith that was moralistic, ecumenical, and non-dogmatic. Indeed, Abbott thought all preachers ought to learn from Sunday's example "how to apply [Christian] truths to the daily business and social life of the American people." It is possible to interpret what an interventionist like Abbott was doing in 1917 merely as a tactic to mobilize religion for the purposes of mobilizing a nation for modern total war. But even if that was all Abbott was up to and his means to that end so transparent, the way he went about doing so reveals a lot about American evangelicalism and war in the spring of 1917.

In the first place, it reveals the degree to which evangelicalism mixed spiritual and earthly warfare. Second, Abbott claimed not to care about

---

17. Lyman Abbott, "An Evening with Mr. Sunday," *Outlook* 115, 16 May 1917, 98–99.
18. "Billy Sunday Says 'Let Roosevelt Go,'" *New York Times*, 2 May 1917, 7.
19. Lyman Abbott, "An Evening with Mr. Sunday," *Outlook* 115, 16 May 1917, 98–99.

theology as long as a preacher preached directly to man's "spiritual nature," to his "conscience." He named as examples Charles Spurgeon, Henry Ward Beecher, Phillips Brooks, D. L. Moody, John Wesley, and the French Catholic preacher Jean-Baptiste Massillon who avoided dogma in favor of morality. What mattered was the simplicity of Christ's message of love of neighbor (and Abbott intended no irony as America mobilized for war). So commendably "untheological" was Sunday's preaching that his message was acceptable to Catholic and Protestant, Jew and Christian. The Jew could not join Sunday's exaltation of "Jesus Christ as a living, present, personal, intimate friend." But that impediment was minimal because of the way Sunday treated this faith in Jesus. The evangelist "did not argue for this faith nor define it, nor even state it. He employed it without defining it, and his appeal was forceful to those who believed in Christlikeness of character whether or not they believed in the historical Christ as the supreme manifestation of that character." In that spirit, Sunday presented Christianity "as a life of heroic service," a life not to argue people into but to be lived out. It was nothing less than "applied Christianity," once a catchphrase of the social gospel movement since Washington Gladden had popularized it back in the 1880s as a call for social and economic justice in industrial America. Sunday preached not so much about Christianity as a "doorway to a future heaven" but as a religion focused on "this life," on "a life of righteousness here and now." The point here is not that Sunday would have necessarily agreed with Abbott's list of his virtues. The point is that Abbott—the advanced theological liberal—went so far in his warm embrace of Sunday in the weeks immediately following America's entry into the war.

The massive mobilization of public opinion conducted during the war by the United States government, private–public cooperatives like the national, state, and local Councils of Defense, the Red Cross, the Boy Scouts, advertising agencies, film producers, and churches, among other agencies, may well have drowned in a sea of voices something as small and momentary as the clergy's "No False Peace" manifesto. If so, a more widespread and populist manifestation of wartime civil religion's ability to submerge theological differences came with promotion of "The Battle Hymn of the Republic." Julia Ward Howe's Civil War hymn, sung to the tune of "John Brown's Body," had been used during the Spanish–American War of 1898 to justify the United States' humanitarian crusade in Cuba and the Pacific as an extension of its self-evident divine mission. Theodore Roosevelt had proposed the song's adoption as a national anthem in 1908. And it was called up for duty again the instant the United States declared war on Germany in 1917. The song's most optimistic proponents praised its capacity to reunite North and South in a common cause to "make men free" and downplayed, ignored, or forgot its history and theology to use it to unite the forces of democracy to defeat autocracy and emancipate the world. The American Rights League again did its part by distributing sheet music for "The Battle Hymn of the Republic" at the bargain price of a dollar per hundred to schools, clubs, colleges, and churches. Evangelicals of all kinds promoted "The Battle Hymn" as a mark of true patriotism.

Three names that appeared at the bottom of "No False Peace"—Lyman Abbott, Billy Sunday, and William Moody—promoted "The Battle Hymn of the Republic" in 1917 and 1918. Abbott again used the *Outlook* to push for adoption of "The Battle Hymn" as the national anthem, resurrecting his friend Teddy Roosevelt's movement from a decade earlier, but with the added twist that Howe's poem could also serve the world as an international anthem.[20] Abbott attributed the adaptability and durability of "The Battle Hymn" to the fact that it never explicitly mentions the Civil War. Its verses never name the North or South or even the institution of chattel slavery. That silence or generality pointed to a wider vision. "The Battle Hymn" could serve in a war for democracy. "This battle hymn is not merely for our Republic," he wrote; "it is for all republics. It would be as appropriate to-day as a national hymn for such democratic nations as Russia, France, England, Belgium, or Italy as for the United States. It is an international hymn of liberty." Howe's poem had proven its power to overcome America's sectionalism. It had arms wide enough to embrace all sections, all peoples, and all sects. It was national, international, and ecumenical. Indeed, "It is pervaded by a religious spirit, but is wholly free from sectarian or theological phraseology. It is equally fitted to express the spiritual faith of Roman Catholic and Protestant, Jew and Christian, conservative and liberal, and is as beautiful in its poetic form as it is inspiring in its elevated and catholic spirit." Abbott praised the American Rights League's efforts to make "The Battle Hymn" available to every patriot, and invited Canadians, Australians, Englishmen, and "all English-speaking peoples" to sing along. He ended by quoting the five verses of "The Battle Hymn."

---

20. Lyman Abbott, "An International Battle Hymn," *Outlook* 116, 27 June 1917, 321. Abbott's editorial gained wider circulation when most of it was reprinted in "Our 'Battle Hymn' for the Allies," *Literary Digest* 55, 14 July 1917, 26–27.

Billy Sunday had been using "The Battle Hymn of the Republic" since at least his Philadelphia revival campaign in 1915. Reportedly, a Sunday afternoon crowd of 20,000 started singing "The Battle Hymn" spontaneously at the end of his sermon.[21] In 1916, at his Boston crusade, Sunday combined the American flag and "The Battle Hymn" with the fight against Satan. One newspaper described the scene: "Demanding that Bostonians rally to the colors and do battle with the devil, he picked up a chair, climbed on his pulpit and yelled: 'Let's show the devil we don't know how to retreat.' The choir sang 'The Battle Hymn of the Republic.'" The irony here was that Sunday was well known for denouncing the liberal theology of the Unitarians in his sermons and yet his chorister Homer Rodeheaver led the choir and congregation in singing the Unitarian Julia Ward Howe's hymn. Moreover, one disgruntled Unitarian minister complained that Sunday railed against Unitarians on the west coast but then met cordially at Second Church, Boston, with 200 Unitarian ministers. The pastor, who was present, claimed that Sunday paid "tribute" to the memory of the Unitarian patriarch William Ellery Channing and said, "We may differ about the Deity of Jesus, but we shall not quarrel." In spite of Sunday's record of verbal abuse, the Unitarians welcomed him warmly.[22] When America entered the war in 1917 at the time of Sunday's New York City spring campaign, he told the large audience, "Our flag has never been furled, and it is now unfurled for the liberty of the world." The press report continued, "Uttering this last sentence with one foot upon his chair and one upon the pulpit, he suddenly seized an American flag and waved it back and forth, while his hearers cheered frantically and finally burst out into singing: 'My County, 'Tis of Thee,' followed by 'The Battle Hymn of the Republic,' to which they kept time with a Chautauqua salute"—the waving of thousands of white handkerchiefs in the air.[23]

While Billy Sunday indulged in these pulpit antics, the more subdued Moody Bible Institute of Chicago also promoted "The Battle Hymn of the Republic," and it did so with an enthusiasm on a par with Lyman Abbott's. In the *Christian Workers Magazine* (soon to be renamed *Moody Monthly*), editors James M. Gray and J. H. Ralston urged "The Battle Hymn" on evangelicals with extravagant praise. Its Unitarian origins were beside the point

---

21. "The 'Sunday' Meetings." *The Christian Advocate* 90, 14 January 1915, 60.

22. "Billy Sunday and Boston," *The Pacific* 66, 23 November 1916, 4–5; and in the same issue, "Mr. Sunday's Attitude toward Unitarians East and Unitarians West," 5–6.

23. "Billy Sunday in New York City," *The Sabbath Recorder*, 30 April 1917, 572–74.

when there was a war on, and the Institute published all the verses of "The Battle Hymn," even the sixth verse Howe had chosen not to publish in 1862. "We reprint this great hymn of Julia Ward Howe as a patriotic duty," the editors explained in August 1917.[24] "It is one of our national classics which many Americans think they know, but which they do not know. There is too much 'religion' in it ever to become our national hymn, but we wish it might be taught to all the boys and girls in our public schools. Mrs. Howe was not an evangelical Christian, her strongest sympathies being with the Unitarians, and yet as one reads the hymn, he is impressed with the fact that the Unitarianism it represents is almost more orthodox than the so-called Evangelicalism of today. A good deal must be read into it to make it a gospel song, but when that is done the singing of it stirs the soul." For Moody Bible Institute, the imperatives of patriotism summoned evangelicals to find the gospel in a Unitarian hymn and promote its use in the nation's public schools. "The Battle Hymn" was good for America, and any evangelical could get behind that cause.

IV

It is conceivable that evangelicals could have signed an alternative to "No False Peace" that avoided the appeal to Christian ideals in justifying war with Germany and as the basis for peace. It is also possible to imagine Woodrow Wilson having delivered a realist war message in April 1917 that kept the conflict with Germany earth-bound and tethered to the ordinary objectives of war and confined to the limits of what war can and cannot achieve in the world of finite knowledge, capacities, and resources. Such a joint statement from the clergy would at least have avoided the mixing of the sacred and secular in the way so common to historic evangelicalism in America, conservative and liberal. But why bother? What distinctive voice would Christians have added to the debate over intervention in 1916 and 1917 through such a joint statement? If Christian leaders in America did not have a distinctive voice to add to the push for intervention, or if there had been no assumption on the part of the American Rights League that the clergy held such cultural authority, then there was really no point in such a manifesto. At its very core, "No False Peace" assumed that Christians had a highly distinctive voice to add, that they could see and publicize the ultimate, transcendent reasons for war, a war waged for the highest, noblest,

24. "The Battle Hymn of the Republic," *Christian Workers Magazine* 17, August 1917, 947.

and most enduring ideals. Mobilized by the American Rights League, these men joined in issuing an insistently "Christian" explanation of the war and of the reasons that compelled America to enter on the side of the Allied Powers and civilization and Christianity against barbarism and the wrong kind of holy wars.

The point of "lumping" evangelicals like Abbott and Sunday into one category and breaking the liberal-fundamentalist continuum is not to obscure differences but to open up the contrast between evangelicals of all stripes on the one hand who fought to perpetuate a cultural and morally Christian America and confessionalists of all stripes on the other hand who had less at stake in the nation's Christian identity. The challenge for historians is to bring to light those pastors, seminary professors, and chaplains on the field who did not grab headlines with their war sermons, books, and editorials. Getting into the headlines is too often the first step to getting into the history books. But historians of American religion need not allow the principle of selection wielded a century ago by publicists, publishers, advertising executives, and journalists to be their own. They can do better. Overcoming the accidents of what evidence happens to have survived from the past in a useable, available, and findable form poses significant challenges and requires considerable ingenuity and fresh questions. Historians have done good work in reconstructing the experiences of racial and ethnic minorities and the stories of certain religious minorities, but the story of confessional Christianity and America's wars remains to be told. Forty years ago, Federick Luebke proved that the story of confessional Lutheran communities could be compelling. That work needs to be extended to American religion more broadly.

Such a study might uncover a group of apolitical preachers who cared for their flock on Sunday, 8 April 1917—the Sunday after Congress declared war—much as they had done every Sunday before, a definable group who carried on preaching from the lectionary or followed their practice of *lectio continua* regardless of the distractions of war and politics. Perhaps they prayed with particular urgency for those in authority in a time of national crisis and met the extraordinary demands of a congregation whose sons had enlisted or would soon be drafted. But they never thought of displaying the Stars and Stripes on or in their churches and certainly not draped across their altars. They never included "The Star-Spangled Banner," "America," or "The Battle Hymn of the Republic" in their order of worship. Instead, they preached on the mission of the church and not the mission of America, took care not to confuse spiritual and physical warfare, and never thought of interpreting God's promises to Israel and to the church as if they were meant for the United States. If such a group could be found for the First World War and all the way back to the Revolutionary War and forward to the War on Terror, and that group turned out to be large, then the entire narrative of American religious history, especially of religion and war, would have to be retold.

BIBLIOGRAPHY

Primary Sources

NEWSPAPERS

The Christian Advocate, 1915.
Christian Workers Magazine, 1917.
Every Week, 1916.
Literary Digest, 1917.
The New York Times, 1915, 1917.
Outlook, 1917.
The Pacific, 1916.
The Sabbath Recorder, 1917.

OTHER

Barton, Bruce F. *The Man Nobody Knows: A Discovery of the Real Jesus*. Indianapolis: Bobbs-Merrill, 1925.
New York Legislative Documents, One Hundred and Forty-Fourth Session, 1921. Vol. 20, no. 50, part 4. Albany: J. B. Lyon, 1921.
"Putnam, George Haven." In *National Cyclopedia of American Biography*, 2:389. New York: James T. White, 1921.

Secondary Sources

Abrams, Ray H. *Preachers Present Arms*. New York: Round Table, 1933.
Du Bois, W. E. B. *The Souls of Black Folk*. 1903. Reprint, Rockville, MD: Arc Manor, 2008.
Gamble, Richard M. *The War for Righteousness: The Progressive Clergy, the Great War, and the Rise of Messianic Nationalism*. Wilmington, DE: ISI, 2003.
Hart, D. G. *The Lost Soul of American Protestantism*. Lanham, MD: Rowman & Littlefield, 2002.

Haselby, Sam. *The Origins of American Religious Nationalism*. New York: Oxford University Press, 2015.

Kleppner, Paul. *The Cross of Culture: A Social Analysis of Midwestern Politics, 1850–1900*. New York: The Free Press, 1970.

Luebke, Frederick C. *Bonds of Loyalty: German-Americans and World War I*. DeKalb, IL: Northern Illinois University Press, 1974.

Marsden, George M. *Fundamentalism and American Culture: The Shaping of Twentieth-Century Evangelicalism: 1870–1925*. New York: Oxford University Press, 1980.

Mott, Frank Luther. *A History of American Magazines: 1865–1885*. Cambridge, MA: Harvard University Press, 1938.

3

The First World War and Catholics in the United States

Patrick Carey

Between the outbreak of the European war in 1914 and President Woodrow Wilson's congressionally approved declaration of war on 6 April 1917, Catholics, like others in the United States, supported American neutrality with respect to the war. That American Catholic neutrality existed alongside of Irish and German Catholic opposition to the British and Allied war against Germany. With the declaration of war, Catholic neutrality to the war disappeared almost overnight. Catholics began immediately to mobilize efforts in favor of war with very little, if any, organized resistance. After the Armistice of 11 November 1918, the Catholic institutions created during the war continued and initiated post-war programs for social reconstruction.[1] This chapter outlines Catholic responses to the war during these three distinct periods and argues that the new Catholic institutions created during the war had a long-lasting influence upon the development of Catholic life in the United States. The war brought the Catholic Church in the United States into a much more active engagement with American public life than had been common or possible in the nineteenth century.

---

1. The following are some of the best studies on Catholics during and immediately after the war: McKeown, *War and Welfare*; Kauffman, *Faith and Fraternalism*, 190–227; Slawson, *Foundation and First Decade*, 36–85.

AMERICAN CATHOLICS IN 1917

Between 1914 and 1919, American Catholics represented about 17 percent (about 15 or 16 million) of the total American population.[2] It is difficult, if not impossible, to generalize about the attitudes and positions of such a large population because of the absence of any polling data and the lack of sufficient historical studies. What we can say comes mostly from the articulated positions of clerical leaders, intellectuals, journalists, and newspaper editors. Some generalizations, however, can be made about the Catholic population. American Catholicism was multi-ethnic. These ethnic (non-British) Catholics, particularly prior to the American declaration of war, had loyalties to the United States that were conditioned by loyalties to their homelands (whether Ireland, Germany, Austria, Belgium, Poland, Italy, or France) and to the transnational character of the Catholic Church (and to the peace pronouncements of Pope Benedict XV), and by hostilities from the early twentieth-century virulent forms of nativism in the Ku Klux Klan and in journals like the *Menace* that operated somewhat on the fringes of American society.

INITIAL CATHOLIC RESPONSE TO THE WAR

From the beginning of the European War until the Armistice in 1918, some Catholics denounced the horrors of war and its causes. The Louisville-based *Record* declared in 1914 that war "eats at the entrails of modern society" and stems from a lack of mutual charity, contempt for authority (especially divine authority), injustice in the relations of social classes, and the modern desire for the continuous seeking of wealth as the highest human achievement.[3] The editor was echoing Pope Benedict XV whose encyclical *Ad beatissimi apostolorum* (1 November 1914) decried the fact that the combatants came from the "greatest and wealthiest nations of the earth" and because of their wealth and modern military science they were able to devise the "most awful weapons . . . to destroy one another with refinements of horror." The Pope, too, cited four fundamental causes of war.

---

2. Finke and Stark, *Churching of America*, 113, calculated that American Catholics represented about 17 percent (14 million) of the American population in 1906 and thereafter represented about 16 percent up to 1926. Shaughnessy, *Has the Immigrant Kept the Faith*, 172–82, estimated that the Catholic population in 1910 was 16 million (about 19 percent of the American population) and by 1920 had increased to 19 million (about 20 percent of the total population). The more conservative estimate is used in this chapter.

3. As quoted in Crews, *American Holy Land*, 228.

"Thus we see the absence from the relations of men of mutual love with their fellow men; the authority of rulers is held in contempt; injustice reigns in relations between the classes of society; the striving for transient and perishable things is so keen, that men have lost sight of the other and more worthy goods they have to obtain."[4] After the Armistice, Father Francis Patrick Duffy, perhaps the most famous and celebrated American chaplain in the war, wrote of "this rotten business of war." Five years after the Armistice, moreover, he looked back upon his army experience and told an audience: "War is something so opposed to God! It is so full of the Satanic. . . . Most men have seen in war-experience nothing but evil in its nakedness. . . . Forever stand these words which Dante placed over the entrance to Hell—'All hope abandon, ye who enter here.'"[5] Even most of those patriotic episcopal and clerical leaders who supported the war after the American declaration saw war as a necessary evil, even when it was conducted for a good and just cause.

During the period of American neutrality Catholics were divided in their responses to the Great War.[6] The United States government was officially neutral and President Wilson had campaigned during 1916 by crediting himself for keeping the country out of war. Most American Catholics supported the government's neutrality even though they differed among themselves on their European loyalties during the war. As Leslie Woodcock Tentler has shown with respect to the diocese of Detroit, German and Irish Catholics were able in 1914 to support the Central Powers and saw no conflict with their Americanism. The same was true with respect to French, Belgian and Polish Catholics in their support for the Allies.[7] What was true in Detroit was also evident with some variations in other parts of the country. Hyphenated American Catholics were not 100 percent Americans during the period, and they were severely criticized for their lack of enthusiastic support for all things American by editors of the anti-Catholic press; even former President Theodore Roosevelt and President Woodrow

---

4. Benedict XV, *Ad beatissimi apostolorum*, 144.

5. Duffy and Kilmer, *Father Duffy's Story*, 311; quotations also in Flick, *Chaplain Duffy*, 84–85, and Abrams, *Preachers Present Arms*, 236.

6. Historians differ in their interpretations of what constituted that diversity of opinion in Catholic journals and newspapers. For instance, see Esslinger, "American German and Irish Attitudes"; Cuddy, "Pro-Germanism and American Catholicism"; O'Keefe, "America, the Ave Maria, and the Catholic World Respond."

7. Tentler, *Seasons of Grace*, 278.

Wilson periodically admonished those Catholics who favored the Central Powers.[8]

The German Central Verein, originating in 1855 as a well-organized expression of German-American Catholicism, had become by the early twentieth century a voice for German Catholic concerns. When the war broke out in 1914, the Central Verein acknowledged the American Catholic Germans' alliance with "our ethnic kindred" and criticized, as had also a number of Irish-edited periodicals and newspapers, the "anti-German tone of the Anglo-American Press."[9] St. Louis's Philip Kenkel, editor of *Die Amerika*, was "avidly pro-German." Not all Americans of German decent, of course, were pro-German in respect to the war. Most bishops of German decent, well aware of the multi-ethnic character of their dioceses, remained publicly silent on their attitudes to the European war, overtly maintaining American neutrality until the declaration of war. The third-generation German archbishop of Chicago, George Mundelein, was less enthusiastic about things German than his mid-western German-American episcopal compatriots.

Arthur Preuss, a second-generation St. Louis German American and editor of the *Fortnightly Review*, wrote repeatedly in favor of American neutrality, against what he considered to be the pro-British sympathies of a majority of Americans and against the one-sided interpretations of the inhumanity of Germany's conduct in the war. War always brought cruelties and wanton destruction by combatants on all sides. It was the system that was wrong-headed and out of touch with the demands of Christianity. The very fact that neither side in the war listened to Pope Benedict XV's forty or more appeals for peace demonstrated to Preuss, as it did to others, that a Christian sentiment could not prevail in the context of the current war. Preuss, like almost all other Catholic opinion-makers of the period, supported the just war tradition. He was no pacifist but he found it difficult to reconcile his faith with the partisan cries for war and for the military defeat of one's enemy. War was almost always a manifestation of human infidelity to God; greed and materialism were contributing causes of war. Ultimately, however, wars became divinely permitted scourges and punishments for general human sinfulness and not just the sinfulness of the belligerents.[10]

---

8. Gleason, *Conservative Reformers*, 159, 164.

9. Quoted in ibid., 157–58; see also 159–71 for other pro-German acts during the period of neutrality.

10. For Preuss on the war, see Conley, *Arthur Preuss*, 167–72.

Preuss, like only a few others, aligned himself with the German-American community but he was less pro-German during the period of neutrality than many of his mid-western compatriots.

Leadership in the Irish American Catholic community was also somewhat divided in its support for the European war during neutrality. For the same reasons as their German-American fellow bishops, Irish Catholic bishops were for the most part silent about their personal sympathies with the European combatants. The Irish American Catholic press was not as quiet as their bishops with respect to the war. Many in the press were particularly critical of the Allied forces and some outrightly favored the German and Austrian-Hungarian league.[11] In the view of some Irish, Germany and Austria-Hungary had supported Catholicism, England had oppressed it, and France's government had been particularly anti-clerical and hostile to the Church. In 1915, the *Ecclesiastical Review* published a particularly hard-hitting anti-British diatribe by Edward Thomas O'Dwyer, the bishop of Limerick. O'Dwyer called upon the neutral countries to support the Pope's peace messages and argued that England's national hatred for Germany prevented the Pope's message from getting a fair hearing, and in fact many of the leading English journals shaping public opinion interpreted the Pope's calls for peace as a subterfuge for his support and sympathy for Germany and Austria.[12] The anti-British rhetoric increased dramatically after the Dublin Easter Uprising in April 1916 and especially after the British government's executions of the ringleaders of the rebellion. The Irish resentment toward England on both sides of the Atlantic was also tied to the British government's war-time support for the self-determination of small nations like Belgium and Poland and its delay of Irish Home Rule and emancipation.[13] Even after the American declaration of war against Germany, Irish Catholic clerics who supported the American entry into the war found it difficult to justify England's resistance to Irish Emancipation. One priest, William A. Keefe, in a flag-raising ceremony at St. Francis Xavier Church in Waterbury, Connecticut, shortly after the declaration of war, told his Catholic audience: "Let no man question our [Catholic] loyalty to America when we demand that England now practice what she

11. In their opposition to the Allied forces, American Irish differed considerably from Canadian Irish who supported the British Empire. See, McGowan, "We are all involved."

12. Edward Thomas O'Dwyer, "The Pope's Plea for Peace," *Ecclesiastical Review* 3, no. 6, 1915, 629–36.

13. On Irish–American opinion after the Easter Rebellion, see Wiel, *Catholic Church in Ireland*, 240–46.

preaches by granting now to heart-broken, down-trodden Ireland—the land of our forefathers—the same 'right of self-determination and home rule' that Woodrow Wilson and Lloyd George demand for Poland and Belgium and Serbia."[14] Hostility toward England was pronounced in a number of American Catholic newspapers and journals, but a few, like the *Catholic World*, whose editor was Irish American, were decidedly pro-British during neutrality and thereafter.

CATHOLIC RESPONSE AFTER THE DECLARATION OF WAR

The period of American neutrality ended on 6 April 1917 when the United States declared war on Germany. The declaration, however, came as no surprise to most observers, because the Wilson administration had been preparing for war for over a year. President Wilson outlined the multiple reasons for going to war in his 2 April 1917 War Message to Congress. Because of the unprincipled and ruthless submarine warfare, the sinking of American ships and killing of United States citizens, and, among other reasons, German espionage attempts, Wilson asserted that neutrality was no longer feasible or desirable. The United States, he emphasized, had no quarrel with the German people, but only with their government. The United States was not seeking revenge or material gain or conquest or dominion; it was seeking peace, justice, and freedom. The country was going to war to make the world safe for democracy, for freedom, and for the right, which was more precious than peace. The lofty reasons for going to war would be repeated frequently by the American Catholic episcopate, priesthood, and laity, as was evident in *War Addresses from Catholic Pulpit and Platform*, the first address of which was Wilson's War Message, which the editor entitled "Why We Went to War." Almost immediately after the declaration, American Catholic leadership endorsed the war and began to mobilize Catholic efforts in support of it—leaving behind former hostilities to the Entente Powers and, to some extent, the papal exhortations to peace (although they tried to reconcile the papal declarations with the "right reasons" for going to war).

On 5 April 1917, three days after the War Message and a day before the declaration of war, James Gibbons, the octogenarian cardinal archbishop of Baltimore and the leading national Catholic spokesman, released a

---

14. Keefe, "Unfurling of Service Flag at St. Francis Xavier's Church, Waterbury," 236.

statement to the press calling upon all Americans to do their civic duty and support the president and Congress. He emphasized the need for "absolute and unreserved obedience" to the country's call to war. What Congress decided, he admonished, "should be unequivocally complied with" because Congress was the instrument of God in guiding Americans in their civic duties.[15]

Cardinal Gibbons met with the fourteen archbishops of the United States on 18 April 1917, and together they drafted a letter of support to President Wilson, promising "our most sacred and sincere loyalty and patriotism."[16] Wishing that the country could have been spared war, they nonetheless accepted the legislative declaration of war and bowed in obedience to "bear our part in it with fidelity, with courage and with the spirit of sacrifice" that was required by loyal citizens. They pledged, too, that they and all American Catholics would "cooperate in every way possible with our President and our national government, to the end that the great and holy cause of liberty may triumph. . . . Our people, as ever, will rise as one man to serve the nation." Such was the beginning of a constant stream of patriotic rhetoric during and after the war years.

American Catholic leaders were adamant in their patriotic rhetoric during the war and after the war they saw to it that their witnesses to patriotism were published in *War Addresses*, a collection of talks given by sixteen bishops from all geographical areas of the country, twenty-four priests from various parishes, and two laymen. The publication was part of a long-standing attempt to defend Catholic patriotism, expressions of which ranged from the unnuanced to the discriminating. Most addresses appealed to American Catholics to do their civic duty, to sacrifice freely for the common good, and to join with all other Americans in the pursuit of justice, peace, and democracy. Patriotism, as bishop Charles Warren Currier told his Catholic audience, knew no religious or racial (i.e., German or British) lines. All Americans were in the war for a common purpose.[17] Cardinal John Farley of New York spoke of "America's Duty in the World War" and asserted that Catholics owed "unswerving allegiance to the American government." Catholics ought to obey the laws because they were founded "in the natural and divine law." Nonetheless, he cautioned, in civil matters one owed obedience to the laws "provided his lawgivers do not contravene

15. Quoted in Ellis, *Life of James Cardinal Gibbons*, 2:239.
16. Letter published in Williams, *American Catholics in the War*, 3–5.
17. Currier, "Sermon Delivered at Field Mass," 121.

the laws of God."[18] Many of the patriotic speeches invoked support for the war even though many realized that even a just war was inherently tragic or a necessary evil to ensure eventual justice and peace.

Bishop John Glennon of St. Louis made it clear to his mixed Irish and German audience that the war was a struggle over principle, not over race (German versus Anglo-Saxon supremacy) or language.[19] The war rhetoric, however, could at times lose balance as it did when Father James J. Dean in Philadelphia asserted that "we are now fighting in the holiest cause the world has known since the first Crusade; fighting, not for glory nor for empire, but fighting for justice and humanity."[20] Another priest, Edward Flannery, gave his religious interpretation of the war, asserting that "God is behind the strife, purifying the race to Himself to make His subjects a royal type and a priestly people."[21]

Eleven of the patriotic *War Addresses* took place at flag-raising events that parishes sponsored to honor the soldiers and to raise funds for the war. All members of the local communities were evidently invited to take part in these flag-raising events and to listen to the discourses of parish pastors or prominent Catholic laypeople. General as well as diocesan histories of American Catholicism pay no attention to these parish flag-raising ceremonies.

In their patriotic addresses and support for the war, many bishops and priests had to try to reconcile that support with Pope Benedict's repeated calls for arbitration and peace. Shortly after the United States declared war, the Pope issued his seven-point plan for peace in an apostolic exhortation addressed to the heads of the belligerent peoples.[22] Cardinal Farley of New York, for example, like many other bishops, defended the Pope's calls for peace and countered press reports and some politicians' claims that the Pope's peace overtures favored Germany and Austria. The Pope was the spiritual father of all his children, Farley argued, and therefore could not side with any of the belligerents. He wanted arbitration to end the war not military conquests. Farley then went on to say that, like the Pope, he favored peace, but he supported the war because "the higher principles of

18. Farley, "America's Duty in the World War," 11.
19. Glennon, "Discourse Delivered at a Military Solemn High Mass," 65.
20. Dean, "Solemn Military Mass," 200.
21. Flannery, "The Value of Sacrifice," 206. See also Farley, "America's Duty in the World War," 19; Keefe, "Unfurling the Service Flag," 236.
22. Benedict XV, *Dès le début*.

international justice [had] to be considered."[23] Even the very ultramontane cardinal archbishop of Boston, William O'Connell, was able to reconcile his patriotic support for war with the Pope's calls for peace. After President Wilson proclaimed 13 May 1918 a day of public humiliation, prayer and fasting, O'Connell declared that "the spirit of God is working in Woodrow Wilson" and connected Wilson's statement with the Pope's advocacy of peace.

> I am proud and happy as a Catholic to be able to join these two influences together. There is the influence of the Holy Father who is constantly pleading for peace... but he remains impartial towards all the world and asks God to grant peace to the sufferers.... But as an American, our President stands by his side... But both stand there on the same dais, and well may the Holy Father say from the bottom of his heart: God bless the President of a country who can make a statement so sublime, so profound, so true, so religious and so eminently Catholic as that, as the leader of a people who if they will pray to God in that spirit can never fail.[24]

Cardinal Gibbons, too, found disconcerting the opposition and biased interpretations of the Pope's peace proposals, and wrote a major statement on the Pope's war policy addressed to the tolerant and fair-minded democratic peoples of the United States. He, too, reconciled American Catholic spiritual loyalty to the Pope and their temporal loyalty to the President.[25]

These bishops and others who supported Pope and President were able to do so because they distinguished between the Pope's spiritual and the President's civic authority. Their powers paralleled one another and both ultimately came from God. A later generation of Catholics would find this interpretation of church-state relations a bit too comfortable and accommodating. But the later generation of Catholics, living in a more ecumenical age, did not always have to defend their patriotism and loyalty to the

---

23. Farley, "America's Duty in the World War," 19.

24. O'Connell, "Address at State Convention of the Knights of Columbus," 33, or other episcopal attempts to reconcile Pope and President. See Carroll, "Christianity and the War," 98; Currier, "Sermon Delivered at Field Mass," 123; Robison, "Patriotic Address," 271.

25. James Cardinal Gibbons, "The War Policy of the Pope," *America*, 23 Feb, 1918, 487–88. See also the non-Catholic George Harvey, "The Hun and the Pope," *North American Review's War Weekly*, 21 September, 1918, 12–13, where he argued that the Pope was not pro-German and that his actual statements ought to be fairly and favorably interpreted.

country. The bishops' patriotism came perilously close to what Columbia University's historian Carlton J. H. Hayes, a Catholic, called "nationalism." In fact, Hayes argued that one of the first effects of the Great War was the growth of the principle of nationalism, or what he referred to as the "flood tide" of nationalism. In 1926, Hayes accused American Catholic bishops and priests of preaching a "very intense nationalism," asserting that they did so as a defense mechanism. Nationalism, as Hayes understood it, was the promotion of "supreme loyalty" to national states, a loyalty that fostered exclusivity. As such, nationalism was something new, having its origins in the eighteenth century and increasing since then and particularly during the Great War.[26] Although the American Catholic clergy came very close to Hayes's nationalism, they never fully identified themselves with the exclusiveness characteristic of what he meant by the term.

The patriotic fervor in the United States drew large numbers of Catholic young men to the armed services. New York's Fighting Sixty-Ninth, a predominantly Irish and Catholic regiment with Father Duffy as its chaplain, was among the first regiments sent to France, leaving New York on 25 October 1917, arriving in Le Havre on 15 November 1917, and fighting in the trenches by March 1918. It is difficult to determine precisely how many Catholics went to war. During the war most Catholic leaders estimated that about 30 percent of the army and as high as 50 percent of the navy were Catholic. The bishops' and clergy's *War Addresses* in particular regularly asserted that Catholic participation in the war far exceeded their proportionate numbers in the general population. The very high estimates seem to have their source in Secretary of War Newton Baker's 22 September 1917 report indicating that "the Catholic denomination . . . will constitute perhaps thirty-five percent of the new army."[27] A fairer estimate might be that Catholics represented about 17.6 percent of the armed services—that was at least the percent of the funds of the United War Work Campaign allotted to the National Catholic War Council (NCWC).[28] American Catholic participation in the war was substantial (between 800,000 and one million

---

26. Hayes, *Brief History of the Great War*, 396; Hayes, *Essays on Nationalism*, 59, 61, 76, 245.

27. Williams, *American Catholics in the War*, 90; see also 86, 207, 476. Hutchinson, "Service Flag Address," 217.

28. The United War Work Campaign was a national fund drive to support all the welfare organizations (including also the YMCA, YWCA, NCWC, Jewish Welfare Board, War Camp Community Service, American Library Association, and the Salvation Army) that served during the war.

in the armed services) even though some estimates of that participation were excessive during and immediately after the war. That participation was at least proportionate to the Catholic percentage of the American population. The war-time Catholic preoccupation with numbers intended to demonstrate patriotism in the face of charges of divided allegiance. But the numbers involved also raised the need for massive mobilization of Catholic efforts to serve the social and spiritual welfare of those Catholics in the army and navy.

Two major themes run throughout the Catholic literature during and immediately after the war: patriotism and ministry to the troops. One can find isolated pacifists and warmongers, but for the most part Catholic leaders did not curse war or the enemy but focused on ministry to the troops.[29] After the declaration of war, Catholics organized institutionally to coordinate efforts to meet the material and spiritual needs of the troops. As odd as it might seem to the present generation, the American Catholic Church was not well organized in 1917 for any concerted joint national action. Since 1890 the archbishops of the country had been meeting annually, but those meetings had very little effect on the national church or on public life. In 1900, hundreds of Catholic lay fraternal and ethnic benevolent societies had organized the American Federation of Catholic Societies (AFCS) to present a unified Catholic voice on various public issues and to disseminate Catholic social and moral teachings. The AFCS, however, was internally divided and lacked the unanimous support of the hierarchy. By the beginning of the war it was in no condition to meet the needs of Catholics in the war.

The need for a cooperative national Catholic response to the war was met by the Knights of Columbus, the NCWC, and the Chaplain's Aid Association. The Knights, a fraternal and benevolent lay Catholic society formed in 1882, had over 400,000 members at the beginning of the war. The Knights were the only lay Catholic society with the experience and resources to aid the troops in 1917. Like the YMCA, the Knights had experience in 1916 providing American troops on the Mexican border with recreation halls and opportunities for spiritual and sacramental services. After the war declaration, the Knights supplied the same services to the preparatory war camps in the United States and to the troops once they landed in Europe. On 21 June 1917 the Secretary of War officially recognized the Knights as a government-approved Catholic institution cooperating with the government in aiding the troops. As such it had the same government-approved

---

29. Piper, *American Churches in World War I*, 11.

status as had been earlier granted to the YMCA, which was primarily a Protestant institution serving the troops. The Knights raised at least 14 million dollars on their own and received from the government-sponsored war fund drive another 25 million. Those resources helped the Knights establish about 360 recreation centers in the United States and an equal number in Europe, staffed by about 2000 paid secretaries and 27,000 volunteers. The Knights served Catholic soldiers but also all other troops "regardless of creed," as the Knights informed President Wilson in their letter of 23 May 1917. Signs posted over the recreation centers read "All Welcome," and "Everything Free."[30]

THE NATIONAL CATHOLIC WAR COUNCIL

The most significant and long-lasting of the institutions that came out of the war was the National Catholic War Council. In 1917, no Catholic institution in the country was organized to coordinate all the Catholic efforts in response to the war. In June 1917, in response to this perceived need, Father John J. Burke, the Paulist editor of the *Catholic World* and the founder of the Chaplains' Aid Association, met in New York with other socially-minded Catholics to suggest a national organization to coordinate various Catholic efforts in support of the troops and to align them with those of the government and other religious and secular societies. After the meeting Burke presented the idea of a national Catholic organization to Cardinal Gibbons. Gibbons accepted the concept and asked Burke to consult with Cardinals William O'Connell of Boston and John Farley of New York. When they agreed to the advice, the three cardinals asked Burke to send a letter to all the bishops in the country seeking their support for the proposal and asking them to send one cleric and one lay person to a meeting in Washington, DC, whose purpose would be to construct an agreed-upon national plan to coordinate Catholic efforts.

A majority of bishops approved the proposal, and Burke invited members of various Catholic societies and the Catholic press, as well as representatives from the various dioceses, to an August 1917 meeting in Washington. At that meeting the members (representative delegates from 68 of the 100 dioceses, from 27 national Catholic organizations, and from the Catholic press) eventually developed a plan for what was called the

---

30. Kauffman, *Faith and Fraternalism*, 190–227, especially 190, 222.

National Catholic War Council. The meeting voted unanimously to establish the national institution and to begin meeting the needs of the troops.[31]

The NCWC was eventually organized into seven standing committees or departments under the umbrella of a Special War Activities Committee. Burke became the general chairman and eventually general secretary of the NCWC. The names of the seven departments (Finance, Women's Activities, Men's Activities, Chaplains' Aid Association, Catholic Interests, Post-war Reconstruction, and Historical Records) indicated something of the functions that the NCWC would play over the three years (1917–20) of its operations. The departments were chaired by prominent Catholics and advised by a few well-known clerical professors at the Catholic University of America (such as William Kerby, John A. Ryan, John O'Grady, John Montgomery Cooper, Edward Pace, and Peter Guilday).

Under Burke's leadership the NCWC communicated and cooperated with the Secretary of War. In November 1918, the NCWC received official government recognition as a cooperating agency representing the American Catholic Church. The NCWC's secretary also cooperated with other religious and social institutions involved in assisting the troops. In fact, he helped form the ecumenical "Committee of Six" (John R. Mott of the YMCA, Bishop James DeWolf Perry of the Episcopal Church, Dr. Robert E. Speer and Dr. William Adams Brown of the Federal Council of Churches, and Colonel Harry Cutler, head of the Jewish War Commission) to advise the Secretary of War on issues related to the social and spiritual needs of the troops.

Originally the NCWC was a voluntary service institution, approved by the bishops but not directly administered by the national bishops. Since the NCWC was responsible for the spiritual as well as material needs and involved chaplain services, Cardinal Gibbons and some other bishops thought that the institution should come under the administrative direction of the national episcopate. Consequently, Gibbons wrote the nation's bishops in November seeking their approval for putting the Council under an Administrative Committee of four bishops. With the majority of bishops approving, the NCWC, under this episcopal sponsorship, remained a purely voluntary, not a canonical, institution. On 16 January 1918, Burke, as the general secretary, met with the Administrative Committee (Bishops Patrick Muldoon of Rockford, Joseph Schrembs of Toledo, William Russell of Charleston, and Patrick Hayes, auxiliary of New York) to make plans

---

31. Williams, *American Catholics in the War*, 135–36.

for the day-to-day operations in Washington, allowing the Knights of Columbus to continue freely their social services under the supervision of the bishops and leaving the Special War Activities Committee to coordinate other dimensions of the Catholic contribution to the war. From the spring of 1918 until 1920 the NCWC functioned as the national clearing house for these contributions.

The NCWC became the primary national episcopal organization to coordinate the war-time efforts of Catholics. Individual bishops and clergy also supported the war in various ways. They participated and helped organize liberty loan drives, encouraged fasting during Lent and the creation of home gardens as means of conserving food, helped recruit young men into the armed services, and organized campaigns to supply the troops with spiritual reading materials and other religious items: New Testaments, *The Imitation of Christ*, Gibbons' *Faith of Our Fathers*, rosaries, scapulars, holy pictures, and religious medals.

CATHOLIC CHAPLAINS

Developing structures for recruiting, appointing, and supplying religious aids for military chaplains happened rather quickly after the declaration of war. Before the war there were only twenty-four Catholic chaplains in the army and four in the navy. In April 1917, Burke organized the Chaplains' Aid Association in New York to supply chaplains with the materials they needed to conduct their services for the troops. In November 1917, Pope Benedict XV appointed Patrick J. Hayes, auxiliary bishop of New York, as extraordinary bishop (Chaplain Bishop) for the armed services, a new institution that has continued into the present as the Archdiocese for the Military, located in Washington, DC. By the end of the war, 1525 chaplains were serving the troops overseas and a number of diocesan priests had ministered as chaplains in the war preparation camps in the United States.[32]

In April 1918, Bishop Hayes sent a circular letter to all military chaplains outlining the virtues of those who served in "dangerous and heroic circumstances." The chaplain, he wrote, needed to be a person of a "marked spiritual life" for the effectiveness of his ministry and for the "safety of his own soul." Modern warfare demanded military leaders of extraordinary courage and endurance; the chaplain needed to match that kind of leadership by developing his own superior strength and spirituality of character.

32. Sheerin, *Never Look Back*, 38. Waring, *United States Catholic Chaplains*, xv, 347–51, counts 1023 chaplains serving by 11 November 1918.

He had to be an exemplary dispenser of the mysteries of God, especially for those who were "ever on the brink of eternity."[33]

The chaplains' roles in the military were described in three major primary sources, Michael Williams's "Our Chaplains at Home and Abroad," the largest chapter in his *American Catholics in the War*, George J. Waring's *United States Catholic Chaplains*, and *Father Duffy's Story*, authored by Father Francis Patrick Duffy.[34] Williams's chapter published letters from more than twenty chaplains detailing their ministry to the troops and reporting on events during the war. Waring's account is a statistical analysis of chaplains. *Father Duffy's Story*, a series of unrelated portraits of soldiers and military life on the front lines, was intended to depict the sacrifices, dedication, and religious life of the troops Duffy served. Duffy's sometimes-witty account appears to be based on a daily diary he kept during the war.

Letters from chaplains and accounts in *Father Duffy's Story* emphasized the sacramental ministry to the troops and underlined the soldiers' faithfulness to their religious practices. The sacrament of penance was a major part of their sacramental life. Chaplains reported that they heard confessions for hours with soldiers in queue for blocks. Confessions took place in the open on board ships, in town squares in France, and wherever soldiers were congregating prior to battle. Those about to face death in the trenches readily came to confession and, when no priests were available in some regiments, the soldiers asked their commanders to send them priests for confessions. French citizens were amazed, as Duffy reports, that the American soldiers stood in line for hours in the public squares while he heard their confessions in the open air. Before battles, too, when there was no time to hear the confessions of all, Duffy asked those attending his prayer services to repent of their sins and gave them general absolution, a practice allowed in canon law. At Christmas and Easter so many soldiers wanted to go to confession that Duffy had to get French priests to assist him. After one Christmas celebration, Duffy asked a soldier how he liked going to confession to a priest who could not speak English. The soldier responded, "Fine, Father. All he could do was give me a penance, but you'd have given me hell."[35]

---

33. Williams, *American Catholics in the War*, 241–42.

34. Ibid., 235–88; see also 289–301.

35. On confessional practices, see Duffy and Kilmer, *Father Duffy's Story*, 47, 109, 146; Williams, *American Catholics in the War*, 250–51, 255, 258–59, 260, 271, for example.

The celebration of Mass, too, was often in the open air or on the front steps of bombed-out French churches.[36] Thousands of troops attended these services and received communion, especially at Christmas and Easter and St. Patrick's Day. Catholic chaplains also held prayer services for those who were not Catholic, comforted the wounded, gave the last rites to the many who were dying, buried the dead, and wrote thousands of painful letters to the parents and wives of the soldiers who died in their company. One chaplain, Paul Bethel, emphasizing the soldiers' faithfulness to their sacramental practices, gave a statistical report on the ministerial services he provided for the month of February 1919:

Sunday Masses in camp	40
Average Attendance	700
Communions	3800
Confessions	4500
Daily masses	150
Average attendance of daily masses	100
Religious articles distributed	Testaments: 500 Rosaries: 2000 Scapulars: 1000 Prayer Books: 500

Catholic sacramental practices were very public. The visible display of Catholicism seemed to bother no one in the army or navy. In fact, according to Duffy, "the average American likes to see a man practice his religion, whatever it may be."[37]

An ecumenical spirit pervades *Father Duffy's Story*. He asserted that cooperation existed among the various denominational ministers and that "their fundamental interests are absolutely in common" in the face of war and death. He told an Episcopal bishop "that the way the Clergy of different churches got along together in peace and harmony in this Division would be a scandal to pious minds." Ecumenical cooperation during wartime ministry was another recurring theme for Duffy and other Catholic chaplains.[38]

36. Duffy and Kilmer, *Father Duffy's Story*, 82–84.
37. Ibid., 100–101, 230.
38. "Father Duffy's Own Story of the Exploits of the 69th," *New York Tribune*, 30 April

After the Armistice was signed in November 1918, the troops began coming home to celebrate the end of the war. When the Fighting 69th returned to New York City in April 1919, for example, the mayor honored the troops with a gala dinner, followed the day after by a parade up Fifth Avenue. Father Duffy was among those who celebrated and the day after the parade he gave an address on the war at Carnegie Hall, filled to capacity by soldiers and citizens who greeted his talk with loud applause as the newspapers indicated. After Duffy died his friends placed a statue of the famous war-time chaplain in Times Square, where it resides today.[39]

EFFECTS OF THE WAR ON AMERICAN CATHOLICS

The war had some long-standing consequences for American Catholics. The growth of nationalism, identifying transcendental values with national goals, as Hayes noted, resulted from the war and it continued to develop after the war, influencing, with a few exceptions, American Catholics during the next two major wars. German Catholic culture suffered most during the war. Even before the war Americanized Germans were gradually losing their language, but the war hastened that process and with the loss of language came a gradual decline in things German. The ecumenical and cooperative spirit that chaplains noted during the war also disappeared rapidly after the war, as had happened after previous wars.

A period of social reconstruction, already envisioned at the beginning of the war, began even before many troops had returned home. The NCWC's Administrative Committee, for example, published what was called the Bishops' Program of Social Reconstruction (February 1919), a document prepared originally by the moral theologian John A. Ryan. The controversial document proposed a number of progressive social and economic reforms to meet the needs of the post-war world. It called for, among other things, social legislation to secure a living wage, just working conditions and hours, social security programs, unemployment insurance, equal pay for women for equal work, and other specific economic reforms.[40]

1919, 3; "Men in 69th Prayed Nearly Every Night," *New York Times*, 30 April 1919, 7; Williams, *American Catholics in the War*, 261, 266.

39. Duffy and Kilmer, *Father Duffy's Story*, 329; "City Dines Old 69th in Regiment's Home," *New York Times*, 27 April 1919, 12.

40. Ellis, *Documents of American Catholic History*, 2:589–607, 607–13. See also McShane, *Sufficiently Radical*.

Catholic participation in social reconstruction meant, as Catholic leaders contemplated, the continuation of some institution like the NCWC to represent Catholic interests before the government and before the American people. During the war ecclesiastical as well as governmental bureaucracies increased in number and in influence over all areas of American life. That development worried some Catholics. Others, more concerned about the increase of the federal government's powers, wanted to continue their nationally organized efforts to represent Catholic interests in national legislation and public life after the war. With this intention in mind, leaders in the NCWC created in September 1919 the National Catholic Welfare Council (later changed to Conference) to look after post-war Catholic interests, serve as a kind of watchdog over federal legislation, and articulate Catholic social teachings on a variety of public issues (such as education, economic justice, and citizenship).

The war had created multiple problems for those returning from service and the National Catholic Welfare Council/Conference encouraged Catholic institutions to develop programs to help the veterans. The Welfare Council urged Catholic hospitals to create, for the first time, outpatient clinics to provide assistance for the wounded soldiers, schools to develop educational programs for the returning troops, and employment training centers to prepare them for jobs. The Welfare Council also published citizenship pamphlets and established citizenship training programs for first generation immigrant soldiers and the new immigrants. With the support and encouragement of the Welfare Council, the Catholic University of America formed the National Catholic School for Social Services to provide women (primarily) with a scientific understanding of systematic social work. Catholic women had played a major role at home and abroad in providing assistance to soldiers during the war, and after the war many of them enrolled in the new school of social service to continue their post-war social work. Under the direction of the former War Council's historical records department, Michael Williams published an account of Catholic participation in the war as an explicit Catholic apologetic for patriotism. Parish and diocesan societies of women and men, which had been organized nationally under the War Council, continued to represent the voices of lay women and men in the post-war world through newly organized institutions: The National Council of Catholic Women and the National Council of Catholic Men.

The war brought Catholics out of their parishes and dioceses into the national arena where they could, for the first time, contribute as a group to the public welfare and develop national institutions that voiced Catholic concerns in the common life. The bishops in particular gained a national voice, and even though they were not always united on specific issues, they established a platform in Washington, DC that has continued on into the twenty-first century.

BIBLIOGRAPHY

Primary Sources

NEWSPAPERS

America, 1918.
Ecclesiastical Review, 1915.
New York Times, 1919.
New York Tribune, 1919.
North American Review's War Weekly, 1918.

OTHER

Benedict XV, Pope. "Ad beatissimi apostolorum." 1914. In *The Papal Encyclicals: 1903–1939.* Vol. 3, edited by Claudia Carlen, 143–51. Raleigh, NC: Pierian, 1990.

———. "*Dès le début*: Exhortation to the Belligerent Peoples and to Their Leaders" (1 August 1917). Apostolic Exhortation. http://w2.vatican.va/content/benedict-xv/fr/apost_exhortations/documents/hf_ben-xv_exh_19170801_des-le-debut.html.

Carroll, John P. (Bishop). "Christianity and the War." In *War Addresses from Catholic Pulpit and Platform*, edited by Joseph F. Wager, 93–105. New York: Joseph Wager, 1920.

Currier, Charles W. (Bishop). "Sermon Delivered at Field Mass." In *War Addresses from Catholic Pulpit and Platform*, edited by Joseph F. Wager, 121–27. New York: Joseph Wager, 1920.

Dean, James D. (Bishop). "Solemn Military Mass at Our Lady of Lourdes Church, Philadelphia, Pa." In *War Addresses from Catholic Pulpit and Platform*, edited by Joseph F. Wager, 194–202. New York: Joseph Wagner, 1920.

Duffy, Francis P., and Joyce Kilmer, *Father Duffy's Story: A Tale of Humor and Heroism, of Life and Death with the Fighting Sixty-Ninth.* New York: George H. Doran, 1919.

Farley, John Cardinal. "America's Duty in the World War." In *War Addresses from Catholic Pulpit and Platform*, edited by Joseph F. Wager, 11–21. New York: Joseph Wagner, 1920.

Flannery, Edward. "The Value of Sacrifice." In *War Addresses from Catholic Pulpit and Platform*, edited by Joseph F. Wager, 202–15. New York: Joseph Wagner, 1920.

Flick, Ella Mary Elizabeth. *Chaplain Duffy of the Sixty-Ninth Regiment, New York*. Philadelphia: Dolphin, 1935.

Glennon, John (Bishop). "Discourse Delivered at a Military Solemn High Mass, St. Louis, Mo." In *War Addresses from Catholic Pulpit and Platform*, edited by Joseph F. Wager, 64–68. New York: Joseph Wagner, 1920.

Hayes, Carlton J. H. *A Brief History of the Great War*. New York: Macmillan, 1920.

———. *Essays on Nationalism*. New York: Macmillan, 1926.

Hutchinson, David. "Service Flag Address, St. Patrick's Church, New Haven." In *War Addresses from Catholic Pulpit and Platform*, edited by Joseph F. Wager, 215–23. New York: Joseph Wagner, 1920.

Keefe, William A. "Unfurling of Service Flag at St. Francis Xavier's Church, Waterbury." In *War Addresses from Catholic Pulpit and Platform*, edited by Joseph F. Wager, 234–39. New York: Joseph Wagner, 1920.

O'Connell, William Cardinal. "Address at State Convention of the Knights of Columbus of Massachusetts." In *War Addresses from Catholic Pulpit and Platform*, edited by Joseph F. Wager, 28–34. New York: Joseph Wagner, 1920.

Robison, William F. "Patriotic Address at St. Leo's Flag Raising, St. Louis, Mo." In *War Addresses from Catholic Pulpit and Platform*, edited by Joseph F. Wager, 269–78. New York: Joseph Wagner, 1920.

Wagner, Joseph F., ed. *War Addresses from Catholic Pulpit and Platform*. New York: Joseph Wagner, 1920.

Waring, George J. *United States Catholic Chaplains in the World War*. New York: Ordinariate, 1924.

Williams, Michael. *American Catholics in the War: National Catholic War Council, 1917–1921*. New York: Macmillan, 1921.

Wilson Woodrow. "Why We Went to War." In *War Addresses from Catholic Pulpit and Platform*, 1–9. New York: Wagner, 1920.

Secondary Sources

Abrams, Ray H. *Preachers Present Arms: The Role of the American Churches and Clergy in World Wars I and II, with Some Observations on the War in Vietnam*. Scottdale, PA: Herald, 1969.

Conley, Rory T. *Arthur Preuss, Journalist and Voice of German and Conservative Catholics in America, 1871–1934*. New York: Peter Lang, 1998.

Crews, Clyde F. *An American Holy Land: A History of the Archdiocese of Louisville*. Louisville, KY: Ikonographies, 1990.

Cuddy, Edward. "Pro-Germanism and American Catholicism, 1914–1917." *The Catholic Historical Review* 54 (1968) 427–54.

Ellis, John Tracy, ed. *Documents of American Catholic History*. 2 vols. Milwaukee: Bruce, 1956.

———. *The Life of James Cardinal Gibbons: Archbishop of Baltimore, 1834–1921*. 2 vols. Milwaukee: Bruce, 1963.

Esslinger, Dean R. "American German and Irish Attitudes toward Neutrality, 1914–1917: A Study of Catholic Minorities." *The Catholic Historical Review* 53 (1967) 194–216.

Finke, Roger, and Rodney Stark. *The Churching of America, 1776–1990: Winners and Losers in Our Religious Economy*. New Brunswick, NJ: Rutgers University Press, 1992.

Gleason, Philip. *The Conservative Reformers: German-American Catholics and the Social Order*. Notre Dame: University of Notre Dame Press, 1968.

Kauffman, Christopher J. *Faith and Fraternalism: The History of the Knights of Columbus, 1882–1982*. New York: Harper & Row, 1982.

McGowan, Mark G. "'We are all involved in the same issue': Canada's English-Speaking Catholics and the Great War." In *Canadian Churches and the First World War*, edited by Gordon L. Heath, 34–74. Eugene, OR: Pickwick, 2014.

McKeown, Elizabeth. *War and Welfare: American Catholics and World War I*. New York: Garland, 1988.

McShane, Joseph Michael. *Sufficiently Radical: Catholicism, Progressivism, and the Bishops' Program of 1919*. Washington, DC: Catholic University of America Press, 1986.

O'Keefe, Thomas M. "America, the Ave Maria and the Catholic World Respond to the First World War, 1914–1917." *Records of the American Catholic Historical Society of Philadelphia* 94 (1983) 101–15.

Piper, John F. *The American Churches in World War I*. Athens, OH: Ohio University Press, 1985.

Shaughnessy, Gerald. *Has the Immigrant Kept the Faith?* New York: Arno, 1969.

Sheerin, John B. *Never Look Back: The Career and Concerns of John J. Burke*. New York: Paulist, 1975.

Slawson, Douglas J. *The Foundation and First Decade of the National Catholic Welfare Council*. Washington, DC: Catholic University of America Press, 1992.

Tentler, Leslie Woodcock. *Seasons of Grace: A History of the Catholic Archdiocese of Detroit*. Detroit: Wayne State University Press, 1990.

Wiel, Jérôme aan de. *The Catholic Church in Ireland, 1914–1918: War and Politics*. Dublin: Irish Academic, 2003.

4

American Lutherans and the First World War

Mark Granquist

AMERICAN LUTHERANISM WAS ANY number of different contradictions at the beginning of the First World War. It was a family of denominations, some of whose roots stretched back almost 300 years, while other church bodies were recently formed by the swelling tide of European immigrants. It was a large grouping of churches, by that time the fourth largest Protestant denominational family in the United States, yet its overall impact on American life was limited by Lutheran isolation, both geographically and linguistically. American Lutherans had been dealing with the challenges of the new American religious world for a long time, yet they were chiefly concerned with inter-Lutheran struggles and developments that had their origins in Europe. Although they were a large denominational family, they were divided into dozens of different denominational units, separated by language, theology, and geography. Lutherans were also divided generationally, with the older generation trying to hold back the rising tide of change and assimilation, while a newer Lutheran generation of "hyphenated Americans" sought to take full advantage of the new world of which they were now a part.

The First World War dramatically and quickly worked to change most of these contradictions, as the experiences of those years impelled a rapid rate of change within American Lutheranism. The most striking was the linguistic transition from the use of the European languages to English, which also meant that American Lutherans would become more fully engaged in the American religious world. War and nativist suspicions compelled American Lutherans to cooperate with each other, and to begin the long process of institutional re-arrangement and merger. The temporary cessation of immigration (made permanent in the 1920s), and a generational change in leadership, pushed Lutherans to become a truly American religious family. Additionally, the traumas visited on European Lutheranism because of the war thrust American Lutherans into new positions of leadership in world Lutheranism. It is not an overstatement to claim, as one American Lutheran historian has written, that "The years between 1915 and 1920, even between 1917 and 1920, constitute one of the most significant watersheds in Lutheran history in America. Theologically there was little change, but the self-awareness and spirit of the church has never been the same."[1] Simply put, the experiences and changes of the First World War defined and directed American Lutheranism for the century to come.[2]

AMERICAN LUTHERANS BEFORE THE FIRST WORLD WAR

By 1900 there were over 2.1 million baptized Lutherans on the rolls of American Lutheran congregations, and because of a flood of Lutheran immigrants (mainly from Scandinavia) and a high birth rate, the figure was certainly significantly higher by 1914, probably closer to 3 million. For American Lutheran leaders the key issue was finding enough pastors and forming enough congregations to reach out to this burgeoning population. The ethnic Lutheran denominations were always behind the curve on this trend; for a number of reasons the immigrant denominations were only able to formally enroll about 10 to 30 percent of the newcomers from Lutheran Europe.

Not all Lutheran denominations were recent developments; the eastern "Muhlenberg" Lutherans had been in America since the 1650s, and were thoroughly assimilated to the American situation. But even groups like this were deeply influenced (directly or indirectly) by the massive immigration of Europeans (Lutherans included) that stretched from the 1840s down to 1914. It is impossible to know exactly how many Lutherans came to the United States in those years, but more than a million Norwegians

---

1. Meuser, "Facing the Twentieth Century," 391.

2. For the general history of Lutherans in America, see Granquist, *Lutherans in America*; and Nelson, *Lutherans in North America*.

and 1.2 million Swedes arrived during that period of time, and almost all of them were at least nominally Lutheran. It is hard to know how many Lutherans came from Germany and the rest of Europe, but given the size of some of the German-ethnic Lutheran denominations in the United States at the time, an estimate of 5 to 6 million would not be out of line. The chief aim of most of the American Lutheran denominations was to reach out to these immigrants as quickly as possible.

The institutional "shape" of American Lutheranism at the time was akin to that of a barbell, with large significant clusters at each end, and smaller groups strung out across the middle. At one end were the descendants of the colonial (Muhlenberg) Lutherans; the General Synod, the General Council, and the United Synod South. Though those groups had long since acculturated to American life and (mostly) spoke English, their numbers, too, had swelled with the late nineteenth-century immigration. Those three groups united in a merger in 1918 to form the United Lutheran Church in America (ULCA), and collectively numbered about one million baptized members. At the other end of the spectrum were the members of the Synodical Conference, mainly the German Evangelical Lutheran Synod of Missouri (Missouri Synod) and a number of other, much smaller groups. Those groups were still ethnically and linguistically German, and together their baptized membership also numbered about a million. Between those two ends were about sixteen or eighteen different ethnic Lutheran denominations, mostly consisting of newer Lutheran immigrants from Germany and the Nordic countries. Those denominations were Swedish (1), Norwegian (5), German (5), Danish (2), Finnish (2), Icelandic (1), and Slovak (2), and almost all were still predominantly using their ethnic language for worship, preaching, and theology. Collectively they, too, numbered about a million baptized members. Some of these denominations in the "middle" were numerically substantial, while others contained only several thousand members each.

The divisions between those groups were legion, and too complicated to relate here in much detail. Suffice it to say that, in general, the divisions were caused by confessional Lutheran differences that they had brought with them from Europe, and which were exacerbated by the task of establishing their "vision" of Lutheranism within the American religious world. It was a world dominated by Reformed Protestantism, revivalism, and a voluntary religious context, all of which these Lutherans found alien (but sometimes also attractive). The main Lutheran questions concerned their confessional identity, especially around the borders; they asked, "how far could any group go in accommodating itself to American religious culture without losing its claim to being Lutheran?" Their eyes were often on Lutheran Europe, and on the categories and questions established there.

This is not to say, however, that those American Lutherans were totally in sync with their confessional partners in Europe. American Lutherans had received some important assistance from the European churches over the years, though by 1914 this assistance had dwindled. Most American Lutheran pastors were educated and trained in America; very few European pastors from the Lutheran State Churches ever made the transition to the new world. Increasingly, American Lutherans were unsure whether they would even accept European Lutheran pastors, trained in the increasingly liberal European universities, and with little practical experience of the American situation. Some of the immigrant leaders of American Lutheranism had left Europe with a distaste for the Lutheran State Church systems of their homeland; many of these leaders were strongly influenced by the pietist revivals and awakenings within nineteenth-century Lutheran Europe, and leaned toward a more "free" Lutheranism, which they attempted to build in the United States. American Lutherans cooperated with European Lutherans, especially around the support for Lutheran missions in Africa and Asia, but increasingly it seemed that they were on different paths. Although American Lutherans had strong bonds with European Lutherans, especially in terms of a common theology and ethos, it was clear by the beginning of the twentieth century that American Lutherans were constructing a new type of Lutheranism within the American religious context.

But if American Lutherans were building something new and distinctively American in the United States, their English-speaking American Protestants neighbors were not so sure that they recognized it as such. To their old-stock Protestant neighbors, most American Lutherans in 1914 seemed still to be rather foreign and European. Much of this was due, of course, to their continued maintenance and use of their European languages for worship and religious life; outside of the colonial "Muhlenberg" Lutherans, the overwhelming remainder of American Lutherans still used the immigrant languages. But in the wider perception, American Lutherans seemed oddly foreign in ways that went beyond language. To many other Americans, Lutherans seemed religiously to be half-way to Roman Catholicism, especially with their liturgical forms of worship, their emphasis on sacramental theology, and other European customs that seemed out of place. American Lutherans were neither revivalistic nor liberal, and many American Protestants were not exactly sure what they were. To be sure, old-stock American Protestants preferred the Lutheran immigrants to the increasingly numerous immigrants of Roman Catholic, Jewish, or Eastern Orthodox backgrounds; Lutherans were still Protestants and of "Nordic" stock, which counted for quite a bit in those racially conscious times. But American Lutherans seemed to outsiders stubbornly slow in assimilating to American culture and ways, and the fact that many Lutherans preferred to educate their children in the immigrant languages (some in parochial schools) was especially troublesome.

In general, American Lutheran denominations generally avoided taking formal and public stances on the political questions of the day, unless they felt that a particular issue had a direct bearing on their ability to worship and speak as they saw fit. Traditional Lutheran theology predicated a model of the "Two Kingdoms" (of God and of the world), and suggested that, while God had created both realms, he gave them distinct laws that did not overlap. For example, it was not proper to try to write Christian morality into secular law; this was a mixing of church and society in a way that was not good for either. Both realms were under God and directly accountable to God, but Christian laws (such as the Sermon on the Mount) were for the church alone. Of course, the border between these two realms was often unclear, and Lutheran denominations did at times make some public pronouncements, but they often resisted doing so as well.

Ordinary Lutherans lived in both worlds, and as citizens of the temporal world occupied offices of power and responsibility in it. Thus they would have to enforce the laws of the world, and keep the public order, by force if necessary. Lutherans had never been pacifists, and saw little problem governing or serving in the military; Martin Luther wrote an influential pamphlet entitled *Whether Soldiers, Too, Can Be Saved*, and stressed that soldiers had a godly duty to keep the secular peace, by force if they had to. While Lutheran denominations did not often take public stances, it was proper (if not necessary) for individual Lutherans to make their political opinions known, and to exercise their rights and duties as citizens.

In general, up to April 1917, American Lutherans tended to have more sympathy with Germany than with the other countries involved in the war, although this obviously varied from person to person. Many American Lutherans were ethnically German, and even those who were not often had a sympathy for that country; many American Lutherans viewed Germany as one of the great bulwarks of Protestantism, especially against the Roman Catholic and Eastern Orthodox countries of Europe. One Swedish-American Lutheran newspaper editor wrote in 1914: "With its people . . . (and) high culture, and not least its Protestantism, Germany constitutes a wall which has held back the pan-Slavic, semi-barbaric drive toward the West."[3] Fears of Russian expansion and of British imperial aggression were common; perhaps it was not so much that these Lutherans were pro-German as that they were anti-Russian or anti-British. Writing in 1914, an American Lutheran professor, J. N. Lenker, cast the war as a racial struggle between the "Teutons" and the "Slavs" whom he considered a menace to Protestant Europe and peace in general: "Must the Teutonic states of Holland, Belgium, Luxemburg, Switzerland, Denmark, Sweden and Norway be neutral, when all are threatened by being overrun by a union of all the Slavs?"[4] Long-standing German fears of Russian hegemony were certainly involved, as was a deep Swedish resentment of its loss of Finland to Russia at the end of the Napoleonic wars. Obviously, many American Lutherans identified with Germany. Only the Danish-Americans tended to be anti-German, with bitter memories of the German defeat of Denmark in 1864 and the Danish loss of Schleswig-Holstein to the Germans.

If American Lutherans identified somewhat with Germany in this conflict, they certainly did not identify at all with Great Britain, whom they tended to blame for the tensions in Europe and around the world. Many of them claimed that it was Britain's long-standing strategy to force Germany into war; one Eastern Lutheran leader, T. E. Schmauk, wrote in 1914: "This war is the result of the British plan of destroying Germany's foreign commerce and relations, and of doing away . . . with a rival whose influence on the world's markets was asserting itself more and more."[5] Another Lutheran correspondent wrote in 1914 that England was largely responsible for the war; referring to "the plans of France, England, and Belgium to attack Germany. These plans were made already in 1906. This proves the treachery of England toward civilization and Germany. . . . England thought it would be a comparatively easy task to destroy Germany and thus enrich herself."[6] The

3. *Augustana*, 15 January 1914, as quoted in Capps, *From Isolation to Involvement*.

4. J. N. Lenker, "Europe Teutonic or Slavic?" *Lutheran Companion*, 29 August 1914, 6.

5. T. E. Schmauk, "The Great War of Germany against Europe." *Lutheran Church Review*, October 1914, 764. Schmauk came from one of the colonial Muhlenberg denominations; he was no recent immigrant.

6. C. A. Larson, "Which Would You Choose?" *Lutheran Companion*, 5 December

predominance of Lutheran opinion in the first years of the war was mildly pro-German, but very definitely against the British and Russians.

But above all, American Lutherans, like many other Americans, were decidedly isolationist. Lutheran opinions strongly and regularly opposed those in America, especially those in the federal government, who were perceived as attempting to "push" the nation into the war on the side of England and France, or endangering a strict American neutrality in the war. There was a widespread mistrust of President Wilson, even though he ran for re-election in 1916 under the slogan, "He Kept Us Out of War," and especially those within his administration with pro-British sympathies. The Lutheran church press had a long-running debate in 1915 and 1916 about the question of a proposed embargo against the warring parties; some supported the idea, while others suggested that it was simply a backhanded way of supporting Britain and France. But in general, some of the strongest voices expressed their anguish at the human cost of this terrible war, and prayed for its end. Decrying the wanton waste of the war, and of the destruction of "civilized" Europe, one editor grimly observed: "It may be that the eyes of man had to be bathed in blood as never before in order to see the iniquity and folly of war . . . It may be that under the guidance of God that this will be the last great war in the history of the world; that it is the last convulsion of the powers of evil before the coming of the Son of Man."[7] In this way, then, no matter their sympathies with one side or the other, American Lutherans were allied with the general trend of American public opinion.

In 1914 and 1915, during the beginning stages of the war, some Lutherans were willing to voice their support for the German war effort, and at times corporately and in public. At its annual meeting in 1914, one of the smaller German groups, the Wartburg Synod, reportedly included public prayers for Germany, followed by the mass singing of German patriotic songs, including "Deutschland über Alles" and "Die Wacht am Rhein."[8] Although such overt displays of sympathy for Germany were rare, the sentiment behind them was fairly common. Much of the strong language in favor of American neutrality was, probably, motivated by a desire to "level the playing field" and to offset the British advantage in naval superiority. In analyzing the rhetoric of the Missouri Synod during this period, one his-

---

1914, 6.

7. "The Great World War," *Lutheran Companion*, 15 August 1914, 3.

8. Cited in Meuser, "Facing the Twentieth Century," 396.

torian has concluded that the German "orientation" of the group pushed it out of its traditional two-kingdoms stance: "With great vigor it denounced America's arms trade, and through its president voiced the conviction that "anything that touches moral issues is within the sphere of the church."[9] The irony is apparent when it is understood that the same group was simultaneously opposing the movement for the prohibition of alcohol, on the basis of the "two-kingdoms" doctrine.

Much of the attention of American Lutherans in the period 1914 to 1917 was focused on plans to celebrate in very grand and public ways the four-hundredth anniversary of the Lutheran Reformation of 31 October 1917.[10] Though this was the celebration of a historical event, it had a further, contemporary purpose; this was to be a public celebration of the fact that Lutherans had "made it" in America, and a show to the rest of the American public of Lutheran strength and presence. Elaborate plans were developed for Lutheran celebrations in major cities around the country, and though ambitious plans for a national, pan-Lutheran committee to oversee events came to naught (because of inter-Lutheran bickering), well over a hundred local and synodical committees planned events. The most impressive of these groups, the New York Reformation Quadricentenary Committee, sought to harness the powers of the media to highlight the celebrations, and gained a national audience beyond Lutheran circles for its efforts. This committee managed to avoid Lutheran "turf wars" by being composed mainly of prominent Lutheran lay leaders instead of often-fractious pastors and theologians.

AMERICAN LUTHERANS' EXPERIENCE OF THE WAR

In the midst of all these local and national preparations, the entry of the United States into the war in April 1917 drastically changed the course and tenor of those celebratory plans; no longer could it be a major celebration of a *German* reformation moment! As O. H. Pannkoke, one of the leaders of New York group later observed: "The May *Bulletin* [of the New York Committee] voiced the new note: 'The Reformation takes on a solemn air with the solemnity of the times in which it falls. It is no more a festival of light rejoicing. It has become an act of reconsecration to all those principles

9. Nelson, *Lutheranism in North America*, 4.

10. The date in 1517 when Martin Luther nailed his 95 Theses to the Castle Church door in Wittenberg.

of liberty, truth, and humanity that made the Reformation the birth hour of the modern day."[11] All across the country Lutheran celebrations of October 1917 took on that solemn air, with generous servings of Lutheran patriotic displays of loyalty to the United States and to its war efforts.

Almost as soon as President Wilson and Congress declared war on Germany in April 1917, American Lutheran denominations rushed to show their loyalty to the American cause. No matter their previous misgivings about the war and about the motives of America's British and Russian allies, they expressed their whole-hearted support of the American decision and of the war effort. During the spring and summer of 1917, Lutheran groups meeting in their annual conventions passed resolutions of support for the government, and drafted telegrams to President Wilson assuring him of their loyalty. One historian has noted that, in general, the American churches "stumbled all over themselves in their haste to pledge support of the military effort" and that "Lutheran church bodies were no exception, although none endorsed the popular view of a 'holy war.'"[12] Typical was the telegram sent to President Wilson from one of the small Danish Lutheran churches: "The Danish Evangelical Lutheran Church in America . . . sends greetings, heartily endorsing the principles of justice to smaller nations [e.g., Denmark] and liberation of oppressed nationalities so nobly expressed by you. May God, from whom alone comes power and wisdom to wage the battle for justice and liberty, strengthen and guide you."[13] For the next eighteen months, until the end of the war, Lutheran church publications issued a steady stream of articles and advertisements that urged their readers to support the war efforts, conserve food and fuel, support the Red Cross, and buy War Bonds, which American Lutherans did at a generally high level. With the war effort getting into high gear, American Lutherans wanted to show their patriotism and "American-ness."

Efforts to demonstrate their loyalty notwithstanding, many other Americans were still deeply suspicious. They had certainly not forgotten previous Lutheran expressions of support for Germany, criticisms of the British motives, and attacks on the policies and intentions of the Wilson administration, and were deeply suspicious of this "new leaf" in American

11. Pannkoke, *A Great Church Finds Itself*, 52. One permanent result of these celebrations was the transformation of the New York Committee into a permanent organization known as the American Lutheran Publicity Bureau, to continue publicity and educational efforts on behalf of American Lutheranism.

12. Nelson, *Lutheranism in North America*, 6.

13. Quoted in Mortensen, *Danish Lutheran Church*, 175.

Lutheran attitudes. Further, the entry of America into the war had unleashed a strong wave of nativism and xenophobia in the country, and Lutherans were a prime target for such attacks. The fact of their traditional cultural and religious ties to Germany tainted many Americans' opinions of all American Lutherans (German or otherwise). But the chief objection of other Americans to American Lutherans was their stubborn refusal to make the transition to the use of English, and to assimilate into the general culture of America. As mentioned above, at least two-thirds of all American Lutheran denominations were still primarily using German or other European languages for their worship, business, and educational efforts, and there were strong forces within American Lutheranism resisting any transition to the use of English. The very use of non-English languages instantly brought American Lutherans under suspicion of a lack of loyalty to the war effort, no matter their public pronouncements or telegrams to the president.

The non-English-speaking Lutherans, concentrated in the American Midwest, suffered the most directly from a wave of efforts targeting anything foreign, and most especially anything German. Angry popular opinion sought the eradication of anything German; town and street names were changed, foods were relabeled (Sauerkraut became "Liberty Cabbage"), German cultural expressions such as books and music were boycotted, German-language books and publications were banned or even burned, and German-language churches and parochial schools were attacked. This popular wave of anti-German sentiment forced American Lutherans to be on the defensive. Speaking of this surge of nativism, one historian wrote: "No self-devised program could have hastened the divorce of Lutherans from their former cultural loyalties as rapidly as did this antagonism from the superpatriots."[14]

The popular pressures against American Lutherans as potential "fifth columnists" and traitors took strong root in some areas of the country, and led to acts of extreme discrimination and even violence against foreign-language Lutherans. "Superpatriots" formed local Councils of Defense (mainly in the Midwest) to root out cases of supposed disloyalty and to harass those who were seen as less than supportive of the war efforts. German congregations and pastors were harassed, church buildings were vandalized and desecrated, parochial schools were forcibly shut, and individuals

---

14. Meuser, "Facing the Twentieth Century," 397.

were threatened. There were even a few instances of physical violence, such as Lutheran leaders being attacked, and tarred and feathered.

Not all of those attacks were instances of mob vigilantism. In a number of states, especially in the American Midwest, governors and state legislatures proposed and even passed laws attacking non-English-speaking Americans, banning the use of non-English languages in schools, churches, and even in public speech. Stretching back into the late nineteenth century there had already been a deep suspicion in some quarters about the "American-ness" of religious parochial schools, a trend that was magnified by the war. In Nebraska, the legislature passed in 1918 the "Sedition Act," which required preachers and teachers to be licensed by local courts, presumably to assure that none of them were proclaiming treasonous messages in their congregations or classrooms. Of course, those laws and efforts were eventually declared to be invalid or unconstitutional, but the very fact of their coming into existence shows the depth of popular resentment and suspicion against Lutherans as perceived or potential traitors in the midst of the country. One popular rumor that was circulated widely during this time, and even taken up and printed by American newspapers, was the so-called "Oath to the Kaiser," purportedly required of Lutheran pastors in America. The "oath" supposedly bound these pastors in obedience to the German Emperor, and to support of the German war effort.[15] As American troops began to enter the war effort in earnest and reports of American causalities in the fighting circulated back home, tensions were enflamed even further.

American Lutherans resisted those attacks when they could, but they had to be careful that their very resistance was not taken as a further sign of disloyalty. Protests against these nativist attacks were often coupled with fervent support for the war effort, reminders that the Lutherans were strongly showing this support in buying war bonds, and in the numbers of young Lutherans who were enlisting in the armed forces. Lutheran leaders had to walk a fine line; on the one hand they needed to be supportive and patriotic, yet, on the other, theologically, they needed to avoid collapsing the traditional borders between church and state. After taking to task Lutheran critics of such public support for the war efforts, the editor of the Missouri Synod's English newspaper, the *Lutheran Witness*, replied: "We shall add,—only by plainly asserting that we are with our Government and against Germany shall we overcome such doubts as are in the mind of the public concerning our 'loyalty' in the war-time sense, the only sense that

---

15. Ibid., 397–98n21.

now counts."[16] One later historian of the Missouri Synod, a denomination that bore much of the brunt of nativist attacks, suggested that the aspersions of disloyalty were rebutted by the fact that members of the Missouri Synod purchased 94 million dollars worth of war bonds, and made "liberal contributions to the Red Cross."[17]

But assuring the rest of the country of their loyalty by pronouncements and buying war bonds was not the only war concern for American Lutherans; they were also deeply worried about the spiritual welfare of the tens of thousands of young American Lutherans who had enlisted in the American armed forces. The American Lutheran denominations knew that they had to work quickly to develop a program of chaplaincy to Lutherans in the military, but faced large obstacles to doing so. The Missouri Synod was large enough to organize its own ministry to the troops, the Army and Navy Board, which cooperated with other groups within the Synodical Conference.[18] But most of the rest of the American Lutheran denominations felt that common efforts in this area were vital, so in the fall of 1917 they pooled their individual efforts into a newly formed group, the National Lutheran Commission for Soldiers' and Sailors' Welfare (NLCSSW). The formation of this group was driven not only by a desire for the efficiency of cooperative work, but by the fact that the American government, and the local military officials, refused to work with more than a single Lutheran entity. Even the Missouri Synod's Army and Navy Board, though not a part of the NLCSSW, coordinated its efforts with this new group. The NLCSSW developed a coordinated plan of ministry to Lutherans in the armed forces, especially to the military training camps that were springing up around the country, and built and furnished "Lutheran Centers" near the camps and military hospitals, complete with supplies, literature, and pastors (and other workers). The NLCSSW also planned for chaplains to go overseas, but the short duration of the American involvement in the war largely scuttled this. Of course, the big question was how the NLCSSW would be financed, but a national fund-raising campaign was quickly launched that raised 1.35 million dollars (double the initial goal); the Missouri Synod's own appeal raised $560,000 for its own efforts.

16. Theodore Graebner, "Unjustified Aspersions," *Lutheran Witness*, 28 May 1918, 169.

17. Baepler, *Century of Grace*, 266.

18. The Missouri Synod had a very high theological threshold in terms of cooperation with other denominations, even other Lutherans, which for them necessitated their own independent chaplaincy efforts.

The experience of the NLCSSW and it war-time ministry to the Lutheran troops was a radically new effort for American Lutherans, and something that they had been forced into by a combination of events during 1917–18. Traditionally, Lutheran denominations in the United States had maintained their theological and linguistic separation rather strictly, and even when cooperative work with other Lutherans did happen (as it rarely did), it came about by means of painstaking theological negotiations, drawn out over the course of many years. In this war situation time was of the essence, and there was no time for theological niceties. American Lutherans salved their theological consciences by declaring that they were simply cooperating in emergency, external matters, and not the internal, essential elements of the faith; but this theological fiction was a thin one, and no one could definitively delineate the border between external and internal matters. In church life, sometimes a creative fiction, interpreted as each party finds helpful, can accomplish a great deal.

As the war was drawing to a conclusion, the denominations that were cooperating in the NLCSSW realized that continued cooperation would be necessary, both to continue to support the troops, and to deal with other areas of common ministry that none of the member denominations could carry out on its own. In September 1918, the presidents of some of the Lutheran denominations involved in the NLCSSW met in Chicago, and formed the National Lutheran Council (NLC), a permanent cooperative agency that eventually represented two-thirds of American Lutherans (the Missouri Synod and its confederates in the Synodical Conference did not join). As the historian of the NLC stated: "Lutheran statesmen could see that there would be continued urgent needs for a united Lutheran voice vis-á-vis the government, for united Lutheran campaigns for funds and publicity, and for united action in future disasters in America as well as the now looming emergency needs of European brethren."[19] Already the NLCSSW had instituted outreach ministries with workers in defense industries (and affected communities), and there were other needs on the horizon.

THE WAR'S EFFECT ON AMERICAN LUTHERANISM

Obviously, the development of increased cooperation was unprecedented for American Lutherans, but it was just one of a number of changes that

---

19. Wentz, *Lutherans in Concert*, 12.

would transform American Lutheranism during and after the war. There are five ways in which those transformations developed: first, acceleration of the transition from the use of European languages to the predominant use of English; second, effective pressure on Lutheran denominations not only toward cooperation among themselves but also into organic union; third, faster integration of American Lutherans into the mainstream of American Protestant life; fourth, emergence of American Lutherans into leadership in world Lutheranism; and fifth, a change in the theological battlefield for American Lutherans, drawing to a conclusion older confessional battles, but opening new areas of conflict and debate. These five areas of change will be examined in order.

The Language Transition

Because of the continued immigration of European Lutherans into the United States up to 1914, and because of the natural conservatism of the Lutheran denominations themselves, up to 1917–18, many (if not a majority) of American Lutherans worshipped, preached, and did their theological work in the languages of their European homelands. Although there was some internal pressure from younger elements to move toward the use of English, the pace of linguistic change was glacially slow. Proponents of the use of German or the other languages argued that their preservation was necessary to serve future immigrants, and they wondered aloud whether Lutheranism could even be done properly at all in English. Among the Norwegian-American Lutherans in 1917, only 30 percent of congregations held any English-language services at all, while over 80 percent had Norwegian-language worship (some congregations had both); by 1930, the situation was completely reversed, and Norwegian was rapidly endangered as a liturgical and theological medium.[20] Among churches of the Swedish-American Augusta Synod, one historian has written that because of nativist pressures in 1917–18: "Virtually overnight the congregations of the Augustana Synod made the transition from Swedish to English, even though in some parishes neither the pastors nor the congregations were adequately prepared for the sudden change."[21]

In many denominations, by 1930 the language transition was almost complete, and the adherents of the old languages were relegated to tiny pockets of resistance. The nativist pressures toward "100 percent

20. Nelson and Fevold, *Lutheran Church*, 2:250.
21. Arden, *Augustana Heritage*, 246.

Americanism" and the virtual end of European immigration (during and after the war) partially contributed to the accelerated rate of change.

The Push toward Union

There had been sporadic efforts to bring about the unification of Lutheran denominations since 1900 or so, and those efforts increased in the 1910s. The three denominations from the eastern, colonial Muhlenberg traditions (divided in the nineteenth century), came together in a merger in 1918, while most of the Norwegian-American Lutherans joined together into a single denomination in 1917. Four of the Midwestern German-American Lutheran denominations (the Ohio, Iowa, Buffalo, and Texas synods) were also working toward union during this time, though their final efforts were delayed until 1930. The First World War did not cause these mergers, but definitely accelerated them. The war, precipitating a language transition to English, started a general conversation among most American Lutheran groups about further merger. If they were now all going to speak and worship in English, was there any rationale for their continued divisions? Those dynamics would define much of American Lutheranism well into the twentieth century.

Integration into Mainstream America

The war caused a greater integration of American Lutheranism into the mainstream of American Protestant religious life. This development is rather more nebulous than the first two, but equally important, as American Lutherans gradually became more active in the wider sphere of American religious life after the war. It is certainly not true that prior to 1914 American Lutherans were trapped in their immigrant enclaves and blissfully unaware of the rest of the country; from the beginning of their time in the United States they had been keenly aware of the wider American religious and social culture. But in general they were interested observers of those areas, rather than active participants in them. Certainly the overwhelming pressure of building their denominations and congregations and gathering in the torrent of new immigrants was one factor in this; the other was the difference in language. By the end of the war in 1918, these two factors were greatly reduced, and slowly American Lutherans became more involved in their wider religious culture, although much more of this would happen only after the Second World War.

Leadership in World Lutheranism

A greater leadership role for American Lutherans in the world at large emerged, especially within the world-wide Lutheran communion. The First World War had a devastating effect on European Lutheranism, and on its missions overseas, an area in which they had led prior to the war. The war, and attendant economic difficulties after the war, had a deep and negative effect on European Lutheran ministries at home and abroad. Lutheran congregations, especially those in eastern France, Eastern Europe, and Russia were devastated by warfare. Lutheran missions in Africa and Asia were cut off from their European funding and leadership, and when British forces took over former German colonies (such as Namibia, Tanzania, and New Guinea), they interned the German missionaries. It fell to American Lutherans to step in and take up the slack in these areas, adopting these so-called "orphaned" missions, and establishing a much greater, permanent American Lutheran mission presence in Africa and Asia. Prior to the First World War American Lutherans were generally "junior partners" to European Lutherans in these missions, but now the Americans took the lead. In 1919, the National Lutheran Council sent representatives to Europe to survey needs and then direct relief efforts among the Lutheran churches most deeply affected by the war, especially in eastern France, Poland, and Russia. The NLC also coordinated financial campaigns among American Lutherans to fund these efforts. After the war, American Lutherans also took the lead in organizing periodic Lutheran World Conventions, meetings where Lutherans from all over the world came together for discussions and common work; the first of those was held in 1923 in Eisenach, Germany.

Reconfiguring Theological Battlegrounds

Finally, there was the redefinition of the theological battlegrounds for American Lutherans. American Lutherans tend to enjoy a good theological battle (something like intramural sports for them), but in the nineteenth century, those battles revolved mainly around questions of Lutheran confessional identity that had been formulated in Europe, and were often carried out in America in the European languages (often, but not always, in the case of Eastern Lutherans). Later battles were fought around the doctrine of predestination (or election). But by the beginning of the First World War those old battles had largely run their courses. With the greater integration of American Lutherans into the American religious world, American Lutherans found new questions to concern them and to fight about, especially the question of the nature of biblical authority. This time period saw the peak of the American Protestant battles over biblical authority, and over the infallibility and inerrancy of the Bible, often referred to as the Fundamentalist-Modernist controversy. As American Lutherans started doing their theology in English in the 1910s and 1920s, they quickly came to wonder just how to express in English their understanding of biblical authority. This had not really been an issue for them in the nineteenth century, but immediately after the First World War it started to be a major issue, beginning in 1919 and 1920 with theological debates over the role of the National Lutheran Council and the future direction of American Lutheran merger efforts.

CONCLUSION

Certainly, the cultural and religious changes within American Lutheranism around the time of the First World War were accelerated by the war itself, and by social upheaval at home. In at least these five ways American Lutheranism was dramatically changed over the period from 1914 to 1920. Not all of the changes happened at once, nor did they happen with the same speed in all American Lutheran groups. But on the whole, the experiences of the First World War, at home and abroad, permanently redirected the trajectory of American Lutheranism moving into the twentieth century. Prior to the war it had been a large and growing family of denominations, but one that was somewhat insular, and preoccupied with its own pressing, internal needs. The experience of the war jolted them out of their concerns and put them into a larger national and international arena, where they quickly learned to take an important role. Having many of their fellow Americans call into question their American identity caused them to greatly accelerate movement into the mainstream of American life, both linguistically and religiously. And given the large number of pressing wartime needs, they were forced to work together and to develop permanent structures to enable them to respond quickly and efficiently to a myriad of issues. Clearly, those few years in the early part of the twentieth century dramatically and irrevocably changed American Lutheranism, and set its course for the rest of that century.

BIBLIOGRAPHY

Primary Sources: Newspapers

Lutheran Church Review, 1914.
Lutheran Companion, 1914.
Lutheran Witness, 1918.

Secondary Sources

Arden, G. Everett. *Augustana Heritage*. Rock Island, IL: Augustana, 1963.
Baepler, Walter A. *A Century of Grace: A History of the Missouri Synod, 1847-1947*. St. Louis: Concordia, 1947.
Capps, Finis Herbert. *From Isolation to Involvement: The Swedish Immigrant Press in America, 1914-1945*. Chicago: Swedish Pioneer Historical Society, 1966.
Granquist, Mark. *Lutherans in America: A New History*. Minneapolis: Fortress, 2015.
Meuser, Fred W. "Facing the Twentieth Century." In *The Lutherans in North America*, edited by E. Clifford Nelson, 359-449. Philadelphia: Fortress, 1975.
Mortensen, Enok. *The Danish Lutheran Church in America*. Philadelphia: Board of Publication of the Lutheran Church in America, 1967.
Nelson, E. Clifford. *Lutheranism in North America, 1914-1970*. Minneapolis: Augsburg, 1972.
———. *The Lutherans in North America*. Philadelphia: Fortress, 1975.
Nelson, E. Clifford, and Eugene Fevold. *The Lutheran Church among Norwegian-Americans: A History of the Evangelical Lutheran Church*. 2 vols. Minneapolis: Augsburg, 1960.
Pannkoke, O. H. *A Great Church Finds Itself: The Lutheran Church between the Wars*. Quitman, GA: n.p., 1966.
Wentz, Frederick K. *Lutherans in Concert: The Story of the National Lutheran Council, 1918-1966*. Minneapolis: Augsburg, 1968.

5

As Citizens of Heaven

Peace, War, and Patriotism among Pentecostals in the United States during the First World War

ZACHARY MICHAEL TACKETT

WITHIN A DECADE OF the 1906 Los Angeles Azusa Street revival, Pentecostals in the United States voiced contrasting perspectives on pacifism and patriotism. The war in Europe during the early twentieth century challenged Pentecostal perspectives on peace, patriotism, and war. As Americans took up arms, most leaders within emerging Pentecostalism called upon the government to recognize the Pentecostal commitment to peace and to validate their constituents' right to claim conscientious objector status. American Pentecostals were not consistent, however, in their objections. Many advocated pacifism; some did not. Historians Jay Beaman and Paul Alexander have shown that, on the whole, Pentecostals during the First World War expressed a commitment to pacifism.[1] Yet, as social ethicist Murray Dempster has shown, pacifism was far from universal among America's Pentecostals. In the Assemblies of God (AG), pacifism was a controversial position among denominational officials, pastors, and constituents.[2]

---

1. Beaman, *Pentecostal Pacifism*; Alexander, *Peace to War*.

2. See the following articles by Dempster, "Peacetime Draft Registration"; "Review of *Pentecostal Pacifism*"; "Crossing Borders"; "Pacifism in Pentecostalism."

Three types of response by Pentecostals to the war in Europe may be observed. First, a prophetic community of some Pentecostals opposed the war. Second, others attempted to simultaneously embrace nationalism and oppose the war in Europe. Third, Pentecostals who upheld the *status quo* either failed to oppose the war or accepted that Pentecostals, like all Americans, should fulfill their patriotic duty by participating in the war effort.

THE CHALLENGE OF THE PROGRESSIVE ERA

Jonathan Hansen identifies two distinct types of Americanism that emerged during the Progressive Era.[3] The first group advocated for a homogenous American society that elicited the image of a smelting pot, where all people would be unified through Anglo-American ideals. An alternative group valued American idealism, but rejected homogeneity in favor of a multi-cultural society. Those proponents valued the contributions of those who were marginalized by the dominant political, economic, and social power structures due to gender, race, servitude, or ethnicity.

The first group, represented strongly by Theodore Roosevelt, emphasized a homogenous community from English and northern European stock. He contended that those who did not fit the Anglo-American mold must be re-formed; all persons from the various ethnic and social communities were to be smelted into an Americanized expression of English and northern European values. This ideal devalued the politically marginalized, the poor, persons of color, recent immigrants from southern and eastern Europe, immigrants from Asia, Native Americans, persons of Jewish and of Catholic heritage, and the first Spanish immigrants to the Americas. However, Roosevelt's smelting pot concept of the American ideal became the politically and culturally dominant concept of Americanism. Furthermore, in Roosevelt's thoughts, war functioned as an ideal crucible for his homogenized view of America. Historian Gary Gerstle interprets Roosevelt's conclusions: "the stress and dangers of combat generated pressures [that served] to unify [in a way] that no peacetime initiative could simulate."[4]

The contrasting ideal of Americanism valued the contributions of multi-ethnic, multi-cultural communities. Supreme Court Justice Louis Brandeis (and other intellectuals and social scientists like W. E. B. Du Bois, Horace Kallen, Randolph Bourne, and John Dewey) argued that the identity

---

3. Hansen, "True Americanism." The Progressive Era (ca. 1890–1920) was a time of optimistic social and political reform.

4. Gerstle, *American Crucible*, 6.

and strength of America should be found in the variety of its immigrants—immigrants past, present, and future—in order to develop a diverse and unified community. According to Brandeis, "Immigrants must be brought into complete harmony with our ideals and aspirations and cooperate with us for their attainment . . . [and] possess[ion] [of] the national consciousness of an American."[5] Unlike Roosevelt, Brandeis looked forward to the contributions of future immigrants who would provide an incipient value to American culture. Hansen summarizes Brandeis: "[prejudice] and industrial dependence, not cultural diversity, threatened American democracy. It was the duty of all true Americans to safeguard equal opportunity and fair play."[6] Therefore, America should not extirpate from the new immigrants that which was distinctive, but "must preserve for America the good that is in the immigrant."[7]

Those conflicting goals concerning American diversity reflected vastly differing proposals for the American ideal. It was in this world that American Pentecostals carved out not only their relationship to nationhood, but also their relationship to the global Christian community. Not least among the issues related to nationhood, these Pentecostals would have to grapple with participation in times of war.

TRAJECTORIES OF PENTECOSTAL PACIFISM

According to Beaman, although Pentecostals had emerged shortly before the First World War as a sect that rejected the *status quo*, they eventually accommodated to the emerging American middle class. Early Pentecostals rejected American cultural expectations through their pacifism, an expression of a sectarian, anti-cultural commitment, but over time their desire to embrace the mainstream led Pentecostals to accept the dominant American culture and reject pacifism.[8]

Paul Alexander, author of *Peace to War*, traces the AG shift from being a peace church during the First World War to being a church that by the Vietnam War had come to recognize war as a legitimate means of resolving international conflict. Alexander demonstrates how the AG came to see pacifism as the venue of the individual, rather than the voice of the church as a community. In 1917, the AG declared to the government that

---

5. Hansen, "True Americanism," 74; Brandeis, "True Americanism," 4–5.
6. Hansen, "True Americanism," 74.
7. Ibid.
8. Beaman, *Pentecostal Pacifism*, 107.

the fellowship would be opposed to armed conflict and contended that all AG members who claimed conscientious objector status should be recognized. This position was affirmed by the vote of the General Council, the highest governing body of the AG, in 1927 and again in 1947.[9] However, Alexander acknowledges that the presbytery may not have allowed the initial statement in 1917 to be voted on by the General Council because leaders feared that the proclamation might not have had the support of the full constituency. Nonetheless, argues Alexander, "If pacifism was not the majority position in the early Assemblies of God, the statement would surely have been changed after World War I—but was not. . . . This retention of the statement even after World War II points to its majority status in at least the first generation of the Assemblies of God."[10]

During the Vietnam War, the AG revisited its policy on combatant and conscientious objector commitments. The denomination declared that individual conscience was the AG perspective toward war; moreover, this had always been its perspective toward war.[11] Murray Dempster rejects the notion that this was not a change in AG policy, but argues that "[s]uch a claim arbitrarily revises history." The revised 1967 statement by the AG was "an unacknowledged banishment of the pentecostal heritage."[12] He particularly lamented his church's failure to engage Scripture when revisiting the statement on peace and war.

> Apparently, the pentecostal believer's conscience on war no longer needed to be formed specifically by biblical teaching but was now to be informed by knowledge of certain political, theological and ethical propositions. . . . The poverty of explicit biblical thinking in this rationale is an utter embarrassment to people who give first priority in a "Statement of Faith" to affirming the authority of Scripture.[13]

Dempster continues: "[W]ill the church model the importance of forming its own moral conscience under the authority of Scripture and of speaking

---

9. Alexander, *Peace to War*; Beaman, *Pentecostal Pacifism*, 21, 73; Robins, "Chronology of Peace," 23.

10. Alexander, *Peace to War*, 37–38.

11. Minutes of the Thirty-Second General Council of the Assemblies of God (1967).

12. Dempster, "Peacetime Draft Registration," 2.

13. Ibid., 3.

a prophetic word to others in accordance with 'the clear teachings of the inspired Word of God which is the sole basis of our faith?'"[14]

In later writing, Dempster emphasized his appreciation to Beaman for highlighting shifts in the Pentecostals' acceptance of war; Beaman's work in 1989 was "a cause for celebration . . . a fresh and illuminating perspective, highlighting the fundamental change in pacifistic belief that has occurred among pentecostals during their short history."[15] However, Dempster challenged Beaman's theory of why Pentecostals made such a shift. According to Dempster, American Pentecostals during the First World War did not reject American cultural expectations, as argued by Beaman, but viewed "pacifism as part of the church's redemptive witness to the world."[16] Thus, early Pentecostals advocated transforming American cultural expectations. Dempster points to Pentecostals such as Arthur S. Booth-Clibborn, his son Samuel H. Booth-Clibborn, Frank Bartleman, Stanley Frodsham, and Charles Parham who challenged the dominant voice of American nationalism during the war. Those pacifists advocated "a moral authentication of the universal truths of the gospel."[17] Pentecostals who engaged this prophetic voice built their case upon the following themes: pacifism provided a moral sign of a restored New Testament apostolic church, pacifism provided a critique of social evil, and pacifism affirmed the value of human life. Moreover, pacifist Pentecostals were not rejecting American culture but were challenging the dominant expression of Progressive Era Americanism. Contributing to the national discussion on the nature of Americanism, Pentecostals framed their critique of the social evil of war in the intrinsic value of humanity given by God to all. "[P]acifism provides a moral authentication of the universal truths of the gospel."[18]

Pentecostal Pacifists as Prophets

"War is madness" shouted the elder Booth-Clibborn.[19] War destroys order in society. Booth-Clibborn was particularly strident against nations that called themselves Christian while using warfare to achieve their imperialist objectives. Nations that backed up their call for peace and political man-

---

14. Ibid., 9.
15. Dempster, "Crossing Borders," 63.
16. Ibid., 64.
17. Ibid.
18. Ibid.
19. Booth-Clibborn, *Blood against Blood*, 12.

dates with weapons of war did not exhibit the principle of peace exhibited by Jesus. Peace talks among nations that were backed by naval fleets and armies were not intended to develop peace but to inspire respect and imperialism: "this wilfully blind and narrow spirit is the seed of war."[20]

Another strident voice against war was the Azusa participant-chronicler, Frank Bartleman. According to Dempster, Bartleman identified war as "institutionalized evil that reflected the sinful power structure of the world system."[21] Europeans were militaristic colonialists who were being judged by God: "Belgium for her Congo atrocities. France for her infidelity and devil worship. Germany for her materialism and militarism. England for her hypocrisy, bullyism over weaker nations, and her overwhelming pride."[22] According to Bartleman, England deserved primary criticism for the war. England was using political and economic power to subjugate humanity, advance colonialism, and further the European caste system.[23] "England, whose religious pretensions are the greatest today, has stolen most of her possessions from the weaker nations. She is the greatest of sea pirates."[24] The United States likewise, did not escape Bartleman's critique. Prior to American entry into the war, Bartleman challenged the American claim to neutrality. He wrote a scathing critique of Americans' outrage at the hostile sinking of the Lusitania prior to the United States officially taking up arms. "A torpedo bored its way into the bowels of the great vessel loaded with ammunition and arms for the destruction of the Germans. . . . The ammunition came from America. And yet we complain because Americans were killed. . . . Judgment time has come."[25]

Bartleman was clear, however, that he was not taking sides with Germany and its allies. To the contrary, "The sins of Germany are many,"[26] particularly in regard to Germany's commitment to imperialism. "Germany no doubt is ambitious to rule Europe."[27] Yet Bartleman had better things to

20. Ibid., 26.
21. Dempster, "Pacifism in Pentecostalism," 38.
22. Frank Bartleman, "Present Day Conditions," *Weekly Evangel*, 5 June 1915, 3.
23. Frank Bartleman, "The European War," *Weekly Evangel*, 10 July 1915, 3.
24. Frank Bartleman, "What Will the Harvest Be?" *Weekly Evangel*, 7 August 1915, 1.
25. Frank Bartleman, "Present Day Conditions," *Weekly Evangel*, 5 June 1915, 3.
26. Frank Bartleman, "What Will the Harvest Be?" *Weekly Evangel*, 7 August 1915, 1.
27. Frank Bartleman, "The European War," *Weekly Evangel*, 10 July 1915, 3.

say about Germany than England. "In German cities even the vacant lots are all planted with vegetable gardens. Every foot of ground is utilized and developed to the utmost. Germans have built their nation with the sword in one hand and trowel in the other."[28] Nonetheless, in the case of Germany and England, along with their allies, they had failed to recognize that faithfulness both to God and to nationalism produced conflicting objectives. "Patriotism has been fanned into a flame. The religious passion has been invoked, and the national gods called upon for defense in each case. What blasphemy! . . . It is simply wholesale murder. It is nothing short of hell. And yet they glorify it."[29]

A third example of a prophetic voice is that of Augustus J. Tomlinson, leader of the Church of God (CG) in Cleveland, Tennessee. Like Booth-Clibborn and Bartleman, Tomlinson contended that war was wrong because it took human life and destroyed society. "Much is said now of patriotism and going to war in defense of our beautiful country, but we have a higher and nobler calling than this."[30] He believed that commitment to heavenly citizenship, engaging an eschatological ethic, must supersede nationalist commitments. "Jesus loves the world. This takes in Germany as well as America. If we are Christ's, then we love the world too, and our love is not limited to our own native country."[31] Using the actions of Jesus as a model, Tomlinson argued, "[D]o we see Him slaying the multitudes because they were trampling upon His rights? It is pride and selfishness usually that leads to war."[32] War also takes the lives of husbands, fathers, and sons, devastating their families at home. Tomlinson laments: "The home is left desolate as wife and children think of husband and father out on the bloody battle field. Weary, hungry, cold, wounded and bleeding, dying, dead, at the hand of the cruel war. Homes broken up never to be united again."[33]

Janette Keith observes that conscription procedures during the war gave preferential treatment to the wealthy, the middle class, and politically

28. Frank Bartleman, "What Will the Harvest Be?," *Weekly Evangel*, 7 August 1915, 1.

29. Frank Bartleman, "The European War," *Weekly Evangel*, 10 July 1915, 3.

30. Augustus J. Tomlinson, "Beautiful Light of Pentecost," *Church of God Evangel*, 12 May 1917, 1.

31. Augustus J. Tomlinson, "The Awful World War," *Church of God Evangel*, 24 February 1917, 1.

32. Ibid.

33. Augustus J. Tomlinson, "President of United States Calls the People to Prayer," *Church of God Evangel*, 26 September 1914, 2.

connected families. "Under the rubric of fairness," notes Keith, "the Selective Service System favored industrial workers, middle-class fathers, and established religious bodies and in doing so fastened a disproportionate burden on the southern rural poor."[34] Tomlinson and the CG would have felt this injustice. One of Tomlinson's primary concerns during the war, in addition to the actual destruction of human life, was the emotional and economic destruction of the family. Sons, husbands, and fathers were taken from the home for the duration of the war and possibly forever.

Tomlinson charged that a commitment to the church and Christian ideals should supersede all other commitments, including nationalist concerns. "[W]e owe our first and best to God. Our first duty is to the church. We obligate [ourselves] to be loyal and true [to God]. This, then, is our first duty. The war demon may try to persuade you that your first duty is to the stars and stripes, but this is a delusion."[35] Tomlinson believed that Pentecostals should reject government-endorsed war by refusing to participate; bravery was not found in the taking up of arms, but in refusing those arms. Bravery was found in challenging the war in Europe by declaring conscientious objector status.

The economics of everyday life also demanded indirect contribution to the war effort. As Augustus J. Tomlinson declared, "We cannot fight [in combat] and we are sometimes at a loss to know just where to draw the lines. We are helping in the war by paying high prices for food and clothing, but these are necessities and we cannot refuse to purchase them.... It makes scarcely any difference what one engages in now[,] he is helping in the war more or less in some way."[36] Postal workers contributed to the war. Coalminers, common in Appalachia, provided the government with needed energy to propagate the war. Farmers supplied food to the soldiers. Tomlinson identified the end result of passive participation in war: "indirectly we are lending our assistance in the very thing our conscience condemns. We are helping to pull the triggers that fire the guns that take the lives of our fellowmen. We do not want to do this but it is forced upon us."[37] Finally, Tomlinson concluded that Pentecostals had a responsibility

---

34. Keith, *Rich Man's War*, 83.

35. Augustus J. Tomlinson, "The Awful World War," *Church of God Evangel*, 24 February 1917, 1.

36. Augustus J. Tomlinson, "Days of Perplexity," *Church of God Evangel*, 26 January 1918, 1.

37. Ibid.

to pursue an eschatological ethic, rather than nationalist concerns: "We are in the world, but not of the world. While we are here we must obey the laws of the country to which we live so long as those laws do not require us to disobey God, then God must be first even if the penalty is inflicted upon us. This is God's world. Here is where we must stand."[38]

Patriotic and Pacifist

In contrast to the absolute pacifists, other Pentecostals either supported the war or provided little objection to the war. For those Pentecostals, ethics and nationalism were compatible. In 1917, although the AG had adopted a pacifist stance, the AG passed a motion that discouraged its ministers from taking actions that might undermine American nationalism. A resolution passed by the Texas District and affirmed by the General Council warned preachers that if they spoke against the government they would be censured; their ministerial credentials would be revoked.[39] The General Council extended the provision, "Such radicals [who object to nationalism] do not represent this General Council."[40]

Thereafter, in January 1918, the editor of the *Weekly Evangel*, E. N. Bell, published the following report: "The General Council has always stood for law and order. So at our last Council Meeting we took a strong stand for Loyalty to our Government and the President and to the Flag. Let all note this and be duly warned."[41] Absolute opposition to United States involvement in war was not acceptable. Bell declared, "It is one things [*sic*] to be in our own faith opposed personally to taking human life, even in war, but quite another thing to preach against our Government going to war. . . . It is none of our business to push our faith as to war on others or on the Government."[42] Bell further admonished "[p]reachers who are excused from war, old or young," to "show their gratitude to God and the Flag for such religious liberty and prove this by extra service and sacrifices to the good of mankind, to the Government and to God."[43]

It is also noteworthy that Bell stated that those final comments reflected his personal stance, not the position of the AG. But, as editor of

38. Ibid.
39. Dempster, "Pacifism in Pentecostalism," 47.
40. As cited in ibid.
41. E. N. Bell, "Preachers Warned," *Weekly Evangel*, 5 January 1918, 4.
42. Ibid.
43. Ibid.

the *Weekly Evangel*, the official organ of the AG, and as the first leader of the fellowship, his words would have been received by many constituents as the official position of the AG. "[T]he General Council cannot and will not try to help any preacher who willfully disobeys the laws of the land," asserted Bell, "So let all our preachers be duly warned not to do anything *rash*, like these other preachers, that will land them in a Federal Penitentiary, or up before a shooting squad for Treason to the Country."[44] Grant Wacker observes:

> Bell was on a roll. In the succeeding weeks he encouraged AOG members to buy Liberty Bonds, remember that Jesus paid taxes to the Roman government, and keep in mind that civil authority was ordained by God. . . . In the summer of 1918 he ordered the destruction of all copies of Frank Bartleman's antiwar broadside, *Present Day Conditions*, which the Evangel had printed back in 1915 and later reprinted in tract form.[45]

Later that year, Bell published what Robins refers to as a "blatantly non-pacifistic" response to the question of whether it was morally acceptable to kill in battle: "Our faith leaves this with the conscience of each man . . . But everyone must keep personal hatred out of his heart."[46] Ironically, following Bell's 1918 article in which he warned AG pastors not to oppose the federal government's commitment to war, the next page gave full articulation of the resolution of the AG advocating pacifism. The editor, presumably Bell, printed the pacifist statement of the AG and articulated the criteria required of a petitioner for conscientious objector status.[47]

Still other Pentecostals and their communities remained silent concerning participation in the war. Such is the case of G. F. Taylor and the Pentecostal Holiness Church (PHC). In June 1917, Taylor stated to his constituents that while the United States was preparing for war, Christians should prepare for spiritual warfare.[48] Taylor seems to have recognized the

---

44. Ibid.

45. Wacker, *Heaven Below*, 246. Wacker cites Bell in *Weekly Evangel*, 26 January 1918, 9; *Weekly Evangel*, 23 February 1918, 6; *Christian Evangel*, 11 June 1918, 8. Wacker indicates that Bell was probably speaking for S. A. Jamieson and A. P. Collins in *Christian Evangel*, 24 August 1918, 4.

46. Robins, "Chronology of Peace," 22–23, citing Bell "Questions and Answers," *Christian Evangel*, 19 October 1918.

47. E. N. Bell, "The Pentecostal Movement and the Conscription Law," *Weekly Evangel*, 5 January 1918, 5.

48. G. F. Taylor, "Preparedness," *Pentecostal Holiness Advocate*, 7 June 1917, 8. Taylor

tension provided by commitments to heavenly citizenship and American citizenship. Christians were "citizens of the cross, as most of my readers are [also] citizens of the United States."[49] Taylor encouraged readers to shift their focus to evangelism. Readers were to view the war in Europe as an admonishment to focus upon "a mighty conflict in the heavenlies," in which "souls are hanging in the balances of their eternal destinies, and the call of the hour is to save them before it is too late."[50] Taylor called ministers to evangelism: "while the nations of the earth are preparing themselves for war, let us be as wise as they, and prepare ourselves for the fight against sin."[51] Later publications in the *Advocate*, the official newsletter of the PHC, instructed preachers, but not laity, how to apply for conscientious objector status. The PHC position followed the standard government exceptions to conscription in which ministers could declare as conscientious objectors.

The PHC did state that soldiers should receive the support of their churches. One advertisement in the *Advocate* encouraged readers to purchase New Testaments that had been edited specifically for soldiers and sailors: "Give one to your son or neighbor's son when he has to leave home."[52] On another occasion, a church member, Joseph F. Barnett, indicated that he was scheduled to appear before the conscription board: "I do not know what will be the end of this, but this one thing I know, I must hold God up everywhere I go." Barnett did not appear eager to serve, but did see military life as an opportunity for Christian service.[53]

Pacifists in Support of American Idealism

Some Pentecostal leaders opposed the war. Other leaders saw themselves as committed to America, even if that meant going to war. A third voice challenged the war, but saw that challenge as consistent with the ideals of Americanism. Two leaders who advanced this third perspective included Charles H. Mason, bishop of the Church of God in Christ (COGIC), and

---

was editor of the *Advocate*. While the article does not include a byline, the assumption is made that Taylor, as editor, either wrote the article or approved the article.

49. Ibid.

50. Ibid.

51. Ibid., 9.

52. Joseph F. Barnett, "Army and Navy Testament," advertisement, *Pentecostal Holiness Advocate*, 25 October 1917, 5.

53. Joseph F. Barnett, "Testimonies," *Pentecostal Holiness Advocate*, 16 August 1917, 11.

Stanley Frodsham in his later writings, when he was working in the role of Secretary of the AG. Although Mason and Frodsham were pacifists, they contended that pacifism could be engaged while remaining faithful to the ideals of Americanism. Frodsham viewed combatant service as acceptable for those whose conscience allowed such service. Mason argued that war was particularly harmful to America's poor and persons of color, yet maintained that he and the COGIC were faithful to the United States and could support the nation financially through the purchase of war bonds.

Mason rejected the killing that war required: "We believe the shedding of human blood or taking of human life to be contrary to the teaching of our Lord and Saviour, and as a body, we are adverse to war in all its various forms," stated the Mason-endorsed COGIC statement of faith.[54] At the same time, Mason called upon COGIC members to buy Liberty Bonds: "I have loaned [to] the government, and have succeeded in raising for the help of the government more than three thousand dollars, in taking out bonds, and as far as I am concerned the spiritual injunction stands. I have loaned, hoping [to receive] nothing in return."[55] Mason considered the purchase of Liberty Bonds by his members on a par with giving to the needy.

Public opinion generally considered conscientious objectors not as advocates for peace, but advocates for Germany.[56] Mason attempted to counter the popular notions that pacifists were enemies of the state and that African Americans were susceptible to influence from German sympathizers.[57] The recently established Bureau of Investigation developed an extensive investigative report on Mason and other African-American leaders. Mason and various colleagues spent time in prison because they supported the right of conscientious objection.[58] The report of the Bureau, often reflecting a bias against African Americans, argued that Mason was an advocate for Germany. Mason is reported to have stated, "Germany is going to whip the United States for the mistreatment accorded the negroes, if for no other reason."[59] To the contrary, Mason confirmed his commitment to

---

54. "In Re: Rev. Charles Harris[on] Mason," held by Special Collections, University of Memphis Libraries, Tolbert-COGIC collection, box 9.

55. Mason, "Kaiser," 40.

56. Kornweibel, "Race and Conscientious Objection," 60–62; *Investigate Everything*, 76–117.

57. Kornweibel, "Race and Conscientious Objection," 61–62.

58. Michael Clark, "FBI File Reveals Endurance," *The Commercial Appeal* (Memphis, TN), 10 November 1983.

59. See "In Re: Rev. Charles Harris[on] Mason."

the United States by placing the responsibility of the war on the German Kaiser. Mason proclaimed, "They tell me the Kaiser went into prayer and came out and lifted up his hands and prayed, and afterwords [sic] declared war." If the Kaiser "had been praying for peace he would not have declared war."[60] The Kaiser acted upon imperialist commitments, "attempting to gather to himself all nations and to rule all people."[61] Mason concluded his sermon by praying that the Germans would be driven back and the independence of Belgium would be restored. This did not mean, however, that Mason advocated war as a solution in Europe. Instead, the church was looking forward to the coming of the Prince of Peace after which all peoples would beat their swords into plowshares and study war no more.[62]

The most vocal and observable pacifist voice within the AG was Stanley Frodsham. He contended that a Christian's priority should rest in a commitment to the eschatological kingdom of God and to heavenly citizenship. His earliest objections to war carried an intense prophetic edge. Yet, in his later and more moderate correspondence to President Wilson, he reported that the AG affirmed loyalty to the president and to the United States. Frodsham assured President Wilson that he would receive "loyal support at this time of national crisis" and "we will do all in our power to uphold your hands." Attached to the letter was a resolution committing the AG to pacifism. "[W]hile purposing to fulfill all the obligations of loyal citizenship, [we] are nevertheless constrained to declare [that] we cannot conscientiously participate in war and armed resistance which involves the actual destruction of human life."[63] At the same time, the document allowed non-combatant participation, stating "any service of a non-military character, not out of harmony with the Resolution attached, that we can give to our country at this time, will be gladly rendered."[64] The document stated further that should some Pentecostals choose to serve as combatants, the AG would not object.[65] J. W. Welch, Chair of the General Council, interpreted the position of the AG, as "not intended to hinder anyone from taking up arms who may feel free to do so, but we hope to secure the privi-

---

60. Mason, "Kaiser," 36.
61. Ibid., 38.
62. Kornweibel, "Race and Conscientious Objection," 62, citing Mason, "Kaiser," 62.
63. "The Pentecostal Movement and the Conscription Law," *Weekly Evangel*, 4 August 1917, 6.
64. Ibid.
65. Ibid.

lege of exemption from such military service as will necessitate the taking of life for all who are real conscientious objectors."⁶⁶

Frodsham's conclusions in his earlier writings had resonated with the absolute pacifists, such as Bartleman, who rejected any form of nationalism that would supersede heavenly citizenship. However, as the United States entered the war, Frodsham relented. This shift places Frodsham in closer agreement with E. N. Bell, who wrote a fiery admonishment to AG ministers warning them not to speak ill of the United States.

CONCLUSION: CITIZENS OF HEAVEN AND/OR EARTH

Straightforward conclusions concerning American Pentecostals and pacifism defy an easy answer. The evidence demonstrates that early American Pentecostals articulated three nuanced positions concerning military participation during the First World War, and at the heart of them all was the tension surrounding the intersection of Pentecostal convictions with American citizenship. The first response was a prophetic voice that called for absolute pacifism, expressed through leaders such as Frank Bartleman, Arthur Booth-Clibborn, and A. J. Tomlinson. Those Pentecostals challenged Roosevelt's contention that war unites the peoples. Instead, war and nationalism destroy society. They believed that the church should call the nations to peace and recognize that all people are equal and valuable. Their challenge was not a rejection of the American ideal, but a prophetic call to recognize the value of all persons, including those who had been labeled as the enemy. From their perspective, American Pentecostals were neither rejecting nor retreating from culture, but calling for a healing of society. This prophetic voice decried a type of Americanism that marginalized many based upon race, gender, ethnicity, or economics. That prophetic voice of Pentecostalism called all to prioritize heavenly citizenship. However, the Pentecostal commitments to heavenly citizenship were not consistent, and Pentecostals struggled with what it meant to be Christian and American. The second approach was from those who were careful in their support of the war, choosing not to challenge the war effort. As such, Pentecostals should make the best of the situation and use it as a means for evangelism. The prominent E. N. Bell represents a conflicted position; pacifist yet staunchly American as he vacillated between voice of the AG and personal commentator. Others such as G. F. Taylor stated that Pentecostals should be concerned not about earthly combat, but prepare for spiritual warfare.

66. J. W. Welch, "An Explanation," *Weekly Evangel*, 19 May 1917, 8.

Those Pentecostals were not avoiding interaction with culture but saw them as expecting to have to participate in war as all Americans. The final approach may be found in those who saw war as destructive, but wanted to maintain patriotic commitments. "This is a rich man's war," stated Bishop Mason. Nonetheless, he thought the COGIC members should readily contribute to American ideals through purchasing Liberty Bonds and by rejecting the claim that African Americans were pawns of foreign governments. Frodsham desired to put the AG on record as rejecting war while recognizing that some of the members of the AG might choose to take non-combatant roles; some might even participate as combatants. Though such proponents did not view war as an appropriate means of resolving global problems, they viewed Pentecostals as faithful Americans, not retreating from society, but fully participating. Following the First World War, Pentecostals continued the struggle individually and collectively to identify their various alignments. Whether in a time of peace or war, questions concerning participation in military service remained intricately connected to questions concerning the degree of allegiance to nationhood.

BIBLIOGRAPHY

Primary Sources

NEWSPAPERS

Weekly Evangel
Christian Evangel
Church of God Evangel
The Commercial Appeal
Pentecostal Holiness Advocate

OTHER

"In Re: Rev. Charles Harris[on] Mason," held by Special Collections, University of Memphis Libraries, Tolbert-COGIC collection, box 9.
Minutes of the Thirty-Second General Council of the Assemblies of God (1967).

Secondary Sources

Alexander, Paul. *Peace to War: Shifting Allegiances in the Assemblies of God.* Telford, PA: Cascadia, 2009.

Beaman, Jay. *Pentecostal Pacifism: The Origin, Development, and Rejection of Pacific Belief among the Pentecostals.* Eugene, OR: Wipf & Stock, 2009.

Booth-Clibborn, Arthur Sidney. *Blood against Blood.* 3rd ed. New York: Charles C. Cook, 1916.

Brandeis, Louis D. "True Americanism." In *Brandeis on Zionism: A Collection of Addresses and Statements by Louis D. Brandeis*, 3–11. Westport, CT: Hyperion, 1942.

Dempster, Murray W. "'Crossing Borders': Arguments Used by Early American Pentecostals in Support of the Global Character of Pacifism." *EPTA Bulletin: The Journal of the European Pentecostal Theological Association* 10, no. 2 (1991) 63–80.

———. "Pacifism in Pentecostalism: The Case of the Assemblies of God." In *Proclaim Peace: Christian Pacifism from Unexpected Quarters*, edited by Theron F. Schlabach and Richard T. Hughes, 31–58. Champaign: Illinois University Press, 1997.

———. "Peacetime Draft Registration and Pentecostal Moral Conscience." *Agora* 3, no. 4 (1980) 2–3.

———. Review of *Pentecostal Pacifism*, by Jay Beaman. *Pneuma: The Journal of the Society for Pentecostal Studies* 11 (1989) 59–64.

Gerstle, Gary. *American Crucible: Race and Nation in the Twentieth Century.* Princeton: Princeton University Press, 2001.

Hansen, Jonathan. "True Americanism: Progressive Era Intellectuals and the Problem of Liberal Nationalism." In *Americanism: New Perspectives on the History of an Ideal*, edited by Michael Kazin and Joseph A. McCartin, 73–89. Chapel Hill: University of North Carolina Press, 2006.

Keith, Jeanette. *Rich Man's War, Poor Man's Fight: Race, Class, and Power in the Rural South during the First World War.* Chapel Hill: University of North Carolina Press, 2004.

Kornweibel, Theodore, Jr. *"Investigate Everything": Federal Efforts to Compel Black Loyalty during World War I.* Indianapolis: Indiana University Press, 2002.

———. "Race and Conscientious Objection in World War I." In *Proclaim Peace: Christian Pacifism from Unexpected Quarters*, edited by Theron F. Schlabach and Richard T. Hughes, 58–81. Champaign: Illinois University Press, 1997.

Mason, Charles H. "The Kaiser in the Light of Scriptures." In *The History and Life Work of Bishop C. H. Mason.* Compiled by Mary Mason, 36–40. Memphis: Church of God in Christ, 1987.

Robins, Roger. "A Chronology of Peace: Attitudes toward War and Peace in the Assemblies of God: 1914–1918." *Pneuma: The Journal of the Society for Pentecostal Studies* 6 (1984) 3–25.

Wacker, Grant. *Heaven Below: Early Pentecostals and American Culture.* Cambridge, MA: Harvard University Press, 2001.

6

Mennonites and the Great War

PERRY BUSH

WARTIME, THE FIRST WORLD War antiwar critic Randolph Bourne observed in 1918, works powerful effects on democracies. During eras of peace, "the republican state has almost no trappings to appeal to the common man's emotions." Yet when a democracy enters a war, he reasoned, it works powerful nationalistic effects. It assumes a purpose and meaning absent in duller times, and fills its citizens with an emotionally dominating and regimenting patriotism. "War," Bourne summarized famously, "is the health of the state."[1]

In ironic ways, war is also the health of pacifists. Peacetime commonly induces pacifists to deemphasize principles that otherwise set them apart from their fellow citizens; it can anesthetize their convictions. Wartime, however, works opposite effects. While it can separate pacifists from the mass of their fellow citizens, even in uncomfortable and sometimes dangerous ways, it tends to sharpen their convictions.

This paradox was never truer than for American Mennonites during the First World War. For an acculturating people who had been gradually moving towards full acceptance into American society, the war reminded them that they could never fully fit in. Indeed, the trauma associated with the war—including the horrible violence directed at conscientious objectors—lingered for decades. Yet at the same time, while accentuating their separation, in the end the war provided both an ideological revitalization of

---

1. Bourne, "War Is the Health of the State."

Mennonite principles and a means for Mennonites to legitimate themselves as citizens. Through it, the historian James Juhnke has argued, Mennonites "gained a new balance between civic alienation and civic responsibility."[2]

In order to grasp these dynamics, it is first necessary to understand something of the considerable ethnic and theological complexity of the American Mennonite world. Scholars such as Juhnke, Leo Driedger, and J. Howard Kauffman have simplified its origins as a "bipolar mosaic," two different migration streams that fed Mennonite immigrants to North America. One was a "Swiss/South-German stream" that coursed into the ethnically diverse colonies in Penn's Woods—Pennsylvania—starting in the later seventeenth century. It reinforced Mennonites' socio-cultural isolation from their neighbors with the barriers of German language and a theology that branded outside cultural intrusions as "worldly" and sinful. A Dutch/North-German stream came later, beginning in the 1870s with a flood of immigrants leaving large Mennonite settlements along the Dnieper River in Ukraine. There they had enjoyed comparative autonomy from the Russian government that had lasted for a century, but eventually felt their immunity from military service was threatened. So they packed up and emigrated *en masse*. Entire congregational communities relocated to states and provinces in the Great Plains, some in the Dakotas and Nebraska, but most in southern Manitoba or south-central Kansas. While sharing many basic beliefs with the Swiss/South-German group, those Dutch/Russian immigrants arrived with a profoundly different worldview: stronger institutional proclivities, a greater pattern of involvement with outside society, and a much more pronounced in-group orientation based on a shared folk culture and a Low German (*plautdietsch*) dialect.[3]

By the first decade of the twentieth century, those migration streams had developed into over a dozen different US Mennonite and Amish-related groups. Totaling over 80,000 members, they ranged in size from the Mennonite Church (MC) with about 35,000 members (from the Swiss/South-German stream), to the General Conference Mennonite Church (GCMC or GC Mennonites, from the Dutch/Russian stream), with about 15,500 members. Amish-related groups numbered about 17,000, with nearly 8,000 in the Old Orders.[4] All those different groups were engaged in a delicate

2. Juhnke, *Vision, Doctrine, War*, 209.

3. Juhnke, "Mennonite History," 83–94; Driedger and Kauffman, "Urbanization of Mennonites"; Juhnke, *Vision, Doctrine, War*, 33–38.

4. Homan, *American Mennonites*, 31–32.

process of selective borrowing from outside society and culture, a dynamic that accentuated Mennonite tendencies towards schism but also resulted in a Mennonite/Amish world of remarkable complexity. For some, the borrowing had begun in Europe. For instance, attracted to newfound patterns of Protestant revivalism that permeated southern Ukraine, a second Dutch/Russian group, the 5,000-strong Mennonite Brethren Church (MB), split off from the GCs before coming to America in the 1870s.[5] Other even smaller groups, such as the Mennonite Brethren in Christ, the Holdeman, and the Defenseless Mennonites, split off in the nineteenth century because of their attraction to pietistic Wesleyan Holiness spirituality.[6] By the eve of the First World War, a wide variety of Mennonites from a variety of US groups had begun to borrow liberally from two different—and increasingly clashing—cultural-theological sources: mainstream American progressivism and an increasingly combative Protestant fundamentalism.[7]

Altogether, Mennonites discovered that their ethnic and theological diversity would immeasurably complicate their efforts to offer a coherent response to their government in war. But their shared values would demand a response. What held Mennonites together were key theological commitments such as the necessity of adult baptism, separation from the world, simplicity, humility, and their tradition of pacifist nonresistance. Different Mennonite groups expressed this pacifist tradition in varied ways. Mennonites from the Swiss/South-German stream stressed a wide gulf between the kingdoms of the church and the world, a let-us-alone posture devolving from a fundamental self-understanding as subjects, not citizens. Mennonites from the Dutch/Russian groups, with conceptions of citizenship established in Russia, posited less of a gap between these two kingdoms.[8] Among most Mennonite groups, nonresistance tended to be not fully rationalized. Yet for most Mennonites, pacifism remained, as two scholars have summarized, "central to their identity."[9] In 1914, as the world broke out into war, that identity led Mennonites into a destructive and profoundly traumatic confrontation with their government.

While the war raged in Europe, initial Mennonite responses varied, in part based on their place in this bipolar mosaic. The Swiss-related groups

---

5. Toews, *Pilgrims and Pioneers*, 26–85; Homan, *American Mennonites*, 32.
6. Loewen and Nolt, *Seeking Places of Peace*, 62–64, 145–46.
7. Bush, *Peace, Progress, and the Professor*, 81–84, 163–70.
8. Bush, *Two Kingdoms, Two Loyalties*, 5–12.
9. Driedger and Kraybill, *Mennonite Peacemaking*, 63–64.

east of the Mississippi reaffirmed their opposition to military service and echoed calls for American neutrality.[10] The writings of the important Mennonite historian and peace leader C. Henry Smith are illustrative. A year into the European war, Smith concluded to his fellow Mennonites that "all the nations are to blame, although some are more guilty than others," assigning blame for the war to "Austria, Germany, Russia, France, England, Serbia, [and] Belgium," in that order.[11] Smith called for America to stay out of the fray. Dutch/Russian groups, mostly located in the Great Plains and western states, also reaffirmed American neutrality and Mennonite nonresistance. However, in line with their more recent immigration and stronger immersion in German culture, their German-language denominational papers rang with sympathy for Germany. Both Abraham Schellenberg, editor of the MB paper *Vorwarts* in Hillsboro, Kansas, and editor Carl Van Der Smissen of the GC publication *Christlicher Bundesbote*, denounced stories of German atrocities as pro-war British propaganda and consistently advanced a pro-German analytical line. Schellenberg even rejoiced when German armies penetrated within forty miles of Paris. Both papers collected Mennonite funds for both the American and the German Red Cross.[12]

As American neutrality evaporated and their nation moved to the edge of war, nearly all Mennonite groups moved to strengthen the nonresistant convictions of their young people. But the move was belated and inadequate. "The war caught us unawares," recognized Silas Grubb, the editor of the GC denominational organ *The Mennonite*, in 1918.[13] Mennonite leaders and churches struggled to produce an appropriate response. In April 1917, for instance, immediately after the US declaration of war, delegates from forty-eight of the fifty-two congregations in the GC's Western District Conference met in Newton, Kansas, to consider a response. They created an official "Exemption Committee," with instructions to go to Washington to secure a dismissal of Mennonite young men from the draft. But they left unanswered a host of immediate questions having to do with matters like war bonds and noncombatant service. The delegates quickly

10. Juhnke, *Vision, Doctrine, War*, 210–11; Homan, *American Mennonites*, 39–42.

11. C. Henry Smith, "The Great War: The Immediate Cause of the War," *Christian Evangel*, July 1915, 266.

12. Toews, *Pilgrims and Pioneers*, 325; Juhnke, *Vision, Doctrine, War*, 211–12; Homan, *American Mennonites*, 40, 81.

13. Silas Grubb, "What Is the Message of a Mennonite Minister in War Time?" *The Mennonite* 33, no. 16, 1918, 2.

composed German-language pamphlets on Mennonite nonresistance and worked to spread them widely among church youth. But it was clear that GC Mennonites in Kansas had not given much thought to peace matters since the Spanish-American War.[14]

Conditions were equally uncertain across the Mennonite landscape. Peace convictions, argues a historian of Mennonites in eastern Pennsylvania, had been sorely neglected there. One prominent local Mennonite leader, Maxwell Kratz, had taught in a military academy.[15] A war draftee who had grown up in a prominent Mennonite church north of Philadelphia later admitted that he did not "recall hearing a pacifist sermon in all my life . . . we had no discussions on pacifism that I recall, till the war came. And then, all of the sudden, boy, everyone wanted to be a pacifist."[16] Few Mennonites in Oklahoma had received much teaching about peace matters,[17] and neither had those in Oregon. Church leaders there, in line with popular evangelicalism, had begun stressing a two-track ethic that elevated fundamentalist doctrine over secondary ethical matters like peace.[18] As late as 1919, the MB church had not yet passed an official church statement of nonresistance and lacked any church committee tending to such concerns.[19] Even the MC church, in many ways one of the most disciplined Mennonite denominations on matters of personal deportment, had let nonresistant matters drift. In 1918, the future MC peace leader Harold S. Bender, then a recent graduate from Goshen College, accepted a summer job assembling gas masks at a Goodyear defense plant in Akron, Ohio and received no reprimand from his church.[20]

Even so, with American entry into the war in April 1917, major Mennonite bodies stirred themselves into action. GC conferences deliberated but remained ambiguous in what they wanted from the state. The MC church—and allied bodies such as the Franconia and then the Lancaster Mennonite Conferences—passed strict guidelines, promising to deny communion to members who bought war bonds or worked in munitions plants. In August 1917, at the Yellow Creek Mennonite Church in Indiana,

---

14. Haury, *Prairie People*, 198–201.
15. Ruth, *Maintaining the Right Fellowship*, 439–40.
16. "Eyewitness Accounts: 'Berky,'" 19.
17. Coon, "Being a Peace Church," 151.
18. Lind, *Apart and Together*, 282–83.
19. Toews, *Pilgrims and Pioneers*, 348.
20. Keim, *Harold S. Bender*, 61–62.

the MCs passed a statement signed by 184 delegates—most of them pastors and bishops—"meekly" informing government officials that they could not consent to military service or in other ways cooperate with the war effort. The MC church also created an official War Problems Committee to oversee negotiations with the state about matters like the draft and war bonds.[21]

The most immediate and pressing developments in the spring of 1917 concerned the possible provisions for conscientious objectors (COs) in the emerging draft legislation. Through the summer of 1917, Mennonite and Amish leaders of all stripes sent letters to Wilson asking him to respect their peace commitments and excuse their young men from military participation. The Mennonite ability to influence such matters was deeply hampered because of divisions in their ranks. For example, when the Exemption Committee of the GC's Western District Conference arrived in Washington to press officials for CO recognition, they found their task complicated by the fact that two other Mennonite delegations were already in the capital operating independently from each other. The MB church had sent a delegation and so had a group of more acculturated GC Mennonites from eastern states called the "All-Mennonite Convention." In June the MC church sent officials and two months later so did the Franconia Mennonite Conference (then loosely affiliated with the MC church). Nor were such delegations operating with similar agendas. The All-Mennonite group wrongly informed a number of congressmen that Mennonites would accept any military role except for actually taking up weapons.[22]

In actuality, while various congressmen and senators were sympathetic, their ability to determine CO issues was limited. That task fell to the president, and neither Wilson nor the main official he had appointed to deal with such matters—Secretary of War Newton Baker—had any intention of excusing anyone from service. The fundamental question revolved around how the president would define noncombatant roles. Hotly debated in Congress, the draft bill of 1917 was not signed into law by Wilson until May 18. It contained a clause appearing to vaguely recognize the right of conscientious objection, excusing COs from direct military service but assigning them to a noncombatant role that Wilson—through Baker—would define later. Noncombatant service and not straight exemption from the

---

21. Stutzman, *From Nonresistance to Justice*, 59–60; Ruth, *Maintaining the Right Fellowship*, 440–41; Homan, *American Mennonites*, 52.

22. Homan, *American Mennonites*, 45–46, 52–53; Juhnke, *Vision, Doctrine, War*, 229–30; Ruth, *Maintaining the Right Fellowship*, 440–41.

military were the best that pacifists would get, a realization that came as a deep shock to many Mennonites. "We had not believed that this would be possible in the United States," admitted a prominent GC leader from Kansas.[23]

Nor did meetings with various officials, especially Baker, provide much reassurance about the possible fate of peace Christians in the US military. Mennonite confusion was understandable because Baker was ambiguous, perhaps deliberately, and gave conflicting signals to the various delegations he met. For instance, in late August, Baker affirmed to a delegation of Hutterites (a communal Mennonite group) that their young men would not be forced to violate their consciences. In early September, he seemed to assure the MC's War Problems Committee that their draftees would not be forced into noncombatant ranks, would not have to put on uniforms or engage in military drill, and instead would be given clearly non-military roles. At one point, he jovially tapped the knee of a Mennonite leader and assured him "Don't worry. We'll take care of your boys." Yet when the delegation returned home, Baker wrote the committee that they had misunderstood; there was no provision for non-military work. Meanwhile directives from the War Department in August made it quite plain that all young men had to register and that all draftees, combatant or noncombatant, would be considered in military service.[24]

In retrospect, it was clear that the decision whether to register for the draft and enter military camps—as Baker and other military officials had repeatedly and consistently urged—was the fateful decision for the Mennonite churches. Baker's fundamental agenda was to keep the number of COs low. Once pacifist draftees were in the camps, he believed, they could be persuaded to drop their conscientious scruples and enter military ranks. So he sent private orders to camp officials to treat them leniently. In this, Mennonite historians later charged, Mennonites had been caught in a "conscription trap" by wily governmental officials, using whatever rhetorical devices at hand to incorporate pacifist draftees into the war effort.[25] While the historian Gerlof Homan disputes this view,[26] documents from the time

23. Keim and Stoltzfus, *Politics of Conscience*, 33–36; Homan, *American Mennonites*, 46–49. The Kansas Mennonite is quoted on p. 49.

24. Keim and Stoltzfus, *Politics of Conscience*, 37–44. The quotation of Baker is on p. 40. Homan, *American Mennonites*, 53–55.

25. Teichroew, "Mennonites and the Conscription Trap"; Juhnke, *Vision, Doctrine, War*, 232; Keim and Stoltzfus, *Politics of Conscience*, 46–48.

26. Homan, *American Mennonites*, 54–55.

appear to support it. "I guess in a way the non-resistant denominations have been duped by these politicians," a sorrowful army medic wrote the president of his Mennonite college. He thought noncombatant service a sham. "The best is to stand firm," Harvey Beidler reasoned, and demonstrate to military officials "that the non-resistant doctrine amounts to more than refusing to shoot a man but being willing for somebody else to shoot after we have loaded the gun."[27]

Many Mennonite draftees looked to their church for instruction. They received uncertain answers. The GC church issued their draftees only vague guidelines. In August 1917, it passed an official statement declaring their willingness to "render any service outside the military establishment which aims to support and save life," but prohibited Mennonites from "any work which will result in personal injury or loss of life to others."[28] Offering more than such broad platitudes could be dangerous. As one GC peace leader told a draftee, "You have to have your own views of pacifism because the pressure is too great on us. They can hold us for treason if we advise you to stand firm."[29] The MC Military Problems Committee did what it could to aid Mennonite draftees with these difficult decisions. Its leader, Bishop Aaron Loucks, journeyed thousands of miles from camp to camp to plead with army officials for more lenient treatment. But Loucks soon had to walk softly. Defense officials in Iowa urged his prosecution as a "German agent" and he soon found himself under investigation by the Department of Justice for possible violation of the new Espionage Act.[30]

As a result, Mennonite draftees made a variety of choices. Some joined the military in either noncombatant or straight military roles; a few of the latter died in combat. Depending on the degree of acculturation operative in their home church community, returning veterans could expect to receive little sanction, or even celebration, for such choices. Two Mennonite students at Bluffton College, a GC school in Ohio, found their combat exploits followed with breathless enthusiasm in the school newspaper.[31]

---

27. Harvey Beidler to Samuel Mosiman, August 28, 1917, S. K. Mosiman Papers, I-A-b, Box 12, folder "War, 1917 – 1919," BUASC.

28. "Statement of the General Conference of the Mennonite Church of North America," 1.

29. Haury, *Prairie People*, 201–3; Homan, *American Mennonites*, 124–25, 133, quotation from p. 133.

30. Homan, *American Mennonites*, 125–31.

31. Bush, *Dancing with the Kobzar*, 86.

Another veteran in eastern Pennsylvania took communion in his home congregation while wearing his uniform.[32]

Other Mennonites, however, tried to remain true to pacifist nonresistance in isolated army camps. Some found it an easier course than others. One draftee in Ohio's Camp Sherman, for instance, reported to his uncle that "there are nine or ten of us objectors here and we are treated real nice." He thought that COs in Camp Travis in Texas "went intirely [sic] too far when they said they would do nothing."[33] Many other draftees, however, found efforts to safeguard pacifist consciences a hazardous occupation, especially in western military camps. If a draftee accepted noncombatant status—signified by wearing the uniform, obeying military orders, and engaging in military drill—they were generally free from abuse. Yet great numbers of Mennonite draftees—perhaps as high as a majority[34]—would not accept such roles. "The further you went with military officials the further they demanded one go," reasoned one Mennonite CO. "The further I went the less reason I could give for stopping—so I concluded the best place to stop was at the beginning."[35] Such draftees, as the Mennonite historian Smith summarized in 1920, soon became subjected to "tortures that would have done credit to the medieval Inquisition."[36]

The examples are chilling and numerous; space allows for only a few here. Jesse Hartzler, a MC draftee from Missouri, found himself imprisoned on a bread and water diet, lashed bloody with straps, and held in solitary confinement. He also recalled, decades later, the occasions when soldiers secretly dissented from these brutalities and slipped him extra food and private apologies.[37] Ferdinand Schroeder refused orders to work at Camp

---

32. Ruth, *Maintaining the Right Fellowship*, 444.

33. Lester Smith to "Dear Uncle," C. Henry Smith Papers, June 9 and June 27, 1918. Hist. Mss. 1, Box 8, folder 1, BUASC.

34. Homan estimates that only about 4,000 of 21,000 or so COs drafted during the war remained true to their convictions and refused to be converted to military service. A further 1,700 of those ultimately accepted noncombatant roles. "Most" of the remaining were Mennonites, though the numbers are elusive. Smaller groupings are probably indicative of the larger whole. A historian of Oklahoma Mennonites estimated three quarters of their draftees took a CO position, while Juhnke's work on Kansas Mennonites estimated about 45 percent did so. See Homan, *American Mennonites*, 103–4; Coon, "Being a Peace Church," 150–55; and Juhnke, *People of Two Kingdoms*, 102–3.

35. Quoted in Homan, *American Mennonites*, 106.

36. C. H. Smith, *Mennonites: A Brief History*, 293.

37. H. B. Yoder, *Same Spirit*, 96.

Funston in Kansas and was beaten so badly he lost a tooth.[38] Officers then demanded he rigidly stand at attention, refusing to even grant him permission to wipe off the blood dripping from his chin. When he refused military training at Georgia's Fort Oglethorpe, Elmer Swartzendruber of the Conservative Amish Mennonite Conference was forced to dismantle an outhouse and then was dunked into the open latrine.[39] Soldiers mockingly "baptized" a CO at Camp Greenleaf by emptying a shovel of excrement on his head. Secretary of War Baker may have preferred kinder policies to "persuade" COs to take up military service, but did not make such wishes known widely enough to effect a change in army behavior; nor did he punish abusers. Officers and soldiers alike took their cues accordingly. They forced absolutist COs to dig their own graves and informed them they would be buried alive.[40] When Ora Hartzler arrived at Camp McArthur in Waco, Texas, officers demanded he either accept military work or get down on his knees and pray. Once Hartzler began praying, officers turned him over to prisoners in the camp stockade. They subjected Hartzler to a mock trial, declared him guilty, and sentenced him to a hundred lashes. These they promptly carried out, with the last sixty-five lashes using the buckle end of a belt. After another mock trial, inmates gave Hartzler another 500 lashes, periodically stopping to ask him if he would consent to work now.[41] One Oregon Mennonite, Orie Conrad, was sent to Camp Lewis in Washington where he was daily subjected to cold and hot showers and had his hair roughly sheared off. One Saturday morning he was taken out behind the barracks where soldiers had slung a rope over a tree. Soldiers fixed the noose around Conrad's neck, threw a sack over his head and asked him for his last words. Officers then intervened and pulled the unconscious Conrad down. (Those solders were later court-martialed).[42]

By spring 1918 the abuse ended for many but not all of the objectors. The newly passed Farm Furlough Act allowed them to be directed into farm labor, far from immediate military supervision.[43] At the same time, however, the brutalities continued for others. In April 1918, new War

38. "Eyewitness Accounts: 'Schroeder.'"
39. N. E. Yoder, *Together in the Work*, 149.
40. Homan, *American Mennonites*, 111, 115.
41. Erb, *South-Central Frontiers*, 90.
42. Lind, *Apart and Together*, 287.
43. Keim and Stoltzfus, *Politics of Conscience*, 49–53; Homan, *American Mennonites*, 129–30.

Department regulations permitted the court-martialing of recalcitrant COs. Trials began the next month and intensified through the summer and fall. Mennonites, in the end, comprised 142 of the 504 COs who were court-martialed during the war, in most cases for matters like refusing to obey military orders. Those guilty were awarded obscenely long sentences—half for twenty-five years or more—because, one War Department official openly admitted to a Mennonite leader, they wanted to send a message.[44] Once imprisoned, most commonly at Ft. Leavenworth in Kansas, these absolutist objectors faced ongoing abuse, particularly if they continued to resist military orders on matters like the military uniform. When Albert Voth and forty-four like-minded objectors, for instance, refused the uniform, he was kept confined in an open stockade in the rain and the broiling sun for ten days, and then starved for three more.[45] While most court-martialed objectors were pardoned and released after the war, not all of them made it home. The most famous case was the tragic fate of four Hutterites from South Dakota, brothers David, Joseph, and Michael Hofer, and their brother-in-law Jacob Wipf. As the four determined men refused to don military uniforms and cooperate with other orders, military officials at Alcatraz penitentiary and then at Ft. Leavenworth intensified the tortures. Those four COs were beaten, stripped of clothing, hung from the bars of their cells for days at a time, and denied food and water. When the men finally broke and died and their grieving families received their bodies, they found them dressed in uniforms.[46]

Mennonites soon discovered that such tests of conscience would not be visited only on their young men. The Wilson administration pushed across draconian legislation like the Espionage Act of June 1917 and the Sedition Act a year later, giving the government new powers to restrict drastically American freedom of expression. Following such cues, Americans quickly launched into a vicious, high-strung campaign against a perceived German enemy abroad and also at home. Vigilante groups sprung up to punish perceived lapses in public patriotism, and when authorities refused to crack down on them, they received semi-official sanction. War dissenters were mobbed and lynched across the country, the Attorney General

---

44. Homan, *American Mennonites*, 143–46.
45. *Sourcebook*, 58–59.
46. Stoltzfus, *Pacifists in Chains*; for a shorter summary of this case, see Homan, *American Mennonites*, 152–54.

banned from the mail anything he deemed seditious, and ordinary Americans received jail sentences for dissenting publicly against the war.[47]

As a definably ethnic German group who were also pacifist, Mennonites were doubly suspect, though it was a year into the war before they began to fully realize the limits of public tolerance. Up until mid-1918, Homan relates, denominational newspapers like the *Gospel Herald* of the Mennonite Church and the GC organ *The Mennonite* carried forth determinedly with their peace message. Editor Daniel Kauffman in the *Gospel Herald*, for instance, reminded MC Mennonites in 1917 to remember to keep the commands of God supreme over the state in their consciences, and to be prepared to "stand the test in these trying times." The paper called Mennonites to persist boldly in the cause of nonresistance.[48] By the fall of 1918, however, public animus had increased to the point where many thought better of these public declarations. The *Berne Witness* of Berne, Indiana, previously indifferent to the war and unsupportive of the draft, soon began publishing pro-war cartoons and pushing Liberty Loan sales. The Mennonite German-language press, in particular, thought it politic to soften its tone and message. *Der Herold* of Newton, Kansas likewise printed cartoons supportive of the war and desisted from editorials critical of the US war effort.[49] Editor Schellenberg of the MB denominational publication *Vorwarts* did not back off from his pro-German sympathies. He managed to escape indictment under the Espionage Act but increasingly found himself out of tenor with his constituency and then out of a job.[50]

With the fires of popular patriotism rising to fever pitch, pressures to fly the flag or contribute to the Red Cross became particular flash points. The Red Cross was a morally ambiguous issue. Decent Christians want to alleviate suffering, especially in a world aflame. Why, some Mennonites reasoned, would we not want to contribute to the Red Cross? "A way of combating evil," declared Silas Grubb, editor of *The Mennonite*, in 1918, "is to emphasize the good opposing it." Grubb urged Mennonites to help in every way short of combat. "We only show ourselves loyal citizens," Grubb insisted, "if in this time of suffering we are ready to contribute something

---

47. Kennedy, *Over Here*, 5, 10–11, 24–26, 45–92.

48. Daniel Kauffman, "'Conscientious Objector' and the Issues Involved," *Gospel Herald* 11, no. 17, 25 July 1918, 291; Homan, *American Mennonites*, 60.

49. Homan, *American Mennonites*, 60–61.

50. Juhnke, *Vision, Doctrine, War*, 220–21.

that will bear favorable comparison to the sufferings and sacrifices made by those who serve under the colors."[51]

Others, however, especially from the more nonconformist Mennonite Church, saw a Red Cross deeply intertwined with the program and needs of the US military. Reasoning like that in 1918 could land one in trouble. When Jacob Stehman, a member of a MC congregation in Garden City, Missouri, refused a Red Cross contribution, a mob of fifty men tarred and feathered him and threatened to do the same to his minister. The congregation avoided further trouble by producing a $1,200 contribution. In what appears like a local protection racket, three other area Mennonite congregations likewise deterred mob violence by producing similar-sized payments to the Red Cross.[52] In other areas Mennonite fidelity to principle resulted in painful public humiliation. When an MC bishop in south central Ohio named Samuel Allgyer refused to make a Red Cross contribution, a large mob, including the local state representative, roughly cut off his hair with horse shears. The same thing happened to a Mennonite minister near Kokomo, Indiana at the hands of a local vigilante group called the Loyal Citizens Vigilance Committee. When he refused to make a $100 Red Cross donation, those citizens shaved his head and slathered it with yellow paint.[53] At a Mennonite church in Fisher, Illinois, vandals reinforced proper patriotism by putting up a flagpole and flag and splashing the church with yellow paint. Mennonite churches in Salem and Metamora, Illinois were also hit with yellow paint. In addition, local patriots plastered the outside walls of the Metamora church with large signs reading "We are Slackers," and "We Buy No Bonds." The letters remained visible for years.[54]

It is no coincidence that the Metamora church received criticism about bonds. Liberty bonds were one of the government's direct ways of financing the war and they were structured in such a manner—with massive Liberty Bond drives, celebrity endorsements, and accompanying media frenzy—as to accentuate their function as a major means of war socialization.[55] Many Mennonites concluded they could have nothing to do with them and paid a price. Take the case, for instance, of Charles and Daniel Diener, a father-

---

51. Silas Grubb, "What Is the Message of a Mennonite Minister in War Time?" *The Mennonite* 33, no. 16, 1918, 3.

52. Erb, *South-Central Frontiers*, 99–100; Homan, *American Mennonites*, 83.

53. Homan, *American Mennonites*, 82–84.

54. W. Smith, *Mennonites in Illinois*, 356.

55. Kennedy, *Over Here*, 100–106.

son team who jointly ministered to the MC Spring Valley congregation in south-central Kansas. When they refused to buy bonds in June 1918, they were visited by mobs who, in the end, whipped the two men, smeared them with carbolic roofing paint and feathers, and threatened them with murder. Another mob went to tar and feather another stubborn Mennonite from the same congregation, Walter Cooprider. Finding him ill and old, they agreed to subject his son George to the treatment instead.[56] Another Mennonite, John Schrag, was nearly lynched for his fidelity to nonresistant principles. Journeying from his nearby farm into the town of Burrton, Kansas on Armistice Day 1918, Schrag was grabbed by a mob. When he refused to buy bonds or lead a victory parade, the crowd covered him with yellow paint and made preparations to lynch him before a local sheriff intervened with his pistol.[57] Another Mennonite named John Franz of Bloomfield, Montana, was rescued by a local sheriff from lynching. Franz's principal offense seemed to be that he had dared conduct Bible classes in German.[58]

The wartime persecution took a variety of forms and spread across the Mennonite landscape. Two Mennonite churches, in Inola, Oklahoma and Fairview, Michigan were burned to the ground during the war.[59] In Ohio a politically ambitious federal District Attorney, Victor Wertz, looked to follow up his prosecution and conviction of the socialist Eugene Debs by prosecuting local Mennonites under the Espionage Act. His first target was Samuel Miller, the Mennonite editor of the Ohio Amish newspaper the *Sugar Creek Budget*. Miller's paper had published a letter from an Amish bishop named Manassas Bontrager regretting that some Mennonites had bought war bonds. For that offense, Wertz brought a five count charge, including the charges that Miller and Bontrager had attempted or caused "insubordination, disloyalty, mutiny and refusal of duty in" in the US military and had promoted "the success of the Imperial German Government." The two men ultimately settled in a plea bargain and a $500 fine. Wertz then prepared a prosecution of all of the 181 Mennonite bishops, pastors, and deacons who had signed the Yellow Creek statement of 1917, and might have proceeded to a mass trial had not the war ended.[60]

56. Entz, "War Bond Drives," 7–9; Juhnke, *Vision, Doctrine, War*, 223; Erb, *South-Central Frontiers*, 226, 266.
57. "Eyewitness Accounts: 'Gordon'"; Juhnke, *Vision, Doctrine, War*, 224–25.
58. Juhnke, *Vision, Doctrine, War*, 223–24.
59. Ibid., 218; Homan, *American Mennonites*, 76–77.
60. Juhnke, *Vision, Doctrine, War*, 225–28; Joseph, "The United States v. H. Miller,"

Mennonites protected themselves from further harassment through a variety of stratagems. Some reluctantly bought bonds; others enthusiastically backed the war.[61] This atmosphere especially permeated the GC Mennonites' two colleges, Bethel in Kansas and Bluffton in Ohio. Students and faculty at both schools joined the military in both combatant and noncombatant roles, sold liberty bonds, and raised money for the Red Cross.[62] Partly this was due to conviction. President Mosiman of Bluffton, for instance, told a friend that he had "felt from the very beginning that the allied cause was the cause of righteousness and justice."[63] He resolutely urged Mennonite men to enter into noncombatant roles, counseling Mennonite draftees not to engage in "hairsplitting" over military orders to accept "the uniform and such things."[64] Yet Mosiman and other college officials may have acted partly out of pragmatic considerations of survival. He was also aware, he wrote to one pacifist critic, that one of the newspapers in nearby Lima recently "counseled mob violence against Conscientious objectors at Bluffton."[65] In Mennonite communities across the country, the war rapidly accelerated what had been a slow Mennonite language transition from German to English. Use of German itself became a subversive act in some places; laws were passed against it in South Dakota and Oklahoma.[66] In other places Mennonites did what they had historically done at other times and places to escape public hostility: they left. The war triggered the migration of some 7,000 Mennonite COs (and presumably also many of their parents) to Canada. Following the torture deaths of the Hofer brothers and Joseph Wipf, most of the Dakota Hutterites likewise migrated across the Canadian border.[67]

In the end, this experience of deep wartime trauma produced lasting effects among American Mennonites, though in paradoxical ways. Take,

---

14–18, the quotation is on p. 16.

61. Homan, *American Mennonites*, 61–62, 92–93.

62. Sprunger, *Bethel College of Kansas*, 54–57; Bush, *Dancing with the Kobzar*, 86–87.

63. Samuel Mosiman to C. J. Claassen, June 22, 1918, S. K. Mosiman Papers, I-A-b, Box 1, folder "C. J. Claassen," BUASC.

64. Samuel Mosiman to J. W. Kliewer, April 15 and June 28, 1918, S. K. Mosiman Papers, I-A-b, Box 12, folder "War Committee on Exemptions," BUASC.

65. Samuel Mosiman to Aaron Augspurger, June 11, 1918, S. K. Mosiman Papers, I-A-b, Box 7, folder "Rev. Aaron Augspurger," BUASC.

66. Coon, "Being a Peace Church," 149–50; Homan, *American Mennonites*, 63–64; H. B. Yoder, *The Same Spirit*, 102–3; N. E. Yoder, *Together in the Work*, 149–50.

67. Loewen and Nolt, *Seeking Places of Peace*, 75.

for instance, the intellectual shift it occasioned in the intellectual journey of the influential Mennonite historian and peace leader C. Henry Smith. Before the war, he had consistently promoted Mennonite acculturation into the progressive mainstream. Within a few years following the war, however, his writings and speeches began to take a different turn, worrying about the darker and repressive capacities of the US state and cautioning Mennonites not to enter so willingly and uncritically into American society.[68] To a fair degree, the war induced the same kind of larger transformation in Smith's church. Mennonites emerged from the war with many more recent, vivid reminders of why their Anabaptist ancestors had warned so deafeningly of the dangers of the wicked world and expected the church to be a persecuted, faithful remnant. A Mennonite pastor undoubtedly spoke for many others when he wrote in 1917 that the war had reinforced for him a central lesson: that "there must be a more distinct separation of our people from the world and politics."[69]

On the other hand, as Juhnke has documented, the war ironically helped lower the barriers that Mennonites had erected between themselves and outside society. They began to redefine what it meant to be a Mennonite in a world of pain and need, and push towards new understandings of Mennonite citizenship. With Europe a battlefield, skyrocketing American farm prices had greatly enriched Mennonite communities. In the postwar years they began pouring these surplus funds into a variety of postwar mission and relief programs. This impulse soon resulted in a number of new relief committees set up by different Mennonite groups. Most important was the new inter-Mennonite relief agency, Mennonite Central Committee, created in 1920 to deal with the massive postwar famine engulfing Mennonite communities in southern Ukraine. Such joint efforts fueled nascent new Mennonite efforts at cooperation and created institutional means for developing patterns of Mennonite ecumenicity.[70] Equally importantly, such new relief and mission agencies provided a means for Mennonites to establish their legitimacy as American citizens in a time when their peace commitments closed off a major mechanism towards such legitimacy seized by other ethnic groups: that of battlefield sacrifice. In this manner Mennonite

---

68. Bush, *Peace, Progress, and the Professor*, 80–111, 156–63, 206–10, 217–18, 242–43, 297–304.

69. Juhnke, "Mennonite Benevolence," 17.

70. Ibid., 18–22, 26–28; Kreider and Goossen, *Hungry, Thirsty, a Stranger*, 23–29; Unruh, *In the Name of Christ*, 12–16.

benevolence efforts functioned, Juhnke has argued, as a Mennonite moral equivalent of war.[71]

At the same time and perhaps most importantly, the war also assisted Mennonites in sharpening and further defining their identity as pacifists. This occurred almost simultaneously among a number of different groups. The GC's Western District Conference, for example, refused to dissolve its Exemption Committee immediately upon the end of the war. Soon it began pushing congressional representatives in Washington against new proposals for compulsory military service.[72] An ongoing warlike world convinced the MC church that they could not dispense with their peace efforts. In 1925, their Military Problems Committee gained permanent status and was renamed the Peace Problems Committee. It functioned for the next half century as a major vehicle for this Mennonite denomination to expand and develop their peace convictions. In a like manner, in 1926 the GC church established its own permanent Peace Committee, which, like its MC counterpart, began mounting peace conferences, publishing pamphlets on nonresistance, and engaging in other efforts aimed at rooting Mennonite youth in peace concerns.[73] Stung by the apparent wartime lapses in the peace convictions of many MB young men, in 1919 the Mennonite Brethren Church held a conference in Mountain Lake, Minnesota where they reaffirmed their historic commitment to nonresistance. Out of that conference a new MB Committee on Nonresistance emerged to tend to such convictions in the future.[74]

Through all these avenues, the trials of the war, traumatic as they were, worked in ironic ways to strengthen and deepen the peace witness of the Mennonite churches. The very language they employed in regards to the state, two scholars argue, had undergone subtle but profound reorientation. No longer, they write, were Mennonites "pleading on their knees with hat in hand. Now in the context of World War I, they were using the language of citizens, not subjects."[75] Fifteen years later, as another world war began to loom, they would send representatives straightaway to Washington, where they would work closely with Friends, Brethren, and other pacifist allies to create an official alternative service program to safeguard the consciences

71. Juhnke, "Mennonite Benevolence," 29–30.
72. Haury, *Prairie People*, 204.
73. Bush, *Two Kingdoms, Two Loyalties*, 37–54.
74. Toews, *Pilgrims and Pioneers*, 348–49.
75. Driedger and Kraybill, *Mennonite Peacemaking*, 66.

of their young men in wartime.[76] The legacy of the First World War would reverberate among the Mennonite churches for decades. In sum, as James Juhnke has written, "in paradoxical ways, war was the health of this nonresistant religious subculture."[77]

BIBLIOGRAPHY

Primary Sources

Archive

BUASC = Bluffton University Archives and Special Collections, Bluffton, Ohio.

Newspapers

Gospel Herald, 1918.
The Mennonite, 1918.
Christian Evangel, 1915.

Other

Smith, C. Henry. *Mennonites: A Brief History*. Berne, IN: Mennonite Book Concern, 1920.

Secondary Sources

Bourne, Randolph. "War Is the Health of the State." http://www.antiwar.com/bourne.php.
Bush, Perry. *Dancing with the Kobzar: Bluffton College and Mennonite Higher Education, 1899-1999*. Telford, PA: Pandora, 2000.
———. *Peace, Progress, and the Professor: The Mennonite History of C. Henry Smith*. Scottdale, PA: Herald, 2015.
———. *Two Kingdoms, Two Loyalties: Mennonite Pacifism in Modern America*. Baltimore: Johns Hopkins University Press, 1998.
Coon, Robert. "Being a Peace Church Makes a Difference." In *Growing Faith: General Conference Mennonites in Oklahoma*, edited by Wilma McKee, 145-56. Newton: Faith and Life, 1988.
Driedger, Leo, and J. Howard Kauffman. "Urbanization of Mennonites: Canadian and American Comparisons." *Mennonite Quarterly Review* 56 (July 1982) 269-90.

---

76. Bush, *Two Kingdoms, Two Loyalties*, 69-80.
77. Juhnke, "Mennonite Benevolence," 17.

Driedger, Leo, and Donald B. Kraybill. *Mennonite Peacemaking: From Quietism to Activism*. Scottdale, PA: Herald, 1994.

Entz, Margaret. "War Bond Drives and the Kansas Mennonite Response." *Mennonite Life* 30 (September 1975) 4–9.

Erb, Paul. *South-Central Frontiers: A History of the South Central Mennonite Conference*. Scottdale, PA: Herald, 1974.

"Eyewitness Accounts: 'Berky,' 'Gordon,' and 'Schroeder.'" *Mennonite Life* 30 (September 1975) 19–25.

Haury, David. *Prairie People: A History of the Western District Conference*. Newton, KS: Faith and Life, 1981.

Homan, Gerlof. *American Mennonites and the Great War, 1914–1918*. Scottdale, PA: Herald, 1994.

Joseph, Ted. "The United States v. H. Miller: The Strange Case of a Mennonite Editor Convicted of Violating the 1917 Espionage Act." *Mennonite Life* 30 (September 1975) 14–18.

Juhnke, James. "Mennonite Benevolence and Revitalization in the Wake of World War I." *Mennonite Quarterly Review* 60 (January 1986) 15–30.

———. "Mennonite History and Self-Understanding: North American Mennonitism as a Bipolar Mosaic." In *Mennonite Identity: Historical and Contemporary Perspectives*, edited by Calvin W. Redekop and Samuel J. Steiner, 83–99. Lanham, MD: University Press of America, 1988.

———. *A People of Two Kingdoms*. Newton, KS: Faith and Life, 1975.

———. *Vision, Doctrine, War: Mennonite Identity and Organization in America, 1890–1930*. Scottdale, PA: Herald, 1989.

Kennedy, David M. *Over Here: The First World War and American Society*. New York: Oxford University Press, 1980.

Keim, Albert N. *Harold S. Bender, 1897–1962*. Scottdale, PA: Herald, 1998.

Keim, Albert N., and Grant Stoltzfus. *The Politics of Conscience: The Historic Peace Churches and America at War, 1917–1936*. Scottdale, PA: Herald, 1988.

Kreider, Robert S., and Rachel Waltner Goossen. *Hungry, Thirsty, a Stranger: The MCC Experience*. Scottdale, PA: Herald, 1988.

Lind, Hope Kauffman. *Apart and Together: Mennonites in Oregon and Neighboring States, 1876–1976*. Scottdale, PA: Herald, 1990.

Loewen, Royden, and Steven M. Nolt. *Seeking Places of Peace*. Kitchener, ON: Pandora, 2012.

Ruth, John L. *Maintaining the Right Fellowship: A Narrative Account of Life in the Oldest Mennonite Community in North America*. Scottdale, PA: Herald, 1984.

Smith, Willard. *Mennonites in Illinois*. Scottdale, PA: Herald, 1983.

Sourcebook: Oral History Interviews with World War One Conscientious Objectors. Mennonite Central Committee, 1986.

Sprunger, Keith L. *Bethel College of Kansas, 1887–2012*. North Newton, KS: Bethel College, 2012.

"Statement of the General Conference of the Mennonite Church of North America." *The Mennonite* 32 (Sept. 13, 1917) 1.

Stoltzfus, Duane C. S. *Pacifists in Chains: The Persecution of Hutterites during the Great War*. Baltimore: Johns Hopkins University Press, 2013.

Stutzman, Ervin. *From Nonresistance to Justice: The Transformation of Mennonite Church Peace Rhetoric, 1908–2008*. Scottdale, PA: Herald, 2011.

Teichroew, Allen. "Mennonites and the Conscription Trap." *Mennonite Life* 30 (September 1975) 10–13.

Toews, John A. *Pilgrims and Pioneers: A History of the Mennonite Brethren Church.* Hillsboro, KS: Mennonite Brethren, 1975.

Unruh, John D. *In the Name of Christ: A History of Mennonite Central Committee.* Scottdale, PA: Herald, 1952.

Yoder, Holly Blosser. *The Same Spirit: History of Iowa-Nebraska Mennonites.* Freeman, SD: Central Plains Mennonite Conference, n.d.

Yoder, Nathan E. *Together in the Work of the Lord: A History of the Conservative Mennonite Conference.* Harrisonburg, VA: Herald, 2014.

7

Quakers and World War One

*Negotiating Individual Conscience
and the Peace Testimony*

ROBYNNE ROGERS HEALEY

O N 10 JANUARY 1918, Mary Stone McDowell, a member of the Brooklyn Monthly Meeting[1] and pacifist teacher at Manual Training High School in Brooklyn, appeared before the New York City Board of Superintendents to answer for her refusal to support school programs in favor of the war. At the hour-long hearing McDowell was interrogated by four school board officials who tried to determine whether McDowell's insubordinate behavior was disloyal and warranted charges. Following the hearing, the Board of Superintendents agreed that charges of "conduct unbecoming a teacher" should be brought against her. Her trial, on 15 May 1918, was short, lasting only two-and-a-half hours. After a month of deliberation, board members upheld the charges against McDowell and dismissed her from her position as a teacher in the New York City Public School System. Despite a series

---

1. The basic organizational unit for Quakers, since the seventeenth century, is the Monthly Meeting. It provides direction in the daily lives of Friends. Monthly meetings have the power to accept and disown members, to make marriages official, and to hold property. Two or more monthly meetings constitute a Quarterly Meeting, which, as the name suggests, traditionally meets four times each year. Several quarterly meetings make up a Yearly Meeting, the meeting with the highest level of authority in the Religious Society of Friends. Yearly meetings determine both doctrine and policy for their members and constituent meetings.

of appeals that ended at the New York State Supreme Court in October 1918, the decision of the school board was upheld. The court ruled that "the petitioner was not dismissed because she is a Quakeress. It has simply been found that certain views and beliefs, which she declares are based upon her religion, prevent her from properly discharging the duty she assumed. . . . While the petitioner may be entitled to the greatest respect for her adherence to her faith, she cannot be permitted because of it to act in a manner inconsistent with the peace and safety of the state."[2] It was not until 1923, after the frenzy of war had subsided, that the school board reconsidered her case and voted to reinstate her. McDowell went back to teaching and retired in 1943.[3] Her position on war, her refusal to participate in any events that promoted it, and her efforts to promote peace will be unsurprising to those familiar with the Religious Society of Friends (Quakers) and its historic commitment to non-violence. Indeed, McDowell's expression of Quaker conscience and her suffering that resulted from her conscientious objection can be considered a quintessential expression of the Quaker peace testimony in the Great War.

Was McDowell's experience the norm for Quakers? Apparently not. While accurate and reliable statistics on Quaker enlistment in the First World War are not readily available, it is generally accepted that 50 percent of eligible American Quakers performed military service.[4] Some studies suggest even higher rates of participation.[5] Figures for American Quaker military service are higher than those reported in England, where roughly 30 percent of Quakers enlisted.[6]

What motivated Quakers to volunteer for military service? Consider the experience of Wyatt Acton Miller, a chemical engineer and member of Salem Monthly Meeting in Salem, New Jersey. Miller enlisted on 22 November 1917 in what became known as the First Gas Regiment. He remained a private in this regiment for the duration of the war. Miller could have chosen to do alternative service with the American Friends Service Committee (AFSC), an organization formed in April 1917 to provide

---

2. Matter of McDowell v. Board of Education, 568.

3. Howlett, "Quaker Conscience in the Classroom," 101–10; Howlett and Howlett, "Silent Witness for Peace," 382–89.

4. Valentine, "Quakers, War, and Peacemaking," 372.

5. Hamm et al., "Decline of Quaker Pacifism," 54.

6. Hirst, *Quakers in Peace and War*, 538.

voluntary alternative service opportunities for pacifists.⁷ In fact, his sister, Alice Thompson Miller, worked with refugees in France under the direction of AFSC. Importantly, Miller's decision to enlist cannot be attributed to an insincere faith commitment nor to a betrayal of his beliefs. A Hicksite Friend, he came from a family deeply rooted in Hicksite Quakerism. Indeed, his was a long line of recognized Quaker leaders (ministers, elders, clerks, or overseers), including his own parents, that extended back to the earliest seventeenth-century Quaker presence in New Jersey. He had received an explicitly Quaker education at George School, a Hicksite boarding school; this connected him to a broader Quaker community outside his own meeting. Moreover, his behavior before and after the war suggests an individual with strong Quaker convictions. He used plain speech with his family and, significantly, with his fiancée E. Lucile Duff, who was not a Quaker before the war. After the war, Miller was recognized as an elder in the Chicago Monthly Meeting, he served on the executive committee of AFSC, was a delegate to the 1952 World Conference of Friends in Oxford, and served on the Board of Trustees of Earlham College. His decision to enlist was not one made lightly or quickly; like McDowell's it was a decision of conscience and was representative of the tensions with which Friends individually experienced the war.⁸

The reluctance of yearly meetings to alienate Friends who, on the basis of conscience, had enlisted is an indication of the multiple ways in which American Quakers negotiated the line between individual conscience and the peace testimony. The official stance of all of the Yearly Meetings remained pacifist. Individual Quakers and the local meetings to which they belonged worked out the praxis of the peace testimony in the context of this particular war. This demanded sustained examination of the tradition of Quaker pacifism, the conditions that caused and might prevent war, and the individual and corporate responsibility for the witness to peace making. In this way, the First World War acted as a catalyst for a renewed commitment to peace as well as reconciliation among American Friends themselves.

PRELUDE TO WAR

Quakers are well-known for their faith-based opposition to war and violence. Indeed, this is often seen as a defining feature of the faith. The

---

7. Frost, "Our Deeds," 8.
8. Miller, "Quaker Community," 38–48.

principles outlined in what is today referred to as the Peace Testimony are often presented as the normative expression of Quakerism since 1660 when George Fox and eleven other Quaker leaders affixed their names to a declaration to Charles II. The 1660 declaration states, "all bloody principles and practices, we, as to our own particulars, do utterly deny, with all outward wars and strife and fightings with outward weapons, for any end or under any pretense whatsoever."[9] As clear as the statement appears, and as much as the dissociation from war has remained the official position of the Society, the practice of pacifism has been much more complex than official statements imply. In her study of seventeenth-century Quaker pacifism, Meredith Baldwin Weddle offers an important insight that applies throughout Quaker history: "it is not at all self-evident what behavior flows from pacifist belief. The choices foist themselves anew upon the conscientious in every changing historical circumstance, not because of any situational flexibility of the principles themselves but because there is always a line beyond which consequences and meaning are difficult and ambiguous."[10]

Developments in nineteenth-century American Quakerism created divisions within the Society over pacifism. Separations divided the Society into a number of groups: the first division produced Hicksite Friends and Orthodox Friends; a subsequent schism divided Orthodox Friends into Gurneyite or Evangelical Friends and Wilburite or Conservative Friends. Holiness revivals of the 1870s and 1880s affected Quakers in Indiana, Kansas, Ohio, and Oregon and influenced the primacy of pacifism as a defining feature of Quaker identity.[11] Some evangelical Friends, who absorbed converts from other denominations, even came to consider the peace testimony as superfluous—a quaint, but unnecessary aspect of membership in the Society.[12] In 1900, yearly meetings with Hicksite origins formed Friends General Conference (FGC) and, in 1902, most Gurneyite meetings formed the Five Years Meeting of Friends (FYM). Despite the unifying appearance of these organizations, the impact of holiness revivals and modernist theology divided Gurneyite Quakers in the years before the First World War.[13]

---

9. Quoted in Weddle, *Walking in the Way of Peace*, Appendix I, 234.

10. Ibid., 6.

11. Brock, *Pioneers of the Peaceable Kingdom*, 350.

12. Currey, "Devolution"; Frost, "Our Deeds"; and Hamm et al., "Decline of Quaker Pacifism."

13. Frost, "Modernist and Liberal Quakers," 78–83; and Hinshaw, "Five Years Meeting," 96–98.

The Civil War (1861–65) was particularly disruptive. Quakers were torn between pacifism and their extreme opposition to slavery. Both Hicksite and Orthodox yearly meetings reiterated the importance of the peace testimony, but many individual Friends acted on the belief that the evils of slavery outweighed the evils of war and joined the Union cause, although this was not universal across meetings.[14] Significantly, both Hicksite and Gurneyite meetings were lenient in enforcing the Discipline in these cases.[15] The tradition of pacifism remained strong, but its practice in the face of war and injustice had become less clear by the end of the nineteenth century.

This should not be interpreted as an abandonment of the principles of the peace testimony. A number of peace efforts emerged among Friends at this time. Beginning in 1894, Albert Smiley began hosting an Annual Conference on International Arbitration at his Lake Mohonk resort in New York State.[16] Those conferences "marked the change from nineteenth century meetings about peace to long-lasting campaigns like those against slavery and alcohol."[17] Quakers united in an important turn-of-the-century initiative to renew the peace testimony. For three days at the end of 1901, North American Quakers representing all branches of the Society of Friends gathered in Philadelphia to discuss issues of war and peace. The conference invitation demonstrates both the desire for unity among Quakers and the renewal of approaches to peace itself: "do we not owe it to ourselves, to our history, to our profession before the church and the world, to the American public and to mankind everywhere, to declare ourselves anew today—and in a united way, as we have never done before—on the great and pressing question of the peace of the world, of the rescue of mankind from the awful iniquities and crushing burdens of modern militarism?"[18] The conference was representative; not only were the separate branches of Friends represented, the conference was open to "all interested Friends . . . without

---

14. For instance, Currey, "Devolution," shows that in the relatively small Kansas Preparative Meeting, there was almost no participation in the Civil War (120). Miller, "Quaker Community," notes a similar response in Salem Monthly Meeting, although a number of members did pay for military substitutes, which itself was at odds with the peace testimony (41).

15. Barbour et al., *Quaker Crosscurrents*, 190–94; Hamm, "Hicksite, Orthodox, and Evangelical Quakerism," 71–73; and Miller, "Quaker Community," 41.

16. Barbour et al., *Quaker Crosscurrents*, 241–44.

17. Ibid., 244.

18. *American Friends' Peace Conference*, 4.

the necessity of any official appointment."[19] The conference sustained a grueling pace: forty-three papers were presented in eight sessions over the course of three twelve-hour days. Topics ranged from biblical exegesis on issues of war and peace to historical analysis and theoretical papers on topics like "internationalism" and "militarism." Peter Brock has observed, "The conference had little to say about the economic causation of war or about the clash of rival imperialisms and the search of finance capitalism for overseas markets," that socialist and labor movements of the day identified as the causes of international conflict.[20] Even so, the five-point declaration (the "Declaration of the American Friends' Peace Conference") reaffirmed Friends' historic position on war and denounced its practice: "War, in its spirit, its deeds, the persistent animosities which it generates, the individual and social degeneration produced by it, is the antithesis of Christianity and the negation, for the time being, of the moral order of the world."[21] The declaration heartily endorsed global efforts for arbitration over armed conflict, going as far as identifying the establishment of the Permanent International Court of Arbitration as "one of the greatest events in the history of human society."[22] The Conference marked a notable shift in Quaker approaches to war and their efforts to be activist peacemakers. Isaac Sharpless's closing comments are suggestive of this shift in tone and tactic:

> Friends have not been very active propagandists. The very feeling of their own complete rightness has made many of them slow to take the stump and proclaim the arguments for the good cause. But this is changing. . . . Shall we lose this historic character as we part with the aloofness from the world which perhaps produced it . . . ? Not so, I think, if he comes under the spirit of George Fox; if he is a peace man not because he believes war to be wasteful, and productive of suffering, or contrary to some pet theory of morals, but because down in his heart he feels the warm spirit of divine love and power that takes away the occasion and the desire and the possibility of war and revenge and hatred.[23]

19. Ibid.
20. Brock, *Pioneers of the Peaceable Kingdom*, 358.
21. *American Friends' Peace Conference*, 208.
22. Ibid., 209.
23. Ibid., 232.

Initiatives like the 1901 Peace Conference exposed the peace testimony to sustained examination. Increasingly, as "integrational pacifists,"[24] Quakers eschewed withdrawal from the world, seeking instead to adapt Christian pacifism to the realities of a global arms race and increased militarism, to exert influence on the liberal reform peace movement. This is evident in initiatives like the ecumenical Fellowship of Reconciliation (FOR), in which American Quakers played a prominent founding role. The first chairman was a Friend, all the major offices were filled by Quakers, Friends dominated the early meetings, and a sense of traditional Quaker pacifism dominated the Fellowship's early statements.[25] Cooperating as they did with non-Quakers, Friends remained mindful that their faith remained at the heart of their pacifism. Rufus Jones, one of the most well-known liberal Modernist Quakers of the twentieth century, reminded Friends and others in the FOR that "the movement is so essentially a thing of the spirit that when the spirit is lost the organization is dead."[26] Brock maintains that the FOR "provided a focal point for the thinking and activities of Christian pacifists" but limited its political activities, preferring, instead, to emphasize "personal conscience."[27] Once war had begun, Friends turned their efforts to keeping America out of the conflict and ameliorating the suffering of those caught up in the hostilities in Europe.

WAR

American Quakers remained on the periphery of the main current of the war for its first three years. Nonetheless, they were vocal in their opinions on what had caused it and what might lead to a lasting peace. Shortly after the outbreak of war, the FGC appointed a delegation to present a peace memorial to President Wilson on behalf of Hicksite Friends. The memorial named group hatred, land hunger, and ambition for power as the causes of war, and called for a "Parliament of Nations." According to those Friends, "a World Parliament with a World Court and a World Police to enforce its decisions can maintain peace."[28] In 1915, the Winona Lake Peace Conference of Young Friends, known as the National Peace Conference, offered a similar, albeit much expanded, solution. The conference resolutions called

---

24. Brock, *Pacifism in Europe*, 475.
25. Marchand, *American Peace Movement*, 371–73.
26. Quoted in ibid., 373.
27. Brock, *Twentieth-Century Pacifism*, 29.
28. *Proceedings of FGC*, 1914, 130.

on the president and Congress to convene a conference of neutral nations to consider the establishment of world government to reform, extend, and enforce international law, an international legislature, and an international court. At the same time they called on American churches to work together with Friends to establish "a kingdom of righteousness" that "embraces peace."[29] To Friends throughout America they reaffirmed "the principle, which Friends have always maintained, that war and Christianity are irreconcilable," and provided a list of thirteen practical ways in which Friends could "spread the principle of peace." Finally, the conference provided a template for a letter to members of Congress and asked that all monthly meetings send it to their representatives.[30] Monthly meetings responded to this call for political action.[31] Both the request and the response demonstrate the desire for practical peace initiatives on the part of Friends.

Hicksite Friends returned to the notion of an international court and an international police force at FCG in 1916, where William Hull delivered a paper, "The Quaker Solution to the War Problem." Distinguishing an international police force from a national army or navy, Hull underscored that any international police force had to be subject to "the control of a genuine international court of justice."[32] Not everyone agreed with Hull that these theoretical Quaker solutions were enough; some wanted more action. In the discussion after the presentation, L. Hollingsworth Wood declared, "It is a good deal easier to give your pocket-book than it is your life. It is a good deal easier to stand up and talk than it is to go out and perform; it is a good deal easier to inherit a peace testimony, as we have in the Society of Friends, than it is to think one out for yourself." Wood directed those present to consider the work of the FOR, which was preparing to send an ambulance unit to Mexico to provide assistance to those caught up in the hostilities of the Border War. According to Wood, *that* was the real work of thinking out the peace testimony, "so that the Friend who can say to us 'I offer my life to my country,' shall be met not with platitudes nor theories, but with men and women willing to lay down their lives for their brethren."[33] Even as Hicksite Friends maintained the traditional antiwar

---

29. "The Peace Conference." *Friends' Intelligencer*, Eighth Month 14, 1915, 522.

30. Ibid., 522–23.

31. See, for instance, "New Salem Monthly Meeting Minutes, 2 October 1915" and "Chester Monthly Meeting Minutes, 2 November 1915," in US, Quaker Meeting Records.

32. *Proceedings of FGC, 1916*, 80.

33. Ibid., 81.

position, they were careful to restate their position as a "deep conviction of patriotic duty." On the eve of America's entrance into war, the Friends' National Peace Committee in Philadelphia, a continuation committee of the 1915 National Peace Conference, contended that "true patriotism . . . calls not for a resort to the futile methods of war, but for . . . new methods of conciliation and altruistic service." To ensure that they made their point about courage and loyalty, they asserted, "Unflinching good-will, no less than war, demands courage, patriotism, and self-sacrifice."[34]

FYM convened its 1917 meeting six months after America's entrance into the war. It, too, confirmed its "unaltered faith" in "religious principles which forbid engaging in war." At the same time, it admitted that "[i]n every war-crisis, some of our members have gone along with the prevailing trend and method." Just the same, "the body itself in its meeting capacity has remained through all the years unswervingly true to the spiritual ideal. We have always been and still are a loyal patriotic people, true to the ideals of citizenship, contributing in all possible ways to the promotion of stable and efficient government, and ready to take our full share in the labors, efforts, dangers and perils involved in the maintenance of a true democracy. But we cannot surrender the central faith by which we live."[35] FYM was clear that Quakers' faith-based stance was not license to dodge responsibility. "It is our hope," they declared, "that our entire membership may now and in the future . . . exhibit in this desperate time a Christian faith colored with the red blood of virility and heroism. We must not do less than those who believe that war is necessary and who are ready to fight with carnal weapons, nor can we seek an easier way of life."[36] A just and lasting peace required the hard work of peacemakers. The challenge remained that the praxis of peacemaking—beyond staying out of war—was still unclear.

Numerous Friends disagreed with the official position of the Society on this particular war. Some, like Albert G. Thatcher, spoke as individuals, although he claimed that his 1917 article in *The Advocate of Peace* had been "prepared at the request of several Friends . . . and endorsed as expressing their views as well as those of the writer."[37] Identifying himself as a pacifist,

---

34. "A Message from the Religious Society of Friends (Quakers) in America," *The Friends Messenger* 23, no. 12, Fourth Month, 1917, 7.

35. *Minutes of FYM*, 1917, 188.

36. Ibid., 189.

37. Albert G. Thatcher, "The Quakers' Attitude toward War." *The Advocate of Peace* 79, no. 8, 1917, 238.

but not "a non-resistant," Thatcher equated the circumstances of the First World War with those of the Civil War. Having participated in the Civil War himself, he reminded readers that many Quakers "had the anti-slavery cause so much at heart that it was a vital part of their religion," and they willingly took up arms to bring about its end. Thatcher saw much that was similar between the two conflicts, "convinced that no body of people would suffer more in spirit and probably in person than our Friends, should the barbaric German idea of Kultur win the ultimate victory and subdue the world."[38] Thatcher explained that he was not encouraging the bearing of arms, but did think, minimally that "all Friends should do their utmost to support the Government in all ways short of this." He concluded by assuring Friends who did enlist that he could not condemn them, "being convinced that all such decisions must be left to the court of the individual conscience."[39]

The discrepancy between the official position of the Society and the particular position of some Friends was noted in the May 1918 edition of *The Advocate of Peace*. It reprinted a leaflet, "Some Particular Advices for Friends and A Statement of Loyalty for Others," juxtaposing the statement made in the leaflet to the official statement adopted by the Philadelphia Yearly Meeting at its 29 March 1918 session. The official statement holds no surprises. It includes a statement from the 1660 declaration and the usual reminders and affirmations of Friends' constancy to the declaration over the centuries and their "deep loyalty" to their country and fellow citizens. It concludes with a plea for peace: "For all men, whether they be called our enemies or not we pray that the sacrificial love of Christ, stirring us to repentance, may reconcile and unite all mankind in the brotherhood of His spirit."[40]

Compare this to "Some Particular Advices," placed immediately after the official yearly meeting statement. Signed by one hundred and twenty prominent Quakers, including Albert G. Thatcher, from the Philadelphia and Baltimore Yearly Meetings, it is scathing:

> We do not agree with those who would utter sentimental platitudes while a mad dog is running amuck, biting women and children;

---

38. Ibid.

39. Ibid., 239.

40. "The Society of Friends and the War." *The Advocate of Peace* 80, no. 5, May 1918, 145–46. "Some Particular Advices for Friends and a Statement of Loyalty for Others." *The Advocate of Peace* 80, no. 5, May 1918, 146–47.

with those who would stand idly by quoting some isolated passage of Scripture while an insane man murdered him, ravished his wife, bayoneted his babies, or crucified his friends; with any person who would discuss with some well and contented stranger the merits of various fire-extinguishers while his wife and children are calling to him from the flames of his burning house. We believe that wrong is relative and has degrees; that there are greater things than human life and worse things than war. There is a difference between peace as an end and peace as a means to an end. We do not want peace with dishonor or a temporary peace with evil. We will not equivocate with honor or compromise with wickedness. . . . Believing that it is not enough at this time to be neutral, and that the views of the Society of Friends have not been adequately represented by the official statements of its executives, nor by the utterances of many of its public speakers . . . We therefore deem it consistent with our Quaker faith to act according to the dictates of our own consciences and proclaim a unity with the teachings of Jesus Christ and the messages of the President of our country.[41]

The Advocate of Peace did not offer any commentary on the inconsistency between the two statements. That was unnecessary. Putting them side by side was enough to illuminate the dissension in the ranks.

Friends' ambivalence about the peace testimony and the war was even evident in meetings. Beyond their reluctance to enforce the Discipline, some meetings' minutes admitted to the challenge faced by Friends individually and corporately. Initially American Quakers had tried to keep out of the war and had discouraged war preparations. Once the United States declared war, Friends faced a dilemma. The sentiments of the Peace Committee of the Wabash Monthly Meeting in Indiana spoke for many: "we did not wish to help the German cause by opposing the war. For that reason there has not been anything done in advocating a peace policy." The best the committee chair could report was that he did "think Friends here hold to the principles advocated and believed by early Friends."[42] This was hardly a ringing endorsement of the Society's official position at the local level.

American Quakers opposed to participation in the war were quick to defend their loyalty. No doubt this was a function of the nation's enthusiasm for war once it had entered into hostilities. Both the National Defense Act

---

41. "Some Particular Advices for Friends and a Statement of Loyalty for Others." *The Advocate of Peace* 80, no. 5, May 1918, 146.

42. "South Wabash Monthly Meeting Minutes, 20 July 1918," US, Quaker Meeting Records.

of 1916 and the Selective Service Act of 1917 exempted members of the Religious Society of Friends and other historic peace churches from combatant service on the basis of their well-established religious beliefs.[43] Echoing official statements, individual Friends reminded their co-religionists that exemption from combat was not freedom from sacrifice. Alice Paige White appealed for active service in relief work: "Let us not placidly hide behind our ancient testimony and smugly feel excused from active work, generous giving even to the point of sacrifice and leadership in whatever will be of benefit to the multitudinous victims of this greatest tragedy of the ages." She concluded with a challenge to her co-religionists, "Will we be 'slackers'?"[44] North Carolina Friends, eager to cast their relief work in a patriotic light, created a Peace Medal contest offered to Friends' peace projects that presented the patriotic and heroic side of Quaker service.[45] The AFSC also stressed the patriotism of its work and, as Anthony Manousos points out, "its value for America's long-term interests in the world." Recalling a feeding program in Upper Silesia, AFSC publicist Howard Brinton recollected, "You can imagine with what emotion I saw a group of our children waving American flags they had made themselves and calling out: 'Uncle Sam is our Uncle.' This love for America shrined in the hearts of children will some day be a mighty asset to its object."[46]

The AFSC not only provided an arena for Quaker wartime service, it worked across divisions within the Society itself. Young Friends had expressed concern about the separations among Quakers. At the final session of the 1915 Peace Conference, Samuel Howarth spoke on "The Society of Friends and the Problem." Howarth considered Quaker factions as representative of the problems of international politics: "for the same spirit that causes national and racial divisions acts in our own Society, and causes theological divisions . . . and [Friends] must solve the lesser problem if [they] were to be worthy to help solve the greater."[47] Young Friends were active in the collaborative work of the AFSC.

---

43. National Defense Act of 1916, section 59; Selective Service Act of 1917, section 4.

44. Alice Paige White, "Responsibility of Friends in War Time," *The Friends* Messenger 24, no. 2, Sixth Month 1917, 3.

45. Manousos, "Guilford College," 31–32.

46. Quoted in ibid., 35.

47. "The Peace Conference." *Friends' Intelligencer*, Eighth Month 14, 1915, 521.

The AFSC began as a temporary organization in 1917 to provide alternative service opportunities for pacifists in the early stages of American participation in the war. Jerry Frost argues that, eager as they were to create the organization, AFSC organizers had to move cautiously to satisfy multiple audiences. The first audience was the government that needed to respect religious freedom, but could not be seen to be harboring shirkers. The War Department was a particular challenge. It was hardly going to support pacifism; it might, however, tolerate it. The second audience was the Society itself, which was divided about support for the war. The AFSC needed donors from across the Society. Fortunately, all the yearly meetings came out in favor of pacifism as a central tenet of Quakerism, giving space to pro- and antiwar Friends' support of conscientious objectors (COs) doing constructive work. The bigger challenge was the theological divisions. Organizers needed the backing of conservative and progressive Friends and all those in between. The third audience was the peace community, consisting of other historical peace churches as well as secular pacifists. The AFSC had to garner the support of all pacifists. The final audience was the American public. Some Americans were familiar with Quakers, if they lived in areas with significant Quaker populations. Many Americans knew very little about Quakers, and, as war fever swept across the country, there was little tolerance for anything that hinted of disloyalty.[48]

In order for the AFSC to work, Friends knew they had to pre-empt the government. The timeline was tight: the US entered the war on 6 April 1917, the president signed the Selective Service Act, calling for the registration of all men between twenty-one and thirty, on 18 May, and the first draft occurred on 5 June. In the spring, young Friends had been working on coordinating policies for relief work in Europe, so when members from FYM, FGC, and Philadelphia Yearly Meeting (Orthodox) met on 30 April 1917, they quickly agreed to the formation of the Friends National Service Committee as a clearing house for peace policies, stating, "We are united in expressing our love for our country and our desire to serve her loyally. We offer our services to the Government of the United States in any constructive work in which we can conscientiously serve humanity."[49] The committee immediately prepared a budget and training plans as well as an independent board and a permanent secretary. It consulted with London Friends and the Red Cross, investigated conditions in Europe, and invited

---

48. Frost, "Our Deeds," 3–6.
49. "Among the Peace Organizations," *The Advocate of Peace* 79, June 1917, 190.

Mennonites and Brethren to participate. It also changed its name to American Friends Service Committee and, within a year of forming, created a reconstruction unit and found opportunities for service. Its early success can, in part, be attributed to its ability to organize so quickly. As Frost contends, the AFSC "presented the War Department with a fait accompli before it had resolved what to do with conscientious objectors."[50] As successful as the AFSC appeared in early days, its chair, Rufus Jones, recalled its initial challenges. Uncertain about the nature of the overseas work, the committee was certain it would need workers who were fit and adaptable. The real challenge, though, was discerning the strength of convictions that motivated applicants: "We endeavored as far as possible to have the group composed of men who were conscientiously opposed to war and for that reason unable to engage in it. The problem, however proved to be a very difficult one. Many of the applicants had never faced the question for themselves. They had not thought through the issues involved. They all hated war . . . But here it was an existing fact . . . The situation presented to them was an unescapable rivalry of loyalties." Measuring physical fitness was one thing; "the scrutiny of the inward process of the soul, was, on the other hand, a baffling undertaking."[51]

The value of the AFSC's work in France was recognized by both the Red Cross and the French. In 1917, the Sous-Préfet of the area around Verdun, one of the most heavily damaged areas in France, requested that Friends take charge of post-war reconstruction work in the area. Forty-four villages needed rebuilding. American and British Friends' acceptance of this responsibility changed the nature of the AFSC. Reconstruction work had little to do with pacifism, although it did have to do with healing the ravages of war. Again, religious convictions were translated into humanitarian work. Its importance is attested to by the numbers: there were more AFSC personnel in France in 1919 than during the war.[52] Postwar work added to the AFSC's reputation as a non-political, non-proselytizing relief organization and it became a permanent body in 1924.[53] The work of the AFSC helped American Quakers to see that their theological and political differences did not have to thwart effective action in the war. Despite Jones's assessment that "nothing that our hands can do ever can atone for

---

50. Frost, "Our Deeds," 10.
51. Jones, *Service of Love*, 13–14.
52. Frost, "Our Deeds," 27–29.
53. Ibid., 35–40.

the agony, the losses and the suffering which have fallen upon the innocent during these years of world tragedy,"[54] the AFSC managed to combine patriotism and pacifism to provide space for alternative service of significant importance. The goodwill this generated at home and abroad went a long way toward healing some of the differences among Friends.[55]

In the context of these institutional statements, how did individual Quakers navigate the space between the peace testimony and personal conscience? Many defended their pacifist stance and suffered for it. Mary Stone McDowell, whose story was related at the beginning of this chapter, is one example. Pacifists may have claimed to be loyal, but in some circles they were considered the worst type of American. As one New York City Board of Education member declared, "the teacher who teaches pacifism and that this country should not defend itself is a thousand times more dangerous than the teacher who gets drunk and lies in the gutter."[56] Public sentiment against pacifists was so strong in some areas that Quakers were subjected to violence, harassment, and general suspicion. The peace committee of one monthly meeting felt so besieged that it resolved that "there is little the peace com[mittee] can do under present circumstances except pray."[57] Indeed, the confinement of conscientious objectors in military camps is indicative of how they were perceived by the War Department at least, if not by society as a whole.[58] Remember that the Selective Service Act of 1917 exempted members of the historic peace churches from military service. Importantly, it stipulated that "no person so exempted shall be

54. Jones, *Service of Love*, 265.

55. Frost, "Our Deeds," 47.

56. General Thomas Wingate, quoted in Howlett and Howlett, "Silent Witness for Peace," 374.

57. Hamm et al., "Decline of Quaker Pacifism," 52.

58. Not all COs were Quakers, and a reliable statistical compilation of conscripted Friends is not available. Hirst, *Quakers in Peace and War*, 519, reports that 200 COs were offered by the United States government to Friends Service Committee for reconstruction work in France. Ninety-nine of those were released from military camps; 54 of them were Quaker. Others were given farm furloughs. Of the 527 sentenced to prison, only 13 were Quaker. A "Brief History of Conscientious Objection," cites the following statistics: "One unofficial source states that 3,989 men declared themselves to be conscientious objectors when they had reached the camps: of these, 1,300 chose noncombatant service; 1,200 were given farm furloughs; 99 went to Europe to do reconstruction work for the American Friends Service Committee (AFSC); 450 were court-martialed and sent to prison; and 940 remained in camps until the Armistice was fully enacted." See also Brock, *Twentieth-Century Pacifism*, 52–56.

exempted from service in any capacity that the President shall declare to be noncombatant."[59] Included in this designation was medical, quartermaster, and engineering work. According to Hirst, roughly "two-thirds of the six thousand conscientious objectors accepted this compromise, and according to one estimate the same proportion of Friends to whom the choice was offered," although Yearly Meeting spokespersons, the AFSC, and a number of Friends who had been drafted found the president's compromise unacceptable.[60] Reconstruction work with the AFSC offered an outlet to these Quakers.

What of those who volunteered for military service? Fifty percent of draft-age Quaker men is a sizeable number. Hamm's study of twentieth-century pacifism shows that support for the war was even higher in some cases. At Earlham College, 253 men of military age served as opposed to 47 who can be identified as conscientious objectors.[61] Some monthly meetings had more members in military service than they had draft-age men; some had a high percentage of conscientious objectors; some seemed to have escaped the impact of the conflict.[62] The results, Hamm admits, are difficult to explain. There are neither geographic nor theological patterns. And many Indiana Friends were enthusiastic supporters of alternative service in the AFSC.[63] Hamm concludes that the First World War set a pattern for Indiana Quakers where the Yearly Meeting would maintain traditional positions, but "most of the members would not consider them binding."[64] The role of personal conscience is illuminating. Individual meetings offered sentiments similar to those expressed by the president and board of Earlham College in an address to students: "Each man is answerable before God as to his duty in the situation which now confronts him. Every man ought to be able to find in his own heart his duty in the present crisis."[65]

59. Selective Service Act of 1917, section 4.
60. Hirst, *Quakers in Peace and War*, 518.
61. Hamm et al., "Decline of Quaker Pacifism," 53.
62. For instance, Wabash Monthly Meeting had 20 draft-age men; 29 did military service; none were COs. Amboy Monthly Meeting had 92 draft-age men; 19 did military service; 29 were COs. Duck Creek Monthly Meeting had 30 draft-age men; none did military service; 1 was a CO (Hamm et al. "Decline of Quaker Pacifism," 55). Currey's study of Kansas Quakers points to almost no support for the First World War ("Devolution," 122).
63. Hamm et al., "Decline of Quaker Pacifism," 54.
64. Ibid., 56.
65. Quoted in Hamm et al., "Decline of Quaker Pacifism," 53–54.

Personal conscience is vital to any understanding of Quakerism. A central tenet of Quaker belief is that of the Light Within.[66] The Light Within speaks in each individual's heart, making Quakerism an experiential faith.[67] Disagreements over the authority of the Light Within regarding both Scripture and church tradition have been at the heart of the American schisms. The appeal to personal conscience brought draft-age men face to face with the peace testimony in this war. Rufus Jones outlines the difficult choice "every serious young Friend" faced:

> How far were they under obligation to serve their country in a mission which appeared to conflict with their ideals of right and wrong, and how far did the desperate world-situation which confronted them lay upon them a call to break with the settled teaching and attitude of their type of Christianity?[68]

Undoubtedly, some of the Quakers who enlisted were either not devout in their faith, or were part of a Quaker meeting where pacifism was no longer considered a defining feature of the faith.[69] But, as the case of Wyatt Acton Miller attests, many committed young Friends wrestled mightily with their choice between military duty and alternative service.

Miller corresponded with his parents, Josiah and Marianna, and his fiancée, Lucile, as he worked through the knotty issues. In May 1917, his father reminded him that "this question is one thee must decide for thyself." Josiah lamented the impact of the war on Quakers and expressed hope that "we can come through with honor without sacrificing our testimonies." Nevertheless, he admitted, "If there ever was a 'Justifiable' war I believe our entry into this one is as near as ever was known before, yet when confronted by the undoubtable truth that all war is wicked, we are in a dilemma." After confessing that he would probably have enlisted himself if he were younger, Josiah again turned to the peace testimony: "cool sober judgment tells me that there is no possible excuse, on religious grounds, for the man who goes forth to commit premeditated murder, for stripped of its glory, that is what war is—nothing less."[70] In addition to Wyatt's unease

---

66. Spencer, "Quakers in a Theological Context"; and Angell, "God, Christ, and the Light."

67. Spencer, "Quakers in a Theological Context," 141.

68. Jones, *Service of Love*, 14.

69. Currey, "Devolution," 123–26; Hamm et al., "Decline of Quaker Pacifism," 48–49.

70. Quoted in Miller, "Quaker Community," 44.

about his peace witness, by October it appears that social pressures were affecting him. Writing to his mother, he expressed guilt for "doing nothing" while "others are sacrificing themselves." He then enquired, "Thee does not wish me to be a coward or a shirker I am sure . . . It is because I hate war that I wish to enter this one and get it over . . . Mother dear I know it must be hard, hard for thee but doesn't thee want thy son to be a man?"[71] Shortly after this communication, it became apparent to his family that Wyatt was determined to enlist. They encouraged him to join a reconstruction unit, but he explained to his parents that, because "he was not neutral in the conflict, he felt it would be dishonest to pose as a pacifist."[72] Wyatt was not in the theater long before he experienced total disillusionment. "The longer I am over here," he bemoaned to Lucile, "the more I wonder how men can be such fools as to kill each other . . . There is no place for war in the scheme of life . . . You mustn't mind my tirade against military ways. You know that it is only the raving of a peace-at-any-price Quaker." His primary fear, expressed to Lucile in March 1918, was his anxiety that his "spark of divinity is getting dimmer all the time."[73] Wyatt Miller remained in the theater until the war ended and he was discharged. He remained a faithful Quaker to the end of his life. Despite his combat service, he did not betray his beliefs, but felt a sincere calling of personal conscience that led him to enlist. His case is representative of the tension between conscience and testimony with which many Friends experienced the war. The mysticism of Quakerism must be lived out in a world that is often in conflict with Friends' testimonies. The peace testimony remained unchanged, but the atrocities of war demanded that individual Friends negotiate the distance between their conscience and the rule of the Society.

The First World War revealed the horrors of modern industrialized warfare. It also exposed Friends to challenging decisions over their peace witness. Quakers were not alone in their dismay about war, nor had the arguments of pacifists been entirely unheard in society at large. Those in the peace movement had been ridiculed, but the persistence of their arguments coupled with the destructiveness of the war resulted in this war being "the first in which people were widely capable of recognizing and being thoroughly repulsed by those horrors."[74] War had become, as Winston

71. Quoted in ibid., 46.
72. Quoted in ibid.
73. Quoted in ibid., 47.
74. Mueller, "Changing Attitudes towards War," 12.

Churchill observed in 1925, "the potential destroyer of the human race."[75] Quakers, along with other peace advocates, became more determined to create a world in which a just and lasting peace was possible. To that end, Friends had agreed in 1917 to hold a global peace conference of all Quakers when the war ended.[76] The All Friends' Peace Conference of 1920 convened in London to discuss how to go "beyond the formal statement of our Peace testimony to the far-reaching issues of social and international behaviour that belongs to it."[77] Over one thousand Quakers from around the world engaged in sustained discussion about the Quaker position on peace.[78] American Friends were significantly more divided than English Friends. In the years leading up to the conference, American Quakers had publicly debated the peace settlement and the League of Nations in publications like *The Friends' Intelligencer*. After the conference, they remained divided between those who could not support the League of Nations and those who believed it was necessary.[79] As William Witte suggests, these ongoing disagreements demonstrate the ways in which post-war American Quakers had to come to terms with finding "a way to make an absolute principle an operative principle in practical affairs."[80]

Rufus Jones delivered the Swarthmore Lecture at the start of proceedings. Its title, "The Nature and Authority of Conscience," indicates that Friends were attuned to the role of personal conscience in their faith. The conscience, Jones told his audience, "*is the voice of our ideal self, our complete self, our real self, laying its call upon our will.*"[81] Even so, in order "to be sound," individual conscience "must have imbibed the spirit of the social group, past and present, living and dead, in which it was formed."[82] The conference concluded with a "Message to Friends and Fellow-Seekers" and demonstrates the vision Quakers maintained, despite the recent war: "The roots of war can be taken away from all our lives . . . Day by day let us

---

75. Quoted in ibid., 17.
76. Kennedy, *British Quakerism*, 405.
77. *Conference of all Friends*, 31.
78. Hirst, who attended the conference and presented a paper on the historic peace testimony, cites over 1000 attendees (*Quakers in Peace and War*, 521). Kennedy cites 936 official delegates, of which 53 percent represented London Yearly Meeting and 36 percent represented North American meetings (*British Quakerism*, 406).
79. Witte, "American Quaker Pacifism," 87–95.
80. Ibid., 98.
81. Jones, *Nature and Authority*, 71. Emphasis original.
82. Ibid., 72.

seek out and remove every seed of hatred and greed, of resentment and of grudging in our own selves and in the social structure about us . . . Fear and suspicion must give place to trust and the spirit of understanding . . . Surely this is the way in which Christ calls us to overcome the barriers of race and class and thus to make all of humanity a society of friends."[83]

American Friends may have come away from the All Friends' Conference divided over the "operative principles" of the peace testimony. They were united, however, in their commitment to personal conscience and their obligation to transform the world rather than to withdraw from it. The sustained examination of the testimony through extensive dialogue among American Quakers and between American Friends and other Quakers resulted in a Society more acquainted with the history and trajectory of its own peace testimony and more conversant with the realities of global affairs. In this way the war was the catalyst for Quaker renewal in the twentieth century and a commitment to the fundamental place of the peace testimony in Quakerism. Still, within the corporate witness of the Society, individual Quakers were always responsible to the Light Within, as Jones told them: "We owe almost everything to the larger society of which we are an organic part—almost everything, but there is one thing we can never surrender, barter, or disobey at the command of any social authority whatever, *the august voice within us.*"[84]

BIBLIOGRAPHY

Primary Sources

NEWSPAPERS

The Advocate of Peace, 1917–18.
Friends' Intelligencer, 1915.
The Friends Messenger, 1917.

OTHER

The American Friends' Peace Conference Held at Philadelphia, Twelfth Month 12th, 13th and 14th 1901. Philadelphia: Published by the Conference, 1902.

---

83. *Conference of All Friends*, 201.
84. Jones, *Nature and Authority*, 75. Emphasis original.

Conference of All Friends Held in London, August 12 to 20, 1920: Official Report. London: Friends' Bookshop, 1920.

Jones, Rufus M. *The Nature and Authority of Conscience.* London: Swarthmore, 1920.

———. *A Service of Love in Wartime: American Friends Relief Work in Europe, 1917-1919.* New York: MacMillan, 1920.

Matter of McDowell v. Board of Education. 104 Misc. 564 (N.Y. Misc 1918), 564–70. casetext.com/case/matter-of-mcdowell-v-board-of-education. Accessed 10 July 2015.

Minutes of the Five Years Meeting of the Friends in America, held in Richmond, Indiana, Tenth Month 16th to Tenth Month 22nd (Inclusive) 1917. Richmond, IN: Balinger, 1922.

National Defense Act of 1916. http://www.legisworks.org/congress/64/publaw-85.pdf. Accessed 25 August 2015.

Proceedings of Friends' General Conference, 1914. Philadelphia: Supplement to the *Friends' Intelligencer*, 1914.

Proceedings of Friends' General Conference, 1916. Philadelphia: Supplement to the *Friends' Intelligencer*, 1916.

Selective Service Act of 1917. http://www.legisworks.org/congress/65/publaw-12.pdf. Accessed 25 August 2015.

US, Quaker Meeting Records, 1681–1935. http://www.ancestry.com/cs/us/quakers. Accessed 25 August 2015.

Secondary Sources

Angell, Stephen W. "God, Christ, and the Light." In *The Oxford Handbook of Quaker Studies*, edited by Stephen W. Angell and Pink Dandelion, 158–71. Oxford: Oxford University Press, 2013.

Barbour, Hugh, et al. *Quaker Crosscurrents: Three Hundred Years of Friends in the New York Yearly Meetings.* Syracuse, NY: Syracuse University Press, 1995.

Brock, Peter. *Pacifism in Europe to 1914.* Princeton, NJ: Princeton University Press, 1972.

———. *Pioneers of the Peaceable Kingdom: The Quaker Peace Testimony from the Colonial Era to the First World War.* Princeton, NJ: Princeton University Press, 1968.

———. *Twentieth-Century Pacifism.* New York: Van Nostrand Reinhold, 1970.

"Brief History of Conscientious Objection." Conscientious Objection in America. http://www.swarthmore.edu/library/peace/conscientiousobjection/co%20website/pages/HistoryNew.htm.

Currey, Cecil B. "The Devolution of Quaker Pacifism: A Kansas Case Study, 1860–1955." *Kansas History* 6 (1983) 120–33.

Frost, J. William. "Modernist and Liberal Quakers, 1887–2010." In *The Oxford Handbook of Quaker Studies*, edited by Stephen W. Angell and Pink Dandelion, 78–92. Oxford: Oxford University Press, 2013.

———. "'Our Deeds Carry Our Message': The Early History of the American Friends Service Committee." *Quaker History* 81, no. 1 (1992) 1–51.

Hamm, "Hicksite, Orthodox, and Evangelical Quakerism." In *The Oxford Handbook of Quaker Studies*, edited by Stephen W. Angell and Pink Dandelion, 63–77. Oxford: Oxford University Press, 2013.

Hamm, Thomas D., et al. "The Decline of Quaker Pacifism in the Twentieth Century: Indiana Yearly Meeting of Friends as a Case Study." *Indiana Magazine of History* 96, no. 3 (2000) 45–71.

Hinshaw, Gregory P. "Five Years Meeting and Friends United Meeting, 1887–2010." In *The Oxford Handbook of Quaker Studies*, edited by Stephen W. Angell and Pink Dandelion, 93–107. Oxford: Oxford University Press, 2013.

Hirst, Margaret E. *Quakers in Peace and War: An Account of Their Peace Principles and Practice*. London: Swarthmore, 1923.

Howlett, Charles F. "Quaker Conscience in the Classroom: The Mary S. McDowell Case." *Quaker History* 83, no. 2 (1994) 99–115.

Howlett, Patricia, and Charles F. Howlett. "A Silent Witness for Peace: The Case of Mary Stone Howlett and America at War." *History of Education Quarterly* 48, no. 3 (2008) 371–96.

Kennedy, Thomas C. *British Quakerism, 1860–1920: The Transformation of a Religious Community*. Oxford: Oxford University Press, 2001.

Manousos, Anthony. "Guildford College, North Carolina Friends and the First World War." *Southern Friend* 25, no. 1 (2003) 27–38.

Marchand, C. Roland. *The American Peace Movement and Social Reform, 1898–1918*. Princeton, NJ: Princeton University Press, 1972.

Miller, Andrew Thompson. "A Quaker Community in Times of War: Friends in Salem, New Jersey." *New Jersey Folklife* 15 (1990) 37–49.

Mueller, John. "Changing Attitudes towards War: The Impact of the First World War." *British Journal of Political Science* 21, no. 1 (1991) 1–28.

Spencer, Carole Dale. "Quakers in a Theological Context." In *The Oxford Handbook of Quaker Studies*, edited by Stephen W. Angell and Pink Dandelion, 141–57. Oxford: Oxford University Press, 2013.

Weddle, Meredith Baldwin. *Walking in the Way of Peace: Quaker Pacifism in the Seventeenth Century*. Oxford: Oxford University Press, 2001.

Valentine, Lonnie. "Quakers, War, and Peacemaking." In *The Oxford Handbook of Quaker Studies*, edited by Stephen W. Angell and Pink Dandelion, 363–76. Oxford: Oxford University Press, 2013.

Witte, William D. "American Quaker Pacifism and the Peace Settlement of World War I." *Bulletin of Friends Historical Association* 46, no. 2 (1957) 84–98.

8

"We do not love war, but..."

Mormons, the Great War, and the Crucible of Nationalism

J. David Pulsipher

While the First World War functioned as a patriotic litmus test for several American sub-cultures and religions, members of the Church of Jesus Christ of Latter-day Saints (more commonly known as "Mormons")[1] were especially sensitive to the fierce demands of nationalism. For the Latter-day Saints, the first decades of the twentieth century were an era of intense transition. The last remnants of Mormonism's first generation, those with personal experience with its founding prophet Joseph Smith, were rapidly dying off. The church was moving beyond its charismatic roots, articulating a more consistent theology and developing a professional bureaucracy. Most significantly, having only recently discarded the practice of plural marriage and elements of theocracy, the Latter-day Saint community was struggling to shake its long-standing status as one of the nation's most pronounced pariahs.[2] The Great War, exploding at this delicate juncture, thus highlighted the complicated relationship between the Latter-day Saint community and the broader United States, and ac-

---

1. This essay will employ both terms, along with the acronym LDS.
2. For a detailed description of the changes, see Alexander, *Mormonism in Transition*.

celerated a process by which Mormonism ultimately made peace with the nation-state.

AMBIVALENCE WITH AMERICA

Born in the turbulence of the Second Great Awakening, Mormonism initially adopted a "non-statist orientation" towards the nations of the earth. As historian Patrick Mason has pointed out, "Joseph Smith's earliest revelations . . . seemed to operate in a political vacuum. The expectation was of an imminent return of Christ and the establishment of the kingdom of God on the earth. Thus, the primary social unit was the Church, or what became known as Zion . . . [and] the revelations afforded no privileged status to any earthly political unit, including the United States of America."[3] Later revelations described the US Constitution as a legal system God "suffered to be established . . . for the rights and protection of all flesh" and the American founders as "wise men whom [God] raised up."[4] Nevertheless, Latter-day Saints saw their beloved Zion as superior—a spiritual and social phenomenon that might initially develop and flourish within America's religious liberty, but would also eventually supersede all nations including the United States.

This attitude of non-statist detachment became more deeply entrenched through what Mormons perceived as a monumental failure of the nation to live up to its founding ideals and protect their basic rights. Removing themselves to the Great Basin after the assassination of their prophet in 1844, Mormons attempted to build their Zion in isolation. This separatist project, along with their embrace of plural marriage, rendered them anathema to the rest of the country. For the next half century, Latter-day Saints engaged in an epic struggle for survival as the full weight of federal authority was mobilized to force the Mormon community to abandon polygamy and comply with national moral, social, and political standards.[5] Before it was over, federal agents engaged in systematic raids of Mormon households, federal judges imprisoned many Mormon men (and some women), the federal legislature passed increasingly harsh measures that disenfranchised most Mormon men (and all women) and

3. Mason, "Wars and Perplexities," 77. See also Ashurst-McGee, "Zion Rising."

4. *Doctrine and Covenants* 101:77, 80. References to the *Doctrine and Covenants*, a uniquely LDS book of scripture, follows conventions similar to the Bible, with the number of the section (chapter) followed by a colon and verse number(s).

5. Gordon, *Mormon Question*.

confiscated church property, and federal courts upheld these statutes. Through it all, Latter-day Saints maintained a tenacious faith in what they still believed were the constitution's divinely inspired religious protections. But their unorthodox practices and civil disobedience against federal laws left them vulnerable not only to charges of heresy but also to accusations of disloyalty.[6]

Mormon ambivalence regarding the nation led to a detached approach to military conflict. When the United States declared war on Mexico in 1846, Latter-day Saints provided a small battalion for the army, but their decision to participate was dominated by practical concerns, as the government's signing bonuses were paid as a lump sum to the church and used to finance the migration to the West. Furthermore, church leaders hardly believed that they were actually sending their men off to war. To the contrary, the "Mormon Battalion" was officially blessed by Brigham Young with a prophecy that it would never see battle or be required to shed blood, a promise that was fulfilled as the battalion remained far from the front lines. Thus Mormon patriotism and enthusiasm for the conflict might be best characterized as "tepid." Rather than urging the battalion to do the work of the nation, church leaders counseled its members not to "misuse their enemies" nor "spoil their property" because the Mexican people were "fellow human beings."[7]

Likewise, during the Civil War, Mormon-dominated Utah formally declared for the Union but largely sat out the conflict. Indeed, the general attitude of the Latter-day Saints during the great national crisis was one of prophetic critique. Ensconced in their Rocky Mountain refuge, Mormons saw the fratricidal conflict as just punishment for the collective sins of the American nation, not the least of which was its failure to adequately protect their religious liberty. Moreover, in LDS eyes the war seemed to confirm Joseph Smith's prophetic mantle. In December 1832, in the midst of the Nullification Crisis, the Mormon prophet had received a revelation regarding "wars that will shortly come to pass," and subsequent developments seemed to match his predictions that "the Southern States shall be divided against the Northern States," "the Southern States will call on other nations, even the nation of Great Britain," and "slaves shall rise up against their masters [and] be marshaled and disciplined for war." Watching from the sidelines, the Latter-day Saints remained convinced the conflict would

---

6. Pulsipher, "Prepared to Abide."
7. Walker, "Sheaves, Bucklers," 46.

eventually fulfill the revelation's promise that there would come "a full end of all nations."[8]

When this did not happen, and when instead a national anti-Mormon crusade gained steam in the post-war years, the Latter-day Saints became increasingly disenchanted with American society. Still, the pressure of the national anti-Mormon campaign forced the church to make significant accommodations, and the Latter-day Saint community began a process of adapting to national standards. Plural marriage and theocratic politics were publicly abandoned in the early 1890s, and as a result Utah was finally admitted as a state in 1896. Consequently, when war broke out with Spain in 1898, church leaders recognized it as an opportunity to challenge perceptions of Mormon disloyalty, issuing a formal declaration of absolute loyalty to the nation and encouraging enlistments, which proved to be energetic.[9] Despite this general enthusiasm, Mormon support for American militarism remained significantly qualified, and the war's aftermath witnessed the rise of a formal LDS peace movement as the Relief Society (the church's auxiliary organization for women) sponsored annual peace meetings.[10] But rather than functioning as a critique of the nation, those rallies reflected a Progressive ethos that was ascendant throughout the country. In fact, as Latter-day Saints emerged from the shadows of isolation, they discovered that "the stuff of early twentieth-century American life—its values, ideas, habits—was eminently suited to the pursuit of their religion." As historian Matthew Bowman has pointed out, "Joseph Smith's vision of human potential . . . wove nicely into Progressivism's confidence in human effort" and many Mormon leaders "found in Progressive ideas the way to harmonize their faith with their nation."[11]

Yet strong tensions with the nation remained. The 1903 election of apostle Reed Smoot to the US Senate sparked a bitter four-year battle over whether to seat him. Among other potentially disqualifying allegations, Smoot was accused of having sworn a Mormon oath against the United States. Many church leaders were subpoenaed to testify before a Senate committee, and they left the capital with a greater appreciation of how deep suspicions ran regarding Latter-day Saint loyalty.[12] Smoot ultimately re-

8. *Doctrine and Covenants* 87:1–6.
9. Walker, "Sheaves, Bucklers," 48; Quinn, "Mormon Church."
10. Arrington, "Modern Lysistratas."
11. Bowman, *Mormon People*, 153–54.
12. Flake, *Politics*.

tained his seat, but Mormons and the rest of the nation continued to have a strained relationship as they moved into the second decade of the twentieth century. Against this backdrop the Great War exploded, eventually drawing these uneasy compatriots together into the trenches of Europe.

THE DEATH AND MISERY OF MANY SOULS

Latter-day Saints initially watched the outbreak of European hostilities with a detachment reminiscent of the one they adopted during the Civil War, yet this time it carried little sense of watching divine retribution and was instead seasoned with a deep sorrow for those who suffered. Some of the earliest official responses to the European war came from leaders of the Relief Society in its monthly periodical. President Emmeline B. Wells, a strong advocate for peace and international arbitration, noted that the emerging conflict "may be the beginning of the very war that the Prophet Joseph Smith prophesied would cover the earth"—a reference to his aforementioned 1832 prophecy, which also predicted that eventually "war will be poured out upon all nations."[13] Calling on her fellow Latter-day Saint women to prepare to succor those who would be afflicted, Wells pleaded: "We must be on the alert to assist in every possible way and by all the means in our power." For nearly forty years the Relief Society had followed counsel from Brigham Young to store up grain as insurance against future calamity. "In all these years we have not had much need to use the grain stored away for the purpose it was designed," Wells noted, "but with the dark cloud hovering over the world as it now does, we can see the prophetic wisdom of President Young."[14]

Such comments reflected what would become a common pattern in Mormon responses to what was initially a distant war. Latter-day Saints consistently demonstrated deep anxiety about the conflict and empathy for its victims, to whom they were prepared to lend assistance. At the same time, they consistently understood the conflict as a validation of their prophetic heritage, more particularly as a demonstration of Joseph Smith's visionary capacity. This pattern was clearly articulated by the impassioned editor of the *Relief Society Magazine*, Susa Young Gates, whose daughter, a rising opera star, was en route to perform in Berlin when the war began:

---

13. "The Grain Question," *Relief Society Magazine*, September 1914, 1–3; *Doctrine and Covenants* 87:2.

14. "The Grain Question," *Relief Society Magazine*, September 1914, 1–3.

> The Prophet Joseph foresaw this condition and portrayed it plainly. But the hearts of women, looking upon their sons and their sons' sons, have sunk in their bosoms, and they had sought to avert the dread time when this war should be poured out on every nation. ... We may have a child—a son preaching the gospel—or a daughter studying music—out in that vortex of war excitement now in the nations of Europe. Our heart contracts, and we mothers know at once how the mothers of those Serbian, German, French and English soldiers feel at even the suggestion of war. Men may fight and kill, but women must suffer and weep.[15]

With deep sympathy for both sides, Gates did not initially find her identity in citizenship of a particular nation, but rather in a universal solidarity with all women. Similar sympathies for all victims were expressed by church president Joseph F. Smith, a nephew of the church's founding prophet. President Smith knew the costs of violence, being five years old when his father Hyrum and uncle Joseph were assassinated by an Illinois mob. His first public comment came in a September 1914 message to the general church membership:

> The Lord has little if anything to do with this war. He will overrule things so that good will come out of it; but he will not heed the war lords who have transgressed his laws, changed his ordinances, and broken the everlasting covenant. . . . The true religion of Christ, which teaches peace on earth and good will to men, and which would prevent them from engaging in war and slaughter, they have never adopted. While they seemingly acknowledge allegiance to the Christian religion, they are not touched nor influenced by its teachings, for these are fundamentally opposed to war and discord, and look for a final gathering of all mankind into one great brotherhood ruled by love.[16]

Smith's focus on Christian principles of peace and goodwill resonated with similar hopes expressed by other clergy of the day. However, unlike many denominations, Mormonism never experienced the war as a crisis of Christianity as a whole. For the Latter-day Saints, the growing horror of the war did not reflect a failure of Christianity, because they believed other Christian traditions had long since abandoned the "true religion of Christ."

---

15. "War! War! And Why War?," *Relief Society Magazine*, September 1914, 3–5.
16. "The Great War," *Improvement Era*, September 1914, 1075.

Thus, Europe's descent into brutality and self-destruction was interpreted as a natural consequence of such apostasy.[17]

Other church leaders reinforced Smith's assessment that God was not to blame. Charles Penrose, second counselor to President Smith, suggested that God did not stop such evil because he intended this world "to be a world of trial and testing and proving" and he "will not interfere with the agency of man."[18] Apostle James E. Talmage expanded even further, noting that even the "poor devil" was "being unfairly blamed for mankind's misuse of moral agency." "If Satan and his hosts were bound today," Talmage noted, "evil would go on for a long time, because he has very able representatives in the flesh."[19] While neither God nor Satan was fully responsible for the barbarity, President Smith suggested that God might be able to work within and "overrule" the tragic situation "so that good will come out of it," perhaps by granting "more liberty to the masses." Still, the war itself did not reflected God's intention, but was instead an indication of how far the world was out of alignment with divine wisdom. "One thing is certain," he noted, "the doctrine of peace by armed force, held so long and tenaciously by czars, kings and emperors, is a failure, and should without question forever be abandoned. It has been wrong from the beginning. That we get what we prepare for is literally true in this case. For years it has been held that peace comes only by preparation for war; the present conflict should prove that peace comes only by preparing for peace."[20] Moreover, Smith proposed, the only thing that would bring peace "is the adoption of the gospel of Jesus Christ, rightly understood, obeyed and practiced by rulers and people alike."[21]

Thus, in the early years of the war, Latter-day Saints consistently saw the destruction as tragic, even horrifying, but also as validating Mormon exceptionalism. Apostasy led to tyranny and violence. Only conversion to the true gospel—as preached by the Latter-day Saints—would bring lasting peace. In the April 1915 General Conference, as the heavy toll of Europe's conflict was becoming increasingly clear, B. H. Roberts, a prominent

---

17. Ibid.

18. *Conference Report*, October 1914, 42–43. The LDS Church president traditionally serves with two counselors, and together these three constitute the First Presidency, the church's highest governing body.

19. Ibid., 104.

20. "The Great War," *Improvement Era*, September 1914, 1074.

21. Ibid., 1075.

theologian and church historian, declared that because of the great tumult "the stage of the world is being reset for increased opportunities for us to make proclamation of this message."[22] Likewise, at that same conference, President Smith expressed his conviction that an expanded missionary effort would heal both sectarian strife and physical war: "From the moment that a Latter-day Saint learns his duty, he will learn that it is his business to make peace, and to establish good will, to work righteousness, to be filled with the spirit of kindness, love, charity, and forgiveness. . . . Our mission is to save, not to destroy; our aim should be to build up, and not tear down. Our calling is to convey the spirit of love, truth, peace and good will to mankind throughout the world; that war may cease; that strife may come to an end, and that peace may prevail."[23]

STRAINING THE BROTHERHOOD OF MAN

By the early twentieth century, it was common for Social Gospel Protestants to speak of "the fatherhood of God and brotherhood of man."[24] Latter-day Saint theology took this notion literally, proclaiming that every human was an actual spirit child of God, and therefore all people were spiritual sisters and brothers. Mormons thus initially empathized with all of the war's victims, regardless of nationality, whether Serbian, Russian, German, French, Italian, or British. Moreover, many Latter-day Saints had personal ties to Europe. From its earliest years, the church had sent missionaries to European countries, particularly to Great Britain, but also to Scandinavia, Germany, Austria, France, and Italy. Many European converts emigrated to the Mormon heartland in Utah and other parts of the Intermountain West, creating Latter-day Saint communities with significant European origins. But during the war, thousands of church members still remained in Europe, and those who had emigrated watched with increasing anxiety for relatives and friends back home.

According to the 1910 census, over half of the inhabitants in Mormon-dominated Utah were either first- or second-generation immigrants, well above the national average. Nevertheless, while Latter-day Saints had connections to all sides of the conflict, their demographics tilted heavily towards the Allied and Neutral Powers. Almost a quarter of all Utah inhabitants had either personally immigrated or were the children of immigrants

22. *Conference Report*, April 1915, 131.
23. Ibid., 4–5.
24. Wessinger, *Oxford Handbook*, 505.

from Great Britain, while nearly another sixth came from Scandinavia. In contrast, those with immediate ties to Germany, Austria, and Italy constituted less than one twentieth of Utah's population.[25]

The complex nature of Latter-day Saint allegiances is illustrated in the experience of Janne M. Sjödahl, a Swedish convert to Mormonism who emigrated to Utah in the 1880s, became a naturalized US citizen, and was later sent to Liverpool, England, to edit the church's official European periodical, *The Millennial Star*. Writing to American church members after the war's first year, Sjödahl suggested that the devastating bloodshed illustrated that armaments are not the best insurance of peace, and that citizen soldiers were as good as conscripts, proving "how unnecessary are the annual enormous expenditures on standing armies." Moreover, he insisted that blood "flowing like water" verified the "insanity of trying to settle international differences by means of war" instead of arbitration. Yet, despite his express bias against what he called the "fallacy" of militarism and the "insanity" of war, Sjödahl ended his dispatch with a discordant hope that his adopted country might get involved: "We are glad that the United States is spared from actual participation in this struggle; and yet, if our country, by throwing her moral influence and financial and military resources in the balances for right and justice, could shorten the terrible slaughter and help to establish a firmer basis for world peace, we would gladly hasten the day of her advent in the arena. For this is a struggle between right and wrong, tyranny and liberty, Michael and the dragon."[26]

Sjödahl's abhorrence of war, yet preference for the Allies, and his association of their cause with principles of righteousness, reveal forces that were straining at the Mormon commitment to universal kinship, and thus at the community's primary orientation of sorrowful detachment. The longer the war dragged on, the more Latter-day Saints began taking sides, which damaged relationships in congregations with mixed immigrant populations. Elizabeth McCune, a member of the general Relief Society board, reported that her official visit to congregations in Milwaukee in 1915 revealed a growing division between Anglo and German members over the Kaiser.[27] A distant war was stretching the limits of local brotherhood.

25. *US Census Report*, 1910. First-generation immigrants from Great Britain constituted 6.1 percent of Utah inhabitants but only 1.3 percent of national inhabitants, whereas first-generation immigrations from Germany, Austria, and Italy constituted only 2.4 percent of Utah inhabitants but 4.7 percent of national inhabitants.

26. "Reflections from the War Zone," *Improvement Era*, October 1915, 1075–76.

27. Elizabeth McCune, Letter to the Relief Society Board, from New York, 6 December

Moreover, the stress of American nationalism also began to intrude on the Latter-day Saint community. By late 1915, as increasingly vocal elements in the national polity called for military "preparedness," church organizations became targets of patriotic pressure. The Relief Society, for example, received a letter from the Women's Section of the Movement for National Preparedness asking for support for the creation of a "moderate army," a cause which "cannot, as we see it, conflict in any way with the convictions of anyone who loves her country." At the bottom of the stock letter was a hand-written note: "Is not your National Relief Society a patriotic body? If so is it not disposed to stand with us for Preparedness?"[28]

Whether intended or not, such questions carried the sting of old accusations. Regardless, the Relief Society did not respond, and as a whole the LDS Church leadership kept preparedness advocates at arm's length. Church periodicals even published open criticism of the movement. An April 1916 article by John Cuthers recounted a well-known narrative from the *Book of Mormon* in which a whole community buried its weapons to suggest that "some at least of the ancient inhabitants of this continent were averse to the continuous and increased use of weapons of war." Cuthers further argued that "*God's truth* and *not increased armaments* are the only sure foundation upon which *the world's peace and the security of nations* shall be established forever."[29] Such sentiments were expressly in line with those of President Smith, whose public comments continued to emphasize the tragic elements of war and who openly promoted Howard Taft's World Peace Foundation over Teddy Roosevelt's Preparedness efforts.[30]

One notable exception to this rule was an editorial by Susa Young Gates published on the eve of the 1916 presidential election. While Gates had earlier decried the fact that men "fight and kill" while women "must suffer and weep," she now dramatically shifted her gendered ideology. As a staunch Republican who deeply admired Roosevelt, she channeled his "strenuous life" philosophy, asserting that individuals, nations, and churches must develop through "activity, aggressiveness, preparedness." Claiming that all women despised "white-livered, mealy-mouthed apologizers, who

---

1915. Church History Library, Salt Lake City, Utah (Catalog # CR-11-16).

28. Letter from Josephine Bates, Chair of the Woman's Section of the Movement for National Preparedness, to Emmeline B. Wells, undated. Church History Library, Salt Lake City, Utah (Catalog # CR-11-16).

29. John Cuthers, "Book of Mormon Aspect of Preparedness," *Improvement Era*, April 1916, 516–17. Emphasis in the original.

30. *Conference Report*, April 1916, 77–79, and October 1916, 68.

not only turn their third cheek for assaults, but make doormats of themselves for their assailants," Gates proposed that society should prepare for hostilities because "war is not the worst calamity."

> Death, a glorious, honorable death, is far more to be preferred than an ignoble, impure, pusillanimous life.... And if good, true men die on the battlefield, their end will be more glorious than their beginning. Let us, as Latter-day Saint women, pray and hope for honorable peace, but dread dishonor, stultification, inaction, slothfulness, vanity, all lusts of the flesh, and the abominations of the world, for ourselves and for our sons. Let us achieve action, progress, fulfillment of prophecy, expansion, and cultivate the aggressiveness of the gospel of truth and righteousness.[31]

Even for the passionate and mercurial Gates, this brash celebration of militarism represented an outlier sentiment, brought on perhaps by the intensity of a close presidential campaign. The next month, after the Republican defeat and with the year drawing to a close, she was back to form—and in greater alignment with other prominent Latter-day Saints—writing in more plaintive tones of armies marching, women crying, orphans hungry for bread, and a world "circled with a bleeding corslet," and poignantly disclosing: "I long, I yearn, I pray for peace—peace—when there is so little peace."[32]

INTO THE CRUCIBLE

The mixed emotions of Susa Young Gates were harbingers of the ordeal to come. Yet, other than her strident election-time editorial, the substance of official Latter-day Saint rhetoric was remarkably consistent through the early years of the war. There was almost no lobbying for US involvement. Instead, the war was regarded, largely from a distance, as a tragic consequence of an apostate Christianity, as a failure to love and recognize the brotherhood of man, and as a validation of Mormonism's prophetic mission. These tropes persisted into the early spring of 1917, as national rhetoric became increasingly militaristic. In March the *Improvement Era* published a report from Fred L. W. Bennett, a recent convert freshly arrived from the British Isles, who confirmed that the war was "the most demoralizing, hateful,

---

31. Susa Young Gates, "The Church Militant," *Relief Society Magazine*, October 1916, 648–49.

32. Susa Young Gates, "Peace on Earth," *Relief Society Magazine*, October 1916, 710–11.

wicked thing known to mankind" and "a natural result of the wickedness of man as a whole."[33] Likewise, on the eve of President Wilson's war address to Congress, the church's *Juvenile Instructor* opined: "War, indeed, seems probable. But we pray God to so shape the affairs of the world as to keep this peace-loving nation out of the conflict!"[34]

When war officially broke on 6 April 1917, the church was in the midst of its Annual General Conference. In his opening remarks to the conference on the previous day, President Smith, anticipating that war might trigger an adverse transformation among the Latter-day Saints, issued a warning:

> I exhort my friends, the people of our country, especially in this intermountain region, to maintain above all other things the spirit of humanity, of love, and of peace-making, that even though they may be called into action they will not demolish, override and destroy the principles which we believe in, which we have tried to inculcate, and which we are exhorted to maintain; peace and good will toward all mankind, though we may be brought into action with the enemy. I want to say to the Latter-day Saints who may enlist, and whose services the country may require, that when they become the soldiers of the State and of the Nation that they will not forget that they are also soldiers of the Cross, that they are ministers of life and not of death; and when they go forth, that they may go forth in the spirit of defending the liberties of mankind rather than for the purpose of destroying the enemy. If we could convert them to peaceful ways and to the love of peace without destroying them, we would become saviors of men.[35]

Along with the danger of bloodlust, President Smith was deeply concerned about the degeneration of other moral standards. He encouraged potential soldiers to maintain "lives of honor, virtue, purity," and warned those who might remain at home not to mistreat or condemn anyone with ties to Germany, Austria, and Italy—"we must respect them and uphold them in the purest kindness, love and compassion, and with sorrow that their native countries are in the terrible plight that they are, for which they are not responsible."[36]

These concerns, echoed by other speakers during the three-day conference, articulated a general concern that LDS soldiers ought to be good

33. Fred L. W. Bennett, "The Ethics of War," *Improvement Era*, March 1917, 423–25.
34. "Congress to Meet April Second," *Juvenile Instructor*, April 1917, 190.
35. *Conference Report*, April 1917, 3.
36. Ibid., 4, 12.

Christians before they were good Americans, suggesting a deep anxiety regarding the relationship of the Mormon community to the nation as a whole. Having critiqued the war with detachment, trying to stand with prophetic witness above a maelstrom of fiercely competing national identities, the church leadership now anticipated a future in which the main body of Latter-day Saints would be pulled into this vortex as citizens of a nation with whom they had previously had an ambivalent relationship at best. This unease was not explicitly acknowledged at the time, but it was hinted at with comments such as those delivered by President Smith's first counselor, Anthon Lund: "We are a people of peace. We do not love war, but . . . as we are an integral part of the United States, if the United States shall be attacked we will take our part with them in defending our country."[37]

Lund's "but" contained a world of unspoken anxiety. The church's daily newspaper had earlier reported Theodore Roosevelt's sentiments that "poltroons and professional pacifists are out of place in a free republic. . . . No man is fit to be a free man unless he has fitted himself to fight efficiently for his freedom."[38] Consequently, given their past history with the nation, Latter-day Saints knew that even the slightest hesitation might be interpreted as unpatriotic. Over a decade after the war, B. H. Roberts openly admitted the "unique position" in which the Latter-day Saints found themselves in 1917. Given the overwhelming Mormon population of Utah, Roberts noted that "what the state of Utah did, and the spirit in which she did it" in relation to the war would reflect the "spirit" of the Latter-day Saints: "Had Utah as a state acted reluctantly, or had she failed in any respect to proceed as the other states of the Union and as the whole nation did, the reluctance and failure would have been chargeable to the Latter-day Saints. *Per contra*, Utah's promptness in action and the spirit in which she did her part would reflect the patriotism, the intensity of the Americanism of the same people."[39]

Yet passing this patriotic litmus test required shifts in Mormon rhetoric. Many of the familiar tropes persisted. Apostle David O. McKay reiterated that God could not be blamed for the brutal conflict or its misery, but rather represented a force of love.[40] But other leaders, such as Charles Penrose, began highlighting principles reminiscent of muscular Christian-

---

37. Ibid., 12–13.
38. *Deseret News*, 23 November 1916, 8.
39. Roberts, *Comprehensive History*, 6:454–55.
40. *Conference Report*, April 1917, 46.

ity. Speaking on the day war was declared, and building on the premise that "the character of our Lord and Savior Jesus Christ is sometimes misunderstood and misinterpreted," Penrose argued that although the Savior "taught that non-resistance, was right and praiseworthy and a duty under certain circumstances and conditions . . . Jesus was no milksop. He was not to be trampled underfoot." Consequently, Penrose continued, "there are times and seasons . . . when it is justifiable and right and proper and the duty of men to go forth in the defense of their homes and their families and maintain their privileges and rights by force of arms."[41]

Similar themes prevailed at the annual conference of the Young Men and Young Women's Associations in June, an event B. H. Roberts referred to as "the war conference," where Penrose openly recruited young men to enlist. "We want to establish peace," he noted, "but sometimes peace has to be achieved through war." His argument for war focused on the possibility that the US might advance principles of truth, liberty, and human rights to "all flesh," but he also touched on the paradox of Mormonism's divided allegiance: "We desire to show, for a fact, that not withstanding reports that have been circulated . . . we are loyal to our Government, as we desire to be, first of all, loyal to our God and to the truths which He has revealed." Moreover, Penrose exhibited some apprehension about fully embracing national culture, advising young men to join local guard units so they might be "under the direction of officers from our own midst, . . . men of the same faith and the same desires and the same grand intentions."[42]

At that conference, President Smith addressed these themes but maintained a position of greater detachment and prophetic witness. Reiterating with increased fervor that God's hand was not in the war, Smith condemned all the "nations of the earth" for quarreling with each other "for power, for worldly greatness." Arguing that "there is not a nation in the world today that is not tainted with this evil," Smith did not grant an exception to the United States and refused "to trace the cause of the evil, or the greater part of it, to some particular nation"—an orientation quite at odds with the propagandistic images of bloody Huns that were by then prevalent in most corners of the nation. He asserted that God was "striving with certain of the nations of the earth to preserve and protect human liberty"—again, he did not single out the United States—but he also emphatically maintained that

---

41. Ibid., 19–20.

42. Charles W. Penrose, "Where and under What Spirit to Enlist," *Improvement Era*, July 1917, 831–34.

these divinely guided nations were *not* righteous. Indeed, God had "some hard material to work with," including "infidels" and "men who are full of pride and ambition." So he pled with the "soldier boys of Mormondom" to remember their religious training and allegiance to Christ, counseling them to "go out [to the battlefront] as you do on a mission [and] be just as good and pure and true in the army of the United States as you are in the army of the Elders of Israel that are preaching the gospel of love and peace to the world."[43]

Given these official, if somewhat qualified, endorsements of the war effort, Latter-day Saints proved generally eager to pass their patriotic test. Initial enlistments for the state of Utah exceeded its quota by 300 percent, and by the end of the war over 5.4 percent of the population served in the military, 17 percent higher than the national average. Liberty Bonds were oversubscribed in Utah, averaging nearly 50 percent more than their apportionment, with the LDS Church itself purchasing $850,000 and its auxiliary organizations, including the Relief Society, purchasing another $600,000 worth. Moreover, the Relief Society practically donated over 200,000 bushels of its wheat reserves to the war effort.[44]

Still, while the actions of Latter-day Saints exhibited strong support of the nation, the rhetoric from most church leaders, especially from President Smith, continued to retain an element of detachment from overt nationalism, sounding instead notes of caution about embracing bloodlust, sexual immorality, alcohol, tobacco, or (more generally) "apostate" Christianity.[45] Moreover, ambivalence towards supporting the war effort was prevalent enough that at the October 1917 conference Charles Penrose acknowledged: "Some of our people, some that are very pacific, become critical as to our war policy . . . and a few of them feel rebellious in their hearts in regard to it, and think that there is fault in the leaders of the people." Reassuring his audience that God "holds the power of life and of death," Penrose declared that "what he says is right, and what he reveals through his servants the prophets . . . is right, no matter what we may think or feel."[46]

---

43. Joseph F. Smith, "To the Soldier Boys of 'Mormondom,'" *Improvement Era*, July 1917, 823–26.

44. Goddard, *Pertinent Facts*.

45. See, for example, Joseph F. Smith, "Why Apostate Christianity Is Disappointing," *Improvement Era*, September 1917, 1016–18; and "A Message to the Soldiers," *Improvement Era*, January 1918, 261–63.

46. *Conference Report*, October 1917, 20–21.

There were some notable exceptions to this rule—prominent voices who began to embrace the nationalist spirit of the day. B. H. Roberts, at the age of sixty, secured a commission as an army chaplain, the only contemporary LDS General Authority to enlist and serve in Europe. Before being deployed, he confidently declared at the October 1917 General Conference: "No nation in the history of this world ever drew the sword in a more righteous cause and in a more unselfish spirit, and with a greater desire to benefit humanity, than our nation has done in the present instance. If there ever was a holy war in this world, you may account the war that the United States is waging against the Imperial Government of Germany as the most righteous and holy of wars."[47]

Such enthusiastic patriotism presaged Mormonism's future relationship to the American nation-state as the LDS community's traditional ambivalence and detachment were destined to fade. Indeed, as the war drew on, and increasing numbers of Latter-day Saint soldiers were deployed and killed at the front, Mormon rhetoric reflected greater certainty in the righteousness of the American cause. Furthermore, the goals of the nation were increasingly conflated with the mission of the church. By April 1918 many church leaders were speaking about conjoined purposes. Orson F. Whitney was one of the most explicit: "I want my boy, who has enlisted in the cause of our country, . . . to feel that he is a soldier of Jesus Christ. . . . God loves the whole world; he gave his Son to save it; he is using America and her allies as instruments for the spread of the Gospel of Liberty."[48]

As US involvement accelerated, church periodicals published updates from the field, including excerpts of letters from LDS soldiers describing patriotic sentiments and relating spiritual and missionary experiences in the military. *The Improvement Era* printed lists of young men who "died in service" alongside lists of church missionaries who "died in the field."[49] Statistics on the Latter-day Saint war efforts were reported in General Conference.[50] Through it all ran a persistent anxiety about how the church's loyalty was perceived by the rest of the country. Church periodicals touted non-Mormon praise for LDS patriotism, including a letter from Herbert Hoover referring to the Relief Society's wheat contribution as a "generous

---

47. Ibid., 102–5.

48. Ibid., 77.

49. Regular lists of those who "Died in the Service" were published every month from June 1918 to April 1919.

50. *Conference Report*, April 1918, 30; October 1918, 3.

and patriotic act" and expressing his "renewed appreciation of the interest and sacrifice which this action by your church typifies."[51] During the last months of the war the church even took the unusual step of commissioning and publishing a report of "pertinent facts bearing upon Utah's loyalty to the government of the United States" in order to counter what were considered "persistent falsehoods circulated by hireling agitators in the East."[52] What is more, President Smith felt compelled to explicitly reiterate allegiance: "I wish to say this, there isn't a feeling in my soul nor in any fiber of my being that is disloyal to the Government of the United States."[53]

ON THE OTHER SIDE

Joseph F. Smith's personal denial of disloyalty may have been necessary because, despite his love for the US Constitution and broad support for the war effort, and counter to the increasingly public nationalism expressed by other church leaders, Smith remained relatively detached from the patriotic currents that swirled so fiercely around the Latter-day Saint community. A natural reluctance had always informed his responses. As the more enthusiastically patriotic Roberts later put it, "President Smith, preeminently a man of peace, was slow at first to recognize that the hour had struck for the United States to drop the neutral attitude."[54] As the war progressed, he continued to hang back and his rhetoric never climbed the nationalist heights of other church leaders. Indeed, Smith's strongest inclination, especially in the last six months of the war, was to pull even further away from the nationalist vortex and reassert a universal, even other-worldly, perspective of the human condition.

In the spring of 1918, having recently lost a beloved son to a ruptured appendix, Smith's own health began to fail, and he spent the next five months generally secluded.[55] Emerging for the October General Conference, Smith announced: "I have not lived alone these five months. I have dwelt in the spirit of prayer, of supplication, of faith and determination; and I have had my communications with the Spirit of the Lord continuously."

---

51. Roberts, *Comprehensive History*, 6:456–70. For other examples, see "Patriotism," *Improvement Era*, May 1918, 640–41, and "Recognition of Noble Work," *Improvement Era*, August 1918, 917–18.

52. Goddard, *Pertinent Facts*, 1.

53. *Conference Report*, April 1918, 5.

54. Roberts, *Comprehensive History*, 6:467.

55. Tate, "Great World."

He later told other church leaders that he had experienced a rather vivid vision in which he saw "the hosts of the dead, both small and great."[56] Expanding beyond the parameters of earth's national cultures and traditional Christianity, Smith saw another world inhabited by all departed spirits—righteous and unrighteous, believers and unbelievers, just and unjust, some in light, others in darkness—where a resurrected Christ organized the just spirits and "commissioned them to go forth and carry the light of the gospel to them that were in darkness, even to all the spirits of men."[57]

Smith's vision reinforced the theology undergirding Latter-day Saint temple ordinances for deceased ancestors. But it also evoked anxieties about the devastation of disease, war, and other forms of untimely death, providing an avenue of hope for the disconsolate. The end of the vision, in particular, hinted at a potentially bright future for young Latter-day Saints who lost their lives: "I beheld that the faithful elders of this dispensation, when they depart from mortal life, continue their labors in the preaching of the gospel of repentance and redemption."[58] Under such a scenario, and "through the sacrifice of the Only Begotten Son," friends and foes in this life might be reconciled to each other in the next—a fragmented and wounded world made whole again on the other side of the veil.[59]

Smith submitted this revelation to the governing bodies of the church on the last day of October and they endorsed it as authentic. Less than two weeks later, the war abruptly ended, and eight days after that, Smith himself passed away. Both events marked important transitions for Mormonism. With the passing of Smith, the Latter-day Saint community lost its last substantial link to the founding generation and the church's charismatic and separatist origins. The end of the war, on the other hand, signaled successful completion of their patriotic crucible and marked the beginning of drastically improved relations with the nation. The next year, when the church was accused of systematically kidnapping and importing girls from England for polygamy, Herbert Hoover came to its defense, citing the Latter-day Saints' war service as proof of their good character.[60]

Yet more than simply reconciling the nation to Mormonism, the war played a significant role in reconciling Latter-day Saints to the nation-state.

---

56. *Doctrine and Covenants* 138:11–12.
57. *Doctrine and Covenants* 138:30.
58. *Doctrine and Covenants* 138:57.
59. *Doctrine and Covenants* 138:57.
60. Alexander, *Mormonism in Transition*, 253.

Having offered a significant sacrifice of treasure and blood "upon the altar of the nation," the Mormon community emerged from the war more fully initiated into America's civil religion.[61] The Latter-day Saints' trauma was now intertwined with and identical to the nation's trauma. Having jointly passed through the agony of battle, they now faced an uncertain but hopeful future together. As veterans returned, the Latter-day Saints struggled to integrate them in the same ways every other community struggled, and perceived these struggles as fundamentally American rather than Mormon in nature.

Moreover, as the meaning and legacy of the war began to be debated, particularly as the nation mourned the disappointments of Versailles and argued over participation in the League of Nations, the Mormon community demonstrated how thoroughly their community was being integrated into the national polity. Unlike the previously united support of the war effort, Latter-day Saint reactions to the League divided the church leadership along partisan lines, with B. H. Roberts and Reed Smoot leading pro- and anti-league factions, respectively. Both sides marshaled scriptures and theology to bolster their positions, creating concern among top leaders that this divisive political issue would inflict lasting damage on the church unity. But in the end, the tension did not produce lasting schism, and church leaders found ways to both heal relationships and separate religious considerations from political sensibilities.[62]

More significantly, the division itself signaled the new robustness with which Mormons would become integral elements of the nation-state. Having endured a crucible of wartime nationalism, and developed political identities that were becoming as important as their religious identities, Latter-day Saints emerged on the other side of the war arguing more with each other as members of partisan factions than with the nation as a whole. The outsiders were now insiders, or at least more comfortably so than they had been before the war. Previously united as Zion-focused "Saints" arrayed against nationalist "Gentiles," Mormons now engaged the great political issues of the day as Americans first, a transformation of corporate identity that has continued until today.

---

61. The phrase and concept are from Stout, *Upon the Altar*.
62. Allen, "Personal Faith."

BIBLIOGRAPHY

Primary Sources (Mormon Periodicals)

Conference Report of the Church of Jesus Christ of Latter-day Saints, 1914–18.
Deseret News, 1916.
Improvement Era, 1914–18.
Juvenile Instructor, 1917.
Relief Society Magazine, 1914, 1916.

Secondary Sources

Alexander, Thomas G. *Mormonism in Transition: A History of the Latter-day Saints, 1890–1930*. Urbana, IL: University of Illinois Press, 1986.

Allen, James B. "Personal Faith and Public Policy: Some Timely Observations on the League of Nations Controversy in Utah." *BYU Studies* 14, no. 1 (1974) 77–98.

Ashurst-McGee, Mark. "Zion Rising: Joseph Smith's Early Social and Political Thought." PhD diss., Arizona State University, 2008.

Arrington, Leonard J. "Modern Lysistratas: Mormon Women in the International Peace Movement, 1899–1939." *Journal of Mormon History* 15 (1989) 89–104.

Bowman, Matthew. *Mormon People*. New York: Random House, 2012.

Flake, Kathleen. *The Politics of American Religious Identity: The Seating of Senator Reed Smoot, Mormon Apostle*. Chapel Hill, NC: University of North Carolina Press, 2004.

Goddard, Benjamin. *Pertinent Facts on Utah's Loyalty and War Record*. Salt Lake City: The Church of Jesus Christ of Latter-day Saints, 1918.

Gordon, Sarah Barringer. *The Mormon Question: Polygamy and Constitutional Conflict in Nineteenth-Century America*. Chapel Hill, NC: University of North Carolina Press, 2002.

Mason, Patrick Q. "'The Wars and Perplexities of the Nations': Reflections on Early Mormonism, Violence, and the State." *Journal of Mormon History* 38, no. 3 (2012) 72–89.

Pulsipher, J. David. "'Prepared to Abide the Penalty': Latter-day Saints and Civil Disobedience." *Journal of Mormon History* 39, no. 3 (2013) 131–62.

Roberts, B. H. *A Comprehensive History of the Church of Jesus Christ of Latter-day Saints*. 6 vols. Salt Lake City, UT: Church of Jesus Christ of Latter-day Saints, 1930.

Quinn, Michael D. "The Mormon Church and the Spanish–American War: An End to Selective Pacifism." *Pacific Historical Review* 43 (August 1974) 342–66.

Stout, Harry S. *Upon the Altar of the Nation: A Moral History of the Civil War*. New York: Viking, 2006.

Tate, George S. "'The Great World of the Spirits of the Dead': Death, the Great War, and the 1918 Influenza Pandemic as Context for Doctrine and Covenants 138." *BYU Studies* 46, no. 1 (2007) 5–40.

Walker, Ronald W. "Sheaves, Bucklers, and the State: Mormon Leaders Respond to the Dilemmas of War." *Sunstone* 7 (July/August 1982) 43–56.

Wessinger, Catherine. *The Oxford Handbook of Millennialism*. New York: Oxford University Press, 2011.

9

The Bible Students / Jehovah's Witnesses in the United States during the First World War

M. James Penton

IN AN ACCOUNT OF the Bible Student / Jehovah's Witness movement,[1] A. Hugh MacMillan recounted what took place in the autumn of 1914 at Watch Tower Society headquarters in Brooklyn, New York:

> Friday morning (October 2) we were all seated at the breakfast table at breakfast when Russell came down. As he entered the room he hesitated a moment as was his custom and said cheerily, "Good morning all." But this morning, instead of proceeding to his seat as usual, he briskly clapped his hands and announced: "The Gentile times have ended: the kings have had their day." We all applauded.[2]

The Watch Tower Society was the central publishing organization for the Bible Student movement, and Russell was the well-known Pastor Charles Taze Russell who was its president, founder, and the primary theologian of the movement. The reason why he was so elated on the day just described above was that he had long believed that 1914 would mark the battle of

---

1. Although Russell would have preferred to call his followers nothing but "Christians," very early they took the name "Bible Students" to distinguish themselves. Outsiders often referred to them as "Russellites." In 1931, the second president of the Watch Tower Society coined the name "Jehovah's Witnesses" for those Bible Students loyal to him and the society, largely to separate them from dissident Bible Students.

2. Macmillan, *Faith on the March*, 47.

149

Armageddon, the destruction of worldly governments, and the establishment of Christ's millennial reign over the earth. Hence he saw the outbreak of the First World War as the end of the Gentile times mentioned in Luke 21:24.[3]

Of course the war was to end with the Treaty of Versailles rather than the establishment of Christ's millennial kingdom. But during the first two years of warfare in Europe, Russell continued to believe that both the churches of Christendom and human governments would collapse under divine judgment shortly.[4] Not surprisingly, then, he regarded the war as unchristian, and he denounced most clergy for supporting their various countries' bloody military programs. Although he had long held pacifist views, because he regarded the secular "higher powers" of Romans 13:1 as having a temporary divine mandate to govern, he had taught his followers to follow a somewhat impractical course in response to military conscription. In 1904, he had written:

> We may be required to do military service whether we vote or not, however; and if required we would be obliged to obey the powers that be, and should consider that the Lord's providence had permitted the conscription and that he was able to overrule it to the good of ourselves or others. In such event, we would consider it not amiss to make a partial explanation to the proper officers, and to request a transference to the medical or hospital department, where our services could be used with the full consent of our consciences;—but even if compelled to serve in the ranks and to fire our guns we need not feel compelled to shoot a fellow creature.[5]

But from September 1915 through till his death on 31 October 1916, he had come to take a sterner stance against warfare, the production of weapons, and especially service in armed forces. In so doing he specifically repudiated his earlier position outlined above. In answer to a rhetorical statement,

---

3. This was based on a complicated system, which used, among other things, the year-for-a-day method popularized in the early seventeenth century by Joseph Mede. For a complete understanding of Russell's eschatological system, see Russell, *Thy Kingdom Come*.

4. In an "Author's Foreword" published in the 1916 reprint of *Thy Kingdom Come*, he suggested that the living Bible Student saints who would come with Christ to rule the world would be changed to meet him in the air in "perhaps a year or two or three." Then, following the destruction of the churches of Christendom, Christ's kingdom would come to rule the world. See Russell, *Thy Kingdom Come*, i–iv.

5. Russell, *New Creation*, 594–95.

"If one were to refuse the uniform and the military service he would be shot," he responded, "If the presentation were properly made there might be some kind of exoneration; but if not, would it be any worse to be shot because of loyalty to the Prince of peace and refusal to disobey His order than to be shot while under the banner of these earthly kings?"[6]

Because of his enhanced anti-war position, Russell not only condemned militarism, but he especially censured those clergymen who encouraged the enlistment of men into their nations' military and naval forces. Writing in *The Watch Tower* magazine, he remarked:

> Recently in Canada the Editor was astounded by the activity of the preachers there—especially those of the Church of England. One was out in khaki uniform marching through the streets with the volunteers. Asked by a college friend, "Did I see you in the ranks?" he answered, "Yes I wanted to encourage the boys." "And did you think of going to the front, to the trenches?" "Not a bit of it!" He was merely acting as a decoy to get others to the front; just as a bull which they have at one of the Chicago stockyards, meets the animals about to be slaughtered and, tossing his head in the air, becomes their leader up the gangway leading to the slaughter. There he knows his little niche, into which he glides and is sheltered; while the others drive and press one another forward to the slaughter.[7]

Although Russell was denied entry to Canada in the summer of 1916 for his views,[8] his message was not regarded particularly negatively at that time in the United States, where most Americans continued to want their country to remain at peace. In fact, President Woodrow Wilson was elected to a second term in the fall of that year in part for having kept the country at peace. But circumstances changed dramatically on 6 April 1917 when the US Congress declared war on Germany at Wilson's behest. Shortly thereafter Congress passed a number of laws that were to curb civil liberties for

---

6. Russell, "Christian Duty and the War," *The Watch Tower*, 1 September 1915, 260–61. *Watchtower Reprints*, 5754–55. One may ask why Russell waited till the late summer of 1915 to take a more realistic pacifistic stand. The answer may have been that there was no conscription at the time in Britain nor in most of its self-governing colonies, and the United States was still at peace. But there certainly was military conscription on the European continent, and it seems that many German Bible Students served in the German Army with good consciences as they followed Russell's earlier admonition.

7. Ibid., 260. *Watchtower Reprints*, 5754.

8. "Pastor Russsell Is Not Allowed to Enter Canada," *Winnipeg Free Press*, 8 July 1916, 1.

any who opposed the country's war effort. Among those, the most draconian was the Espionage Act of 15 June 1917 that made it illegal to do anything that interfered with the American war effort. Section Three of that act reads as follows:

> Whoever, when the United States is at war, shall wilfully make or convey false reports or false statements with intent to interfere with the operation or success of the military or naval forces of the United States or to promote the success of its enemies and whoever when the United States is at war, shall wilfully cause or attempt to cause insubordination, disloyalty, mutiny, refusal to duty, in the military or naval forces of the United States, or shall wilfully obstruct the recruiting or enlistment service of the United States, to the injury of the service of the United States, shall be punished by a fine of not more than $10,000 or imprisonment for not more than twenty years, or both.

So statements like Russell's quoted above about what was happening in Canada in 1915 were, in the United States in 1917 and 1918, regarded as illegal and "un-American." Even more serious was the fact that a seeming majority of Americans became so captivated by a spirit of extreme patriotism that historian David Kennedy has compared the United States of the First World War to George Orwell's Oceania in his famous novel *1984*. He has written: "The American experience in World War I . . . darkly adumbrated the themes Orwell was to put at the center of his futuristic fantasy: overbearing concern for 'correct opinion,' for expression, for language itself, and the enormous propaganda apparatus to nurture the desired state of mind and excoriate all dissenters."[9] In addition, he places much of the blame on President Wilson himself: "'Woe to the man or group of men that stand in our way,' he warned peace advocates in June 1917. They had small idea, as yet, just how much woe was to befall them."[10]

Thus not only did the government begin to restrict civil liberties, but both social paranoia and vigilantism became rife. For example, hamburgers were renamed "liberty sandwiches" and sauerkraut became "liberty cabbage." The governor of Iowa prohibited the speaking of German on streetcars, on the telephone, or publicly. A politician in the same state asserted, "ninety percent of all men and women who teach the German language are traitors." And mobs began to lynch and manhandle German-Americans.

9. Kennedy, *Over Here*, 62.
10. Ibid., 46.

Perhaps the worst case of such madness occurred in St. Louis, Missouri. David Kennedy states: "In one of the most infamous cases of vigilantism, near St. Louis in April 1918, a mob seized Robert Prager, a young man whose only discernible offense was to have been born in Germany." Although he had tried to enlist in the US Navy, he had been refused for medical reasons. Despite that, he was bound with an American flag, dragged barefoot through the streets, and hanged to the cheers of some five hundred "patriots." When the leaders of the mob were tried for "patriotic murder," a jury of their peers acquitted them in only twenty-five minutes. Concerning the matter, the *Washington Post* remarked: "In spite of excesses such as lynching, it is a healthful and wholesome awakening in the interior of the country."[11]

It was not just German-Americans who experienced the wrath of both the government and a large section of the American public. Any individuals who opposed the war suffered for it. They included Socialists, members of the International Workers of the World, pacifistic feminists, and conscientious objectors.[12] Then, because unthinking patriotism tended to excite nativism, ethnic bias, and racism, foreign immigrants felt excessive pressure to become Americanized,[13] and African-Americans suffered an amazing increase in lynchings.[14]

Like members of all "peace churches," the Bible Students came under attack, and their men of military age were often placed under brutal army control or imprisoned for refusing to be conscripted. Congress had included in the draft law an escape section for conscientious objectors, but that was often ignored.[15] The same happened with members of other anti-war religions. Yet with the possible exception of the Hutterites,[16] the

11. Ibid., 67–68.
12. Ibid., 26–27, 70, 72, 85, 163–65, 284.
13. Ibid., 66–67.
14. Ibid., 283.

15. For a contemporary account of the plight of conscientious objectors in the United States in 1917 and 1918, see the National Civil Liberties Bureau, *Facts about Conscientious Objectors*.

16. The Hutterites suffered persecution in the Dakotas and Montana because of both their pacifism and their use of the German language. Many of their men were drafted into the US Army despite the law granting exemption to religious conscientious objectors. Four of them who were drafted refused to soldier, and were imprisoned and physically abused. Two of the four, Joseph and Michael Hofer, died at Leavenworth Military Prison from torture after the end of the war. As a result of such persecution, most American Hutterites migrated to Canada.

Bible Students probably suffered more than any other American religious community for their unpatriotic stance proclaimed by Charles Russell and his successors.

Charles Russell died on 31 October 1916, and shortly thereafter a three-man "executive committee" was established to oversee the affairs of the Watch Tower Society. The individuals who sat on this committee were Vice President A. I. Richie, Secretary-Treasurer William E. Van Amburgh, and the Watch Tower Society's legal advisor, "Judge" Joseph F. Rutherford.[17] But in January 1917 Rutherford was elected as the second president of the Society in what was a rigged election.[18] Immediately thereafter, he set about enhancing his personal control of the Watch Tower Society, and in later years, was to replace Bible Student congregational governance with what he called "theocratic government" or "the Theocracy," over which he personally spoke for Jehovah and determined what the Almighty wanted.[19]

Rutherford was a tall, powerful man who had been raised as a Baptist in Morgan County, Missouri, and had become a lawyer through the old apprentice system rather than through study at a college of law. After practicing law in Boone, Missouri, where he served as a substitute judge for four days, he became a Bible Student convert and thereafter served for some years as a "pilgrim" or traveling preacher, as well as the Watch Tower Society's lawyer. At the time Russell died, his residence was in California where he had a legal practice. But while on a trip to the eastern United States, he was notified of Russell's passing. As a result, he returned to Watch Tower headquarters in New York where he was catapulted into membership in the above-mentioned executive committee.[20] From that time forward, he

---

17. Rutherford used the title "Judge" throughout his life, a fact many have considered improper. For citations on the data respecting that issue, see note 20 below.

18. As chairman of the election, A. Hugh Macmillan conspired to make certain that only Rutherford would be nominated for the position of president. He practically admitted as much years later when he stated: "A few ambitious ones at headquarters were holding caucuses here and there, doing a little electioneering to get their men in. However, Van Amburgh and I held a large number of votes. Many shareholders, knowing of our association with Russell, sent their proxies to us to be cast for the one whom we thought best fitted for office" (Macmillan, *Faith on the March*, 68).

19. In 1940 the *Consolation* magazine, the predecessor of Jehovah's Witnesses's *Awake!*, proclaimed: "The Theocracy is at present administered by the Watch Tower Bible and Tract Society, of which Judge Rutherford is the president and general manager." (*Consolation*, September 4, 1940, 25).

20. For Rutherford's background and certain activities, see the Transcript of Record of *United States of America* vs. *Rutherford et al.*, pp. 964, 965, 968, 979. Hereafter, this

ignored carrying on business in California and failed to care for his invalid wife who remained there. As a result, he became estranged from her and their son, Malcolm. When he died in 1942, neither attended his funeral.

In his will, Russell had indicated clearly that he did not want a powerful individual to take over the management of the Watch Tower Society when he died; rather, he planned for the creation of a five-man editorial committee that would oversee the publication of doctrinal works and a board whose members would operate collegially.[21] But Rutherford had no intention of letting that happen, and he soon found himself in a bitter struggle with a majority of the board. Supported by Secretary-Treasurer Van Amburgh, he carried on the management of the Watch Tower Society without allowing its board members or even its vice president to examine the society's accounts.[22]

Using a subsidiary organization to the Watch Tower Society called the Peoples Pulpit Association, Rutherford kept the fact from most fellow board members that he had decided on publishing *The Finished Mystery*, a book that two Bible Students, Clayton J. Woodworth and George H. Fisher, had produced. In it they had used numerous quotations from Russell's works, and therefore it was described on its second page as the "posthumous work of Pastor Russell." Significantly too, it was listed on its title page as "Series VII" of Russell's *Studies in the Scriptures*.

The Finished Mystery was released at a mid-day meeting of the Watch Tower headquarters staff on 17 July 1917. The Watch Tower Society and Jehovah's Witnesses have falsely claimed that it was the cause of an attack on Rutherford that resulted in his replacement of four board members who were in opposition to his policies.[23] However, Rutherford admitted under oath in court that this was not the case and that the so-called Seventh Volume had nothing to do with a bitter altercation at the time.[24] What it really did, along with other of the society's publications, was to bring the wrath

---

source will be listed as "Transcript." See also Curran, *Judge*.

21. "Will and Testament of Charles Taze Russell," *The Watch Tower*, 1916, 358–59. *Watchtower Reprints*, 5999, 6000.

22. For an account of the struggle that followed between Rutherford and a majority of the Watch Tower Society's board of directors, see Penton, *Apocalypse Delayed*, 71–79.

23. *Jehovah's Witnesses in the Divine Purpose*, 70–71. *Jehovah's Witnesses: Proclaimers*, 719.

24. When questioned as to whether *The Finished Mystery* was the cause of the "difficulty" that had happened at Watch Tower headquarters, Rutherford stated emphatically: "It was not. Did not include the Finished Mystery in the slightest" (Transcript, 982).

of the US Administration of Justice down on the heads of Watch Tower leaders.

Given the times, the release of *The Finished Mystery* to the Bible Student community and to the general public as well seems to have been an act of sectarian madness. In the first place, after reading it, many Bible Students rejected it as Russell's "posthumous work."[25] But far more serious was the fact that it contained statements that appeared shockingly disloyal to most Americans, who by mid-1917 were already super patriots. For example, Clayton Woodworth wrote:

> Nowhere in the New Testament is Patriotism (a narrow-minded hatred of other peoples) encouraged. Everywhere and always murder in its every form is forbidden; and yet, under the guise of Patriotism the civil governments of earth demand of peace-loving men the sacrifice of themselves and their loved ones and the butchery of their fellows, and hail it as a duty demanded by the laws of heaven.[26]

He then followed this statement with a series of anti-militaristic quotations from the *Watch Tower* magazine that had been published by Russell over the decade prior to the United States' entry into the war. Included in these statements was the one about the Anglican clergyman who had led young men in Canada into the army without himself having personally enlisted.

Of course, practically all of the material in *The Finished Mystery* had been written before the United States had declared war on Germany. But Bible Student leaders seemed to have no concern about distributing the so-called Seventh Volume to both Bible Students and the general public in the fall of 1917 and during the winter of 1918. Furthermore, they published other printed works that condemned the war and attacked the clergy for their support of it in Canada, Great Britain, and the United States. So why did they do so when they knew that their actions might cause them to get into serious trouble with US federal authorities?

Unquestionably, they were distressed over the severe treatment that individual Bible Student men were suffering at the hands of the military for refusing to take up arms in all three countries.[27] Second, they were shocked

---

25. This was certainly true of those who broke with Rutherford following his re-election in 1918. A number of them established two new movements: The Pastoral Bible Institute and The Layman's Home Missionary Movement.

26. Woodworth and Fisher, *Finished Mystery*, 247.

27. For the First World War treatment of Bible Students in Canada and Great Britain,

at the suffering that Bible Student men and women were experiencing in the United States at the hands of mobs, something that will be mentioned briefly below. But even more important was their millenarian belief that the churches of Christendom were soon to be annihilated, followed by the destruction of the nations and their rulers. For example, George Fisher stated in *The Finished Mystery* "that Christendom is smitten by the onslaughts of revolution that might be expected to flash throughout the world on or about 27 April 1918."[28] Later in the volume Woodworth made his agreement with Fisher abundantly clear:

> The clergy are the ones directly responsible for the war in Europe ... They are an entirely unauthorized class—except for themselves; a self-perpetuating fraud. They have brought upon their heads the blood of all the nations of the earth in this world war; and God will require it at their hands. In the spring of 1918, and from that time forward forever, it will be unsafe to tell the lies that have filled Babylon's exchequers as it will be to be a king—Zech. 13:2–6.[29]

Amazingly, in the midst of the flag-waving patriotism that had swept over the United States after Congress's declaration of war against Germany, the Bible Students distributed thousands upon thousands of anti-war, anti-clergy books, magazines, and tracts of which *The Finished Mystery* was by far the most important.

> Through the close of 1917 and into 1918, the Bible Students energetically distributed the new book, The Finished Mystery. By the end of 1917, the printers were busy on the 850,000 edition. *The Watch Tower* of December 15, 1917, reported: "the sale of the Seventh Volume is unparalleled by the sale of any other book known, in the same length of time, excepting the Bible."[30]

Despite their joy over distributing so many pieces of Watch Tower literature, Rutherford and his associates were coming to realize that their position vis-à-vis the American government was fragile. The fact that the

---

see Penton, *Jehovah's Witnesses in Canada*, 56–62. For an account of what took place in the United States, see "Letters of General Interest," 125–26. In these sources, accounts are given of the beatings and torture that Bible Students experienced at the hands of the militaries in all three countries.

28. Woodworth and Fisher, *Finished Mystery*, 530.

29. Ibid., 228–29. For an overview of this teaching, see Wills, *A People for His Name*, 103–6.

30. *Jehovah's Witnesses: Proclaimers*, 69.

Canadian government had banned *The Finished Mystery* and a second publication, *The Bible Student's Monthly*, on 30 January 1918, disturbed and obviously frightened Rutherford greatly. The penalty for anyone possessing either of the banned publications could be a fine of $5,000 and a five-year prison sentence.[31] Therefore, when the American officials objected to pages 247–53 in *The Finished Mystery*, Rutherford had them removed and replaced. Then, when on March 15 the government indicated that it was displeased with the entire book, the Watch Tower president ordered that it should no longer be distributed.[32] But these actions came too late, and on May 7, based on indictments brought forward by a grand jury that had been sitting since April 6, the government had warrants issued for the arrests of the following Watch Tower officials, writers, and staff members: Joseph F. Rutherford, William E. Van Amburgh, A. Hugh Macmillan, Robert J. Martin, George H. Fisher, Clayton J. Woodworth, Frederick H. Robison, and Giovanni DeCecca. All were charged with conspiring to violate the Espionage Act of 15 June 1917, especially interfering with conscription.[33] Their trial was set to begin on June 3.

Yet even while awaiting his and his associates' day in court, Rutherford made further attempts to compromise with the US government. In the *Watch Tower* issues of May 1 and 15, he again asserted publicly that it was not wrong for Bible Students to buy Liberty Bonds to support the war effort. Then, on page 174 of the 1 June 1918 issue of the society's magazine, he called on Bible Students to join in a day of prayer as requested by President Wilson in which he, Rutherford, stated: "Let there be praise and thanksgiving to God for the promised glorious outcome of the war, the breaking of the shackles of autocracy, the freeing of the captives (Isaiah 61:1) and the making of the world safe for the common people—blessings all assured by the Word of God to the people of this country and the whole world of mankind." Most outstandingly, the "Judge" even repudiated his earlier advice to Bible Student men who were denied conscientious objector status. Up until the spring of 1918 he had advised them to refuse orders to be drafted or to serve in the military under any circumstances. But when he personally faced the possibility of incarceration, he started directing them to accept

---

31. The banning of the two Bible Student publications and the assessment of providing penalties for the possession of them was taken under the authority of the Canadian War Measurers Act.

32. Transcript, 965, 966.

33. Ibid., 11–71.

the draft as non-combatants.[34] Evidently, he hoped that by becoming more patriotic he and his associates might escape going to prison; principles that he had formerly held as a faithful follower of Russell and that were clearly outlined in *The Finished Mystery* were then to be ignored.

Not surprisingly, many Bible Students who had accepted *The Finished Mystery* as based on Russell's teachings were shocked, and another major schism, that of the "Standfasters," occurred, particularly in Oregon, Washington, and British Columbia.[35] And despite his efforts to ingratiate himself and the Bible Students with the government, Rutherford's attempts at compromise availed him and his associates nothing. Their trial began on June 3 and on June 21 they were convicted as charged. All but DeCecca were sentenced to twenty years' imprisonment. He was later sentenced to ten years. When they sought bail pending appeal, they were refused[36] and were taken by train to the federal penitentiary at Atlanta, Georgia.

The Bible Students and their Jehovah's Witness descendants have long blamed the arrest and conviction of these men on the clergy of those religious communities—Christian and Jewish—who supported the war against Germany and its allies with fervor. They have argued that the clergy had been enraged by the distribution of the 30 December 1917 issue of *The Bible Students Monthly* called "The Fall of Babylon," which was a bitter anti-clerical, anti-war jeremiad.[37] But in all probability, that played very little part in their indictment; they had far more critics and adversaries than just the clergy.

It also seems clear that Bible Student leaders were brought to court in the spring of 1918 by the civil authorities that were acting in response to what Philip Jenkins has described as the "spy madness" of the period.[38] So, although American authorities were well aware of what was taking place

---

34. This is made clear in a long, fully documented letter from a former Bible Student draft resister that may be found in "Letters of General Interest," in *The Present Truth and Herald of Christ's Epiphany*, 1 August 1931, 125–27. *The Present Truth* magazine is a publication of the Layman's Home Missionary Movement that was then under the editorship of P. S. L. Johnson.

35. Under the primary leadership of Pilgrim Charles E. Heard, the Standfast Bible Students Association was founded at Portland, Oregon on 1 December 1918 in opposition to Joseph Rutherford and the Watch Tower Society. The Standfasters objected strongly to Rutherford's assertion that it was proper for Bible Students to buy Liberty Bonds and to advise Bible Student men to serve in the military forces.

36. Transcript, 1156–69.

37. *Jehovah's Witnesses: Proclaimers*, 647.

38. Jenkins, "Spy Mad?"

with respect to Canadian Bible Students, and the overwhelming majority of American clergy certainly seem to have been openly negative towards all pacifists and the Bible Students in particular, there is no evidence to show that they had any direct part in the arrest and imprisonment of Russell's successors at Watch Tower headquarters. After briefly discussing the general antipathy toward pacifist communities, Philip Jenkins states:

> A much more serious menace was felt to be the Russelites [sic] or Watch Tower Society, the later Jehovah's Witnesses, who were accused of having crossing [sic] the line from anti-war sentiment to actual treason. The movement would long be controversial for its refusal to acknowledge the jurisdiction of earthly governments, and members usually claimed conscientious objector status. In 1918, the FBI and the [Pennsylvania] State Police launched a major investigation of a book entitled *The Finished Mystery*, a continuation of the writings of Charles Taze Russell, the movement's founder. This work included a fierce denunciation of war and nationalism. Two Scranton [Pennsylvania] men had written "the most objectionable and vicious portions of the book," which apart from the WWI tracts was the anti-war item most often singled out for condemnation.[39]

Jenkins goes on to remark that police infiltrated Bible Student meetings, their literature was tracked for distribution, and sale of *The Finished Mystery* was grounds for prosecution under the Espionage Act. "In addition, the German Government was said to have financed publication, enabling the book to be distributed free in large quantities."[40]

What about the Bible Student / Jehovah's Witness claim that Watch Tower leaders were victims of a clerical plot? Many clerics certainly detested the Bible Students. For years they had resented Russell's denial of eternal torment for the wicked, his neo-Arianism, and his hostility to the churches as "Babylon the Great," the harlot of the book of Revelation. Many of them were caustic about his pre-millennial date setting for the establishment of Christ's kingdom on earth. Finally, many had made personal attacks on his character, even suggesting he was an adulterer.[41] But it remains important

---

39. Ibid., 210–11.

40. Ibid., 211.

41. Some of the criticisms of Russell were unfair and extreme. However, his defenders have refused to admit that certain charges against him were true. For a hagiographical defense of him, see *Jehovah's Witnesses: Proclaimers*, 644–47. For a carefully researched view of his personal behavior, see Penton, *Apocalypse Delayed*, 49–65.

to examine the historical record to determine whether the clergy were the root cause of Bible Student travails in the United States or not.

It is true that in Canada many members of the Protestant clergy were eager to see Bible Student publications suppressed in late 1917, and made representations to the civil authorities calling on them to outlaw this literature, which was distributed through the mails and by ordinary Bible Students. For example, Congregational minister E. A. Cooke wrote to the Minister of Militia on behalf of the Vancouver Ministerial Association and stated:

> While we would earnestly deprecate anything in the nature of interference with religious principles, we do believe that in this time of National and Imperial crisis, the dissemination of such literature in Canada is highly detrimental to the best interests of our people, and to the success of the great and righteous cause for which so many of our men have already laid down their lives.[42]

Later, after two Bible Student publications were declared illegal, the Canadian Censor wrote to the Rev. Cooke, and indicated to him "your communication conveying as it did the views of such an influential body as The General Ministerial Association of Vancouver, proved very useful in securing action in this important matter."[43] But why is this information important to what was happening in the United States? The answer is that Canadian action in banning Bible Student publications acted as a catalyst to cause American authorities to take even more drastic actions against members of what was a small but aggressively anti-war religious movement.[44]

Of course it is also true that most American clerics of virtually all non-pacifistic denominations of any and all theological shades were eager to see legal action taken against the Bible Students and anyone else who opposed their country's war effort. As documented by Philip Jenkins, the First World War in the United States had taken on the character of a crusade as it had in practically all of the warring nations of the world.[45] But it is Ray H. Abrams who, through direct quotations, shows just how bellicose many American clergymen were, whether they were religious conservatives or theological liberals. Two examples out of a great many will demonstrate this. The first is that of the famous conservative evangelist Billy Sunday,

---

42. Penton, *Jehovah's Witnesses in Canada*, 52–53.
43. Ibid., 67.
44. Ibid., 45. See also 326n45.
45. Jenkins, *Great and Holy War*.

who is quoted as having stated: "The Christian Pacifists ought to be treated as Frank Little was at Butte [Montana] and then let the coroner do the rest."[46] By this he meant that the they should be kidnapped and lynched as Little had been. For both had opposed the war.[47] The second is that of the liberal, Dean Shailer Mathews of the University of Chicago. While less overtly bloodthirsty in his remarks than Sunday, he nonetheless asserted: "For an American ... to oppose preparation for war, to induce men to avoid draft, and to attack all forms of military preparation for military defense, is not Christian."[48]

Not surprisingly, the Bible Students believed that the clergy were behind the travails they suffered, for they had long been the objects of attacks by certain members thereof and regarded them as their primary enemies. Thus, they have presented supposed evidence to support their belief right up to the present. For example, when Watch Tower president Joseph Rutherford, and the society's secretary-treasurer William Van Amburgh visited a General James Franklin Bell concerning some Bible Students who had been sent to Camp Upton army camp despite having claimed exemption from military service as conscientious objectors, Bell reacted negatively.[49] In describing what happened, A. Hugh Macmillan wrote:

> Bell told about a conference of a large number of clergymen in Philadelphia in 1917. These men had appointed a committee to visit Washington, D.C., to insist on a revision of the Selective Draft Act and the Espionage Law. They selected John Lord O'Brien of the Department of Justice to introduce a bill to have all cases against the Espionage Law tried before a military court with the death penalty imposed as punishment. Bell stated with considerable feeling: "That bill did not pass, because Wilson prevented it; but we know how to get you, and we are going to do it."[50]

The Bible Students therefore felt that they were the victims of a clergy-organized "conspiracy," and they have not been alone in believing this. Ray H. Abrams has written:

---

46. Abrams, *Preachers Present Arms*, 217.
47. For a description of the murder of Frank Little, see Kennedy, *Over Here*, 73.
48. Abrams, *Preachers Present Arms*, 133.
49. The original account of this event may be found in *Consolation* (23 August 1939) 5.
50. Macmillan, *Faith on the March*, 87.

> An analysis of the whole case leads to the conclusion that the churches and the clergy were originally behind the movement to stamp out the Russellites. In Canada, in February 1918, the ministers began a systematic campaign against them and their publications, particularly *The Finished Mystery*. According to the Winnipeg Tribune, the attention of the attorney general had been called to the Russellites, and the suppression of their book was believed to have been directly brought about by "the representations of the clergy."[51]

While it is true that Canadian clerics did much to inaugurate the banning of Watch Tower literature in Canada, and their co-religionists in the United States detested the Bible Students, the evidence is pretty clear that it was police, the secret service, and the military[52] that ultimately moved the US Attorney General's Department to take Rutherford and his associates to court.

What, then, about the nature of their trial? In reading the transcript of record thereof, it is easy to see that Judge Howe's assertion that the Bible Students were devious in their answers to questions from the prosecution has more than a little merit.[53] For example, Rutherford claimed that while the Bible Students where opposed to participating in warfare, they did not take a stand against what the government was doing. Yet in reading the pages of *The Finished Mystery* it is clear that they had considered war, any war, as a machination of the devil. On the other hand, the charge that they were trying to interfere directly with the draft was nonsense. Any reasonable reading of the law should have given their men of conscriptable age automatic exemptions. But what is more outstanding is that the transcript shows clearly that the judge was extremely prejudiced in his attitude towards the Bible Student leaders. For example, in sentencing them, he stated with rancor and hyperbole:

---

51. Abrams, *Preachers Present Arms*, 183.

52. Agents of the US Army Information Department had earlier entered Watch Tower headquarter where its agents found a roof antenna and a stored radio set which they supposedly believed were for the purpose of maintaining contact with the German government. The Bible Students surrendered both the antenna and radio set to the agents who must have been suffering with an extreme case of war-time paranoia; radio had not yet become able to receive messages from long distances and the surrendered (perhaps 77) set could not broadcast. See *Jehovah's Witnesses in the Divine Purpose*, 76

53. Transcript, 1162.

In the opinion of the court, the religious propaganda which these defendants have vigorously advocated and spread throughout the nation as well as our allies, is a greater danger than a division of the German Army. If they had taken guns and swords and joined the German Army, the harm they could have done would have been insignificant compared with the results of their propaganda. A Person preaching religion usually has much influence, and if he is sincere, he is all the more effective. This aggravates rather than mitigates the wrong they have done. Therefore, as the only prudent thing to do with such persons, the Court has concluded that the punishment should be severe. The sentence is that the defendants, Joseph F. Rutherford, William E. Van Amburgh, Robert J. Martin, Fred H. Robison, George H. Fisher, Clayton J. Woodworth and A. Hugh Macmillan, serve a term of twenty years in the Federal Penitentiary at Atlanta, Georgia, on each of the four counts of the indictment, but that the sentences commence and run concurrently; and that they stand committed until the sentence is complied with.[54]

An appeal to the US Circuit Court of Appeals was launched immediately, and on March 21 that court ordered the release of the Watch Tower leaders on bail. On 14 May 1919 it ruled: "The defendants in this case did not have the temperate and impartial trial to which they were entitled, and for that reason the judgement is reversed." Thereupon the court ordered that Rutherford and his associates should be granted a new trial, but on 5 May 1920, the government announced that it was dropping all charges against the Bible Student leaders. The war was long passed and with it wartime hysteria. So there was little possibility of a conviction of the indicted persons.[55]

While the eight Watch Tower leaders had been imprisoned from late June 1918 through to late March 1919, they experienced no long-term harm to themselves except for Rutherford. He suffered some damage to his lungs.[56] In fact, when they returned to Brooklyn, they were welcomed as returning martyrs,[57] something that helped them maintain their positions in the face of criticism from dissident Bible Students. But their original conviction brought a great deal of harm to ordinary American Bible Students

---

54. Ibid., 1164–65.
55. *Jehovah's Witnesses: Proclaimers*, 653–54.
56. Ibid., 75.
57. Ibid.

and even to some of their brethren in other lands. The book *Jehovah's Witnesses: Proclaimers of God's Kingdom* states correctly:

> The spring and summer of 1918 witnessed persecution of the Bible Students, both in North America and in Europe. Among the instigators were clergymen of Baptist, Methodist, Episcopal, Lutheran, Roman Catholic, and other churches. Bible literature was seized by officers without a search warrant, and many Bible Students were thrown into jail. Others were chased by mobs, beaten whipped, tarred and feathered, and had their ribs broken or their heads cut. Some were permanently maimed. Christian men and women were held in jail without trial. Over one hundred specific instances of such outrageous treatment were reported in *The Golden Age* of September 29, 1920.[58]

Like other cases of vigilantism directed at various anti-war groups during the years 1917 and 1918, those actions were the result of excessive crusading nationalism and are a stain on the history of the United States. Thus it seems that Oscar Wilde was right when he stated: "Patriotism is the virtue of the vicious."

BIBLIOGRAPHY

Primary Sources

NEWSPAPERS

Consolation. A publication of the Watch Tower Bible and Tract Society (1939–40).
The Present Truth and Herald of Christ's Epiphany. A publication of the Layman's Home Missionary Movement, 1931.
Watchtower Reprints = *Zion's Watch Tower and Herald of Christ's Presence*, 1879–1907, and *The Watch Tower and Herald of Christ's Presence*, 1908–19. Reprinted in 7 vols. Brooklyn, NY: Watch Tower Bible and Tract Society, 1919.
The Winnipeg Free Press, 1916.

OTHER

National Civil Liberties Bureau. *The Facts about Conscientious Objectors in the United States (Under the Selective Service Act of May 18, 1917)*. New York, June 1, 1918.

---

58. Ibid.

Russell, Charles Taze. *The New Creation*. Brooklyn, NY: Watch Tower Bible and Tract Society, 1904.

———. *Thy Kingdom Come*. Brooklyn, NY: Watch Tower Bible and Tract Society, 1916.

Transcript of record of *United States of America* vs. *Rutherford et al.* in the United States District Court for the Eastern District of New York as appealed to the United States Circuit Court of Appeals under the title *Rutherford et al.* vs. *the United States of America*. 258 Federal Reporter.

Woodworth, Clayton J., and George H. Fisher. *The Finished Mystery*. Brooklyn, NY: Peoples Pulpit Association, 1917.

Secondary Sources

Abrams, Ray H. *Preachers Present Arms: The Role of American Churches and Clergy in World War I and II with Observations on the War in Vietnam*. Eugene, OR: Wipf & Stock, 1969.

Curran, Edward Lodge. *Judge—for Four Days—Rutherford*. Brooklyn, NY: International Catholic Truth Society, 1940.

Jehovah's Witnesses in the Divine Purpose. Brooklyn, NY: Watchtower Bible and Tract Society, 1959.

Jehovah's Witnesses: Proclaimers of God's Kingdom. Brooklyn, NY: Watchtower Bible and Tract Society, 1993.

Jenkins, Philip. *The Great and Holy War: How World War I Became a Religious Crusade*. New York: HarperCollins, 2014.

———. "Spy Mad? Investigating Subversion in Pennsylvania, 1917–1918." *Pennsylvania History* 63, no. 2 (1996) 204–31.

Kennedy, David M. *Over Here: The First World War and American Society*. New York: Oxford University Press, 2004.

Macmillan, A. H. *Faith on the March*. Englewood Cliffs, NJ: Prentice Hall, 1957.

Penton, M. James. *Apocalypse Delayed: The Story of Jehovah's Witnesses*. 3rd ed. Toronto: University of Toronto Press, 2015.

———. *Jehovah's Witnesses in Canada: Champions of Freedom of Speech and Worship*. Toronto: Macmillan of Canada, 1976.

Wills, Tony. *A People for His Name: A History of Jehovah's Witnesses and an Evaluation*. 2nd ed. Morrisville, NC: Lullu, 2006.

10

Military Chaplains in the First World War

Timothy J. Demy

ONCE THE UNITED STATES entered the war, contemporary enthusiasm for it was great and most religious bodies supported the American war efforts from the pulpits and the pews.¹ They reflected the sentiments of those in uniform, and newspapers and magazines routinely reported on religious aspects of the war and the religion in the military with articles such as "Religious Unity in the Army," "Our Neglect of Prayer for Victory," and "The Kind of Religion the Soldiers Want."² Secular media even discussed a topic that knew no national boundaries and was prominent throughout the war—the relationship between sacrifice and salvation. An American example of this can be read in the 14 September 1918 edition of *The Literary Digest*'s article "The Future Reward of the Soldier."³ While there was individual and institutional dissent on the basis of religion, soldiers and civilians alike overwhelmingly supported the American war effort and did so from a faith perspective. Philip Jenkins observes: "Judging from the abundant evidence of letters and diaries, soldiers commonly demonstrated a religious worldview and regularly referred to Christian beliefs and ideas. They resorted frequently to biblical language and to concepts of sacrifice

---

1. Jenkins, *Great and Holy War*, 3.

2. "Religious Unity in the Army," *The Literary Digest* (8 June 1918) 31–32; "Our Neglect of Prayer for Victory," *The Literary Digest* (5 October 1918) 30–31. "The Kind of Religion the Soldiers Want," *The Literary Digest* (5 October 1918) 30–31.

3. "The Future Reward of the Soldier," *The Literary Digest* (14 September 1918) 32.

and redemptive suffering."[4] Sharing the experience of war and ministering to the troops in garrison, at sea, and at the front were military chaplains.

Numerous American military chaplains served with distinction in the First World War. However, the military chaplaincy in the United States Army and United States Navy was organizationally and administratively unprepared for the war and for the number of chaplains needed to minister to troops in the United States and overseas. In both services there was an increase in the number of chaplains providing ministry, but the numbers never reached the total authorized by Congress. The rapid increase in the recruiting of soldiers, sailors, airmen, and marines to whom chaplains were called to minister exacerbated problems of administration, oversight, and ministry of chaplains. Neither the Army nor the Navy had a formal central chaplain corps or a chief of chaplains. The lack of command organization to provide directives, oversight, assignment, coordination, and resources for chaplains created a ministry environment of confusion and uncertainty for individual chaplains. On the national level, confusion regarding chaplains can be traced to the longstanding principle of the separation of church and state derived from the First Amendment and the outworking of it in American politics and religious life throughout the nineteenth century.

In both the Army and the Navy the service of chaplains was built upon a post-Civil-War organization wherein the scope of ministry was defined more by the preference of the individual commanding officer than by law, service regulations, or policy. Further, there was no standardization in the recruitment and appointment of chaplains and denominations had no central authority over chaplains representing them or a mechanism for ensuring quality of ministry and individual capabilities. There was also little attempt at maintaining denominational balance or representation with the services.

By the turn of the century steps had been taken by some religious bodies to centralize endorsement of chaplains. For example, the Protestant Episcopal Church through its House of Bishops, the Roman Catholic Church, the Methodist Episcopal Church, the Lutheran Church Council, the Disciples of Christ, and the Jewish Welfare Board established mechanisms for screening chaplains. In 1913, in response to an appeal by a Navy chaplain before the Federal Council of Churches, a Washington Committee on Army and Navy Chaplains was appointed to approve chaplaincy

---

4. Jenkins, *Great and Holy War*, 4.

candidates.⁵ Denominations and religious bodies not affiliated with the Federal Council of Churches had no such mechanism.

"BE THY STRONG ARM OUR EVER SURE DEFENSE" —US ARMY CHAPLAINS

When America entered the war, US Army (and National Guard) chaplains continued their long tradition of ministry under arduous circumstances. Their most recent involvement had been in the 1916–17 expedition against Mexican Revolutionary General Franciso "Pancho" Villa, along the US–Mexican border. Although they had a strong ministry during the event they were often handicapped in their service by collateral duties that consumed much of their time and detracted from their primary purpose. Indeed, the expedition's leader, General John J. Pershing, later admitted: "Customs in our army . . . had often relegated them to the status of handy men who were detailed to write up boards of survey or operate libraries."⁶ Similar experiences were shared by chaplains in the Navy.

The War Department had at its disposal 213,000 troops, of which 127,000 were regular Army and the remainder National Guard and Philippine Scouts. By the end of the war the Army had surged to more than 3.6 million soldiers, of which about 2 million would cross the Atlantic and fight in the American Expeditionary Forces (AEF). Of these, there would be 106,000 American deaths, including 23 Army chaplains.⁷ Beyond the end of the conflict with the Central Powers on 11 November 1918, US forces and chaplains served from September 1918 to September 1919 in Russia in the Murmansk-Archangel region amidst the Russian Civil War and from August 1918 to April 1920 in Siberia encouraging the Russian "Whites" against the Bolsheviks.⁸ On the day the United States entered the war there were 74 chaplains in the Army, augmented by 72 National Guard chaplains. By Armistice Day, 2,217 additional clergy had been commissioned, and yet there were many places where there where shortages of chaplains.⁹ Honeywell states that "during the period of hostilities 2,363 chaplains held commissions under some component of the Army."¹⁰ Congressional

5. Jorgensen, *Service of Chaplains*, 11.
6. Pershing, *My Experiences*, 283.
7. Stover, *Up from Handymen*, 187–88.
8. See Willett, *Russian Sideshow*.
9. Stover, *Up from Handymen*, 188.
10. Honeywell, *Chaplains*, 180.

authorization in the Act of 25 May 1918 for one chaplain for every 1,200 servicemen did not become law until the United States had been in the war for thirteen months. On Armistice Day there were between 1,250 and 1,300 chaplains with the AEF, but civilian Episcopal Bishop Charles H. Brent, who had been appointed "General Headquarters, AEF. Chaplain" in January 1918, said that the lowest acceptable number should have been 1,800.[11] Insufficient numbers of chaplains and lack of strong organizational support was prevalent throughout the military during the war and created confusion and frustration among chaplains. Although the religious bodies they represented supported the war and their ministries, the rapid growth of the military during the war and the lack of standards and organizations in the prewar Army and Navy were detrimental to the effective delivery of spiritual care to the forces. Though American chaplains ministered to troops facing the same traumas and terrors of trench warfare as their British counterparts, American chaplains were not as well organized or as prepared for the battlefield as were the British, nor was the duration of their exposure as great.[12]

In December 1917, Bishop Brent arrived in France as a representative of the YMCA to assist General Pershing. Pershing requested that Brent, his close friend and family minister, assist him with "moral matters pertaining to the Army."[13] Pershing wanted an AEF corps of chaplains headed by Brent, but Brent persuaded him to appoint a permanent executive board of chaplains to oversee the work of Army chaplains and civic agencies ministering in the AEF. Pershing agreed and appointed a board consisting of Brent, Congregational chaplain Paul A. Moody (son of evangelist Dwight L. Moody), and Roman Catholic chaplain Francis B. Doherty. Brent served as the head of the board and was generally acknowledged as the chief of chaplains of the AEF. Brent served at first as a civilian but after several months was persuaded by Pershing to take a commission and did so as a "major and chaplain."[14] Brent, Moody, and Doherty did much to bring organization and credibility to chaplains in the AEF, and worked intentionally and effectively irrespective of religious differences.

From the transport ships carrying troops to France to the trenches of the frontline soldiers, chaplains provided services to individuals and

11. Stover, *Up from Handymen*, 189.
12. On experiences of British chaplains, see Snape and Madigan, *Clergy in Khaki*.
13. Cited in Stover, *Up from Handymen*, 220.
14. Ibid., 220.

groups. They worked closely with the wounded and dying and served alongside surgeons, ambulance crews, and stretcher-bearers at the first aid stations. Chaplains often rescued wounded men from the battlefield. They were not immune from "going over the top" with their units and twenty-seven chaplains were awarded the Purple Heart, four with Oak Leaf Cluster. Twenty-seven others were awarded the Distinguished Service Cross, and eighteen were awarded the Silver Star, three with Oak Leaf Cluster. Eleven chaplains were killed in action or died from battlefield wounds.[15]

Chaplains' duties in the aftermath of combat were also extremely demanding in the service and ministry to the dead. They helped collect the dead and provided religious burial services for American, French, and German soldiers. Beyond the prayers and burial, chaplains ensured that, when possible, each grave was marked with the decedent's full name, unit, and date of death. Each grave was then reported with map coordinates. Chaplains worked closely with the Graves Registration Service of the AEF. Beyond these efforts was then the task of writing sympathy letters to the next of kin.[16]

For chaplains arriving in France who had not had prior Army chaplain school training at the school established in February 1918 at Camp Zachary Taylor, Kentucky, and later at Fort Monroe, Virginia, there was a ten-day chaplain school established in a chateau at Neuilly-sur-Suize, near Chaumont, in midsummer 1918 near AEF Headquarters.[17]

Although there was a 1:1,200 ratio of chaplains to soldiers authorized, the Army average was 1:1,690.[18] Throughout the war chaplains were hampered by lack of regulations restricting their work to primarily religious functions such that chaplains often ended up being the collateral duties officer. Honeywell notes: "Many were put in charge of the post exchange, a mess, the unit post office, special funds, bond sales, athletics, or the schools established after the cessation of hostilities."[19] Probably the most time consuming of the duties was that of censoring the mail. For some chaplains this accounted for more than half of their time.[20]

15. Ibid., 194.
16. Ibid., 195.
17. Honeywell, *Chaplains*, 174, 180.
18. Ibid., 184.
19. Ibid., 193.
20. Ibid., 193; Stover, *Up from Handymen*, 196–98.

Significantly assisting military chaplains in the provision of ministry to troops were civilian religious organizations such as the YMCA, Jewish Welfare Board, and Knights of Columbus, which sent representatives overseas to and near the front lines to provide ministry. Although there was some initial reluctance on the part of some Army chaplains to engage fully the services of those groups due to longstanding memories of disagreement with members of the private relief agency of the United States Sanitary Commission during the Civil War, this was soon overcome. The YMCA surpassed its outstanding work during the Civil War and Spanish–American War and provided much needed space in the form of its "huts" for religious services and social activities for soldiers. Such efforts attracted the volunteer services of thousands of people (among them, Presbyterian theologian J. Gresham Machen, who served in France throughout 1918).[21]

Corresponding to the military and civilian agency cooperation there were many instances of cooperation across denominations and faith groups by chaplains. It was routine throughout the war for chaplains to minister to those of all faiths and no faith.[22]

When word spread of the cessation of hostilities on the morning of November 11, Chaplain William F. Davitt and his commander made preparations for a celebration and went to get the regimental colors for the festivity. While they were returning, one of the last German artillery shells fell, killing the chaplain, who died with his company's flag in his possession.[23]

"GUARD AND GUIDE THE MEN WHO FLY"
—AIR SERVICE ARMY AVIATION CHAPLAINS

An Aeronautical Division was established in the US Army Signal Corps in 1907, but prewar numbers were too small to warrant the assigning of a chaplain. In 1914, legislation created the Aviation Section of the Signal Corps with an authorized strength of sixty officers and twenty-six enlisted men.[24] By the time the country entered the war, the aviation section had sixty-three officers and 1,080 enlisted men flying fifty-five aircraft. Military aviation in the United States was still in its infancy and the nation ranked fourteenth in military aviation power.[25] These numbers increased signifi-

21. See Machen, *Letters from the Front*. See also Stover, *Up from Handymen*, 214–16.
22. For many examples, see Shay, *Sky Pilots*.
23. Stover, *Up from Handymen*, 195–96.
24. Jorgensen, *Service of Chaplains*, 14.
25. Ibid., 15.

cantly by the time the United States Air Service made its combat record from April to November 1918, but there was no provision for assignment of chaplains to air units until the 16 May 1917 Act of Congress authorized the President to appoint chaplains "at the rate of not to exceed one per each ... Aero Wing."[26] Even so, the Air Service was slow in making any request for chaplains.

When internal Army inquiries were made in December 1917 regarding assigning chaplains to the Air Service, authorities responded that in the United States where units were assigned there were plenty of civilian clergy and church facilities available. Moreover, it was not "deemed necessary or desirable, during the present emergency to have chaplains in this country." Regarding overseas units, the response continued, "If it is deemed desirable by your division to have chaplains assigned to squadrons overseas, it is suggested that they be assigned at the rate of one to each twelve squadrons."[27]

By February 1918, the situation had improved some with respect to chaplains such that the Chief Signal Officer wrote to the Adjutant General: "It is now recommended that one chaplain be furnished ... for each regiment of motor repair troops; for each six service or other squadrons (one Aero Wing); for each six construction squadrons (Spruce); for each six Balloon companies; and for each six construction companies (Bricklaying)."[28] Numbers were increased but still lacked full capacity.

Compounding the difficulty of assigning chaplains to air units was the fact that some leaders in the Air Service thought all officers in aviation units should be flying officer qualified and in a flying status. This resulted in further limiting the assignment of chaplains in Air Service (though at least one chaplain, Calvin Pardee Eerdman, a Presbyterian, did receive flight wings and was dually assigned as a chaplain and flight instructor).[29]

In Europe there was a matrix developed for assigning Air Service chaplains to the various types of commands serving with the American Expeditionary Forces in France, but it was never enacted. Air chaplaincy historian Daniel B. Jorgensen observes: "The net result of the confusion regarding the basis on which chaplains could be authorized in the Air Service, together with the conflicting policy on flying status, resulted in the Air

26. Cited in ibid., 23.
27. Ibid.
28. Ibid. Spruce construction squadrons were remote logging camps in the Northwest responsible for providing spruce for aircraft construction.
29. Jorgensen, *Service of Chaplains*, 24.

Service having insufficient religious coverage for the fields in the United States and almost none for oversea units."[30]

Within the AEF there was belief and policy that the Army ground units should take priority over Air Service units for the assignment of chaplains. The rationale was that because air units were in the rear, safer position, the other units were in more pressing need of chaplains. The General Headquarters Chaplain roster of the AEF for October 1918 lists 790 chaplains known at that time but only two listed in the Air Service. After the war, for December 1918 and April 1919, there were none.

The majority of the ministry provided to Air Service units in France was through chaplains, "camp pastors," and other clergy serving with auxiliary agencies such as the YMCA (there was no USO until 1941), American Red Cross, Knights of Columbus, Jewish Welfare Board, and Salvation Army. Additionally, Army chaplains assigned to other units within the AEF in the same geographic region as Air Service units in France often provided coverage on a voluntary basis.

"FOR THOSE IN PERIL ON THE SEA"
—US NAVY CHAPLAINS

One of the most striking things for researchers to discover on the subject of First World War American naval chaplaincy is the paucity of information available for study. Some of this may be attributed to the brevity of the American experience in the war when compared to that of the British, Canadian, and other Allied nations. Another reason may be the nature of the operations performed by the Navy during the war—mostly convoy duty and troop transport operations—not the type of thing that makes for exciting memoirs. There are no book-length first person accounts by Navy chaplains of First World War service and ministry. The few materials that are available in the US Navy Chaplain Corps archives are limited to portrait photographs and newspaper clippings.

Most of the information that is available comes from the two-volume official history of the US Navy Chaplain Corps written in the 1950s by Dr. Clifford M. Drury. Poor archival administration of official records used in the writing of the history resulted in their subsequent destruction. This loss pertains not just to the First World War era, but to all archival material of the US Navy Chaplain Corps from its founding in 1778 through the

---

30. Ibid., 25.

Korean War era. In the early 1980s I interviewed Drury and he stated that the destruction of the material was so extensive that, if the two volumes and a subsequent volume on the Korean War had not been written and published, the history could no longer be written. Interestingly, and as further confirmation, there is no information on the Chaplain Corps history volumes among the Clifford M. Drury Papers 1932–1958 deposited at the Manuscripts, Archives, and Special Collections, Washington State University Libraries.[31] Available documented history of American naval chaplaincy during the war is limited to forty pages (pp. 162–202) in Volume 1 of Drury's work and much of this pertains to administrative matters pertaining to Navy chaplains.

When the United States entered the First World War in April 1917, naval planners and strategists were politically and strategically unprepared for the ensuing war at sea. Planning had been constrained by President Wilson's stance of armed neutrality that prevented major preparations for readiness in facing the realities of a defensive war against German submarines.[32] In spite of the Naval Act of 1916 that authorized a strong Navy for the postwar era, the only operational plan the Navy had ready for war was War Plan Black, an offensive plan calling for battle-line action against an advancing fleet.[33] Naval historian George Baer writes:

> No serious thought had been given to how much the United States would cooperate with Britain and France, to how many warships would be deployed outside U.S. waters, to how the Navy would change its major focus from sea battle to transport and supply, or to how the inevitable demand of cooperation with the U.S. Army would be met for these tasks. . . . America's isolation from the front and its self-conscious distancing from European politics had encouraged complacency.[34]

In the years preceding the war, the US Navy, like other navies, was in an era of transformation and modernization. Paralleling the growth of what was known as the "New Navy" from 1880–1920 was the development of administrative and personnel policies that began a period of standardization. The same was true for US Navy chaplains. From 1881 to 1900 the

---

31. For the archives, see http://ntserver1.wsublibs.wsu.edu/masc/finders/cg144.htm. Accessed 10 July 2015.

32. Baer, *One Hundred Years*, 65.

33. Ibid., 64–65.

34. Ibid., 66.

number of Navy chaplains was normally at the full quota of twenty-four chaplains, a number that had been set by law in 1842.[35] There was no organized corps of chaplains, no director of chaplains, and matters of pay, uniforms, and rank were perpetual concerns.[36]

Prior to the First World War, US Navy chaplains had last been in war during the 1898 Spanish–American War. The aftermath of the war brought new possessions to the United States in the Far East and West Indies. This, coupled with the election of pro-Navy Theodore Roosevelt as President, brought about a period of growth for the Navy that was sustained through the First World War. The Naval Appropriation Act of 1914 stipulated that there would be a quota of one chaplain for every 1,250 naval personnel.[37] It also began a more structured era for Navy chaplaincy. In 1912, the first chaplain was assigned to the Marines, J. F. Fleming, who was part of the landing party of Marines in Nicaragua. After Fleming, the first chaplain assigned exclusively to Marines was Bower R. Patrick, who was ordered to the Marine Expeditionary Force of the Atlantic Fleet on 21 April 1914.[38]

For the US Navy, the entry of the United States into the war brought primarily concern of the threat of U-boats, the transport of troops to Europe, and the protection of convoys. A squadron of five battleships, the *New York*, *Wyoming*, *Texas*, *Florida*, and *Delaware* joined the British Grand Fleet at Scapa Flow in December 1917 and by the end of the war three others, the *Nevada*, *Oklahoma*, and *Utah* were stationed at Bantry Bay in Southern Ireland. In addition to two large transports, the *Henderson* and *Hancock*, the Navy took over twenty American liners for transporting troops to Europe and more than two million troops were sent to Europe. Naval forces were sent ashore in France to man a number of fourteen-inch rail guns used on the Western Front and more than 30,000 US Marines were sent to France.[39]

Upon declaration of war by the United States on 6 April 1917 there were forty chaplains on active duty in the Navy. Eight others were soon called to active duty from the Naval Militia and National Naval Volunteers. Congress passed the Act of 22 May 1917 that temporarily increased the size of the Navy and Marine Corps. The act also permitted the appointment of

---

35. Drury, *History of the Chaplain Corps*, 62.
36. Ibid., 133.
37. Ibid., 141–42.
38. Ibid., 155.
39. Ibid., 162.

temporary chaplains for the duration of the war.[40] Of the forty chaplains on active duty at the war's outbreak only one of them was serving with the United States Marine Corps. The total number of active duty chaplains increased five-fold during the war to a peak of 201 chaplains and thirteen of them served with the Marines in France.

If the ratio of one chaplain for every 1,250 naval personnel had been upheld, there would have been about 480 chaplains on duty at the peak of naval enrollment just before the armistice. However, the number never neared that, and remained at only 42 percent of authorized strength.[41]

Records of ministry activities at sea during the war are sparse. Drury cites letters and accounts of several chaplains who reported that their time was filled with counseling, troop visitation, and worship services. Chaplains on troop ships often held several Divine Services to allow the opportunity for as many as desired to attend.[42] Battleships often had a ship's band or orchestra that provided music for the services. It was during this era that the term "General Service" came into usage to describe a non-sectarian Christian service that sought to give an opportunity for worship that was non-sacramental and was neither Protestant nor Roman Catholic.[43] Chaplains were also active in and advocates of the distribution of religious literature. The American Bible Society recorded distributing more than seven million copies of Scripture during the war.[44]

Chaplains serving aboard the five battleships that comprised the Sixth Squadron of the British Grand Fleet based at Scapa Flow encountered enemy action when the *Florida*, *New York*, and *Delaware* maneuvered against torpedoes fired by German submarines. Two chaplains were on troop transports that were torpedoed and sunk off the coast of France—Chaplain Grover C. Whimsett aboard the *President Lincoln*, torpedoed on 31 May 1918, and Chaplain Perry Mitchell who was aboard the Covington, sunk on 1 July 1918.[45]

Chaplains with Marines sailed in the first convoy that crossed to France in June 1917. Marines in France came under US Army jurisdiction and each Marine regiment had one Protestant and one Roman Catholic

40. Ibid., 163.
41. Ibid., 172.
42. Ibid., 176.
43. Ibid., 177.
44. Ibid., 182.
45. Ibid., 188.

chaplain.[46] By the end of the war thirteen Navy chaplains served about 31,000 Marines in France. Chaplains serving with Marines during the summer of 1918 German offensive and fighting at Chateau Thierry and Belleau Wood were chaplains Brady, Park, MacNair, Darche, and Beckley.[47] Four chaplains serving with Marines in France were recipients of the Navy Cross.[48]

CHAPLAINS AND THE INFLUENZA EPIDEMIC

For millions of people the capstone of the war was not the November armistice or Paris Peace Talks but the influenza epidemic that broke out in the spring of 1918. The outbreak claimed fifty million casualties, two and a half times that of the war. Wartime censors minimized the ravages of the epidemic to maintain morale.

In the trenches the influenza struck with severity and with the reverse of what normally transpired among civilians. Normally, natural selection of the virus favored a mild strain and the very ill stayed home while those only mildly ill went to work, thus spreading the mild strain. In the trenches, those mildly ill stayed and fought and those with the harsher strain were transported out of the trenches and dispersed to crowed trains, battalion aid stations, and hospitals. This magnified the spread of the more virulent strain and killed many soldiers who, thus far, had survived the ravages of the war.

The devastation was not limited to the ground war. Sailors on ships at sea, especially troop transports headed to Europe, succumbed to the virus as well. One chaplain, F. B. Huske, assigned to the Naval Hospital Norfolk, Virginia, stated that one of his ministries was helping dying sailors sign up for the $10,000 government life insurance policy they had thought too expensive on their recruit pay of $30 a month. By so doing, dying sailors provided some financial assistance to their beneficiaries. Huske recorded that in 1918, he had helped deathbed sailors obtain $4,300,000 worth of insurance.[49] The only chaplain to die of influenza during the war was Simon A. O'Rourke. He had been appointed on 14 June 1918 and died of influenza

46. Ibid., 184.
47. Ibid., 185.
48. Ibid., 187.
49. Ibid., 182–83.

on 21 September in Navy Yard, Boston; he had been on his first week of active duty.[50]

ADMINISTRATIVE ADVANCES

Accompanying the growth of the wartime Navy and the increase in the number of chaplains was the need for greater administration of the chaplains. As a result, the first Director (Chief) of Chaplains, Southern Methodist John B. Frazier, was appointed as head of the Chaplain Corps on 7 November 1917. A chaplaincy manual was produced, reflecting the growth and need for standardization of institutional ministry practices.[51] Organizationally, there were chaplains appointed to the Fleets to oversee broad ministry within the Fleets, and chaplains serving on ships. The first Jewish chaplain, David Goldberg, was commissioned on 30 October 1917.[52] Issues of pay, promotion, collateral duties, and uniform requirements were addressed and became part of the broader growth and administration of the Navy.

CONCLUSION

In many ways what one finds when looking at Army and Navy chaplains during the war is a study in miniature of the challenges facing the US Army and US Navy and the United States, namely, the quest for greater participation in and responsibility for control of surrounding activities. What chaplains sought institutionally, the United States sought internationally. For both, the attainment and outworking of that quest would unfold in the ensuing decades of the twentieth century. During the interwar years, both the Army and the Navy chaplaincy made significant strides in the regulation, organization, and training of chaplains. These were improvements that were much needed and enhanced the role of the chaplain as a professional military officer as well as a religious leader. Such advances were crucial to the ministry of American military chaplains when once again war erupted on a global scale.[53]

---

50. Ibid., 173.
51. Ibid., 164–65, 173–75.
52. Ibid., 168.
53. See Snape, *God and Uncle Sam*.

BIBLIOGRAPHY

Primary Sources

The Literary Digest, 1918.

Machen, J. Gresham. *Letters from the Front: J. Gresham Machen's Correspondence from World War I.* Transcribed and edited by Barry Waugh. Philadelphia, PA: Westminster Theological Seminary, 2012.

Pershing, John J. *My Experiences in the World War.* Vol. 1. New York: Frederick A. Stokes, 1931.

Secondary Sources

Baer, George W. *One Hundred Years of Sea Power: The U.S. Navy, 1890-1990.* Stanford, CA: Stanford University Press, 1993.

Drury, Clifford M. *The History of the Chaplain Corps, United States Navy.* Vol. 1, *1778-1939.* Washington, DC: Department of the Navy, 1969.

Honeywell, Roy J. *Chaplains of the United States Army.* Washington, DC: Department of the Army, Office of the Chief of Chaplains, 1958.

Jenkins, Philip. *The Great and Holy War: How World War I Became a Religious Crusade.* New York: HarperCollins, 2014.

Jorgensen, Daniel B. *Air Force Chaplains.* Vol. 1, *The Service of Chaplains to Army Air Units 1917-1946.* Washington, DC: Office, Chief of Air Force Chaplains, 1961.

Shay, Michael E. *Sky Pilots: The Yankee Division Chaplains in World War I.* Columbia, MO: University of Missouri Press, 2014.

Snape, Michael. *God and Uncle Sam: Religion and America's Armed Forces in World War II.* Rochester, NY: Boydell, 2015.

Snape, Michael, and Edward Madigan, eds. *The Clergy in Khaki: New Perspectives on British Army Chaplaincy in the First World War.* Burlington, VT: Ashgate, 2013.

Stover, Earl F. *Up from Handymen: The United States Army Chaplaincy, 1865-1920.* Washington, DC: Office of the Chief of Chaplains, Department of the Army, 1977.

Willett, Robert L. *Russian Sideshow: America's Undeclared War, 1918-1920.* Washington, DC: Brassey's, 2003.

11

"The accursed partnership of Turk and Teuton"

American Churches and the Armenian Genocide[1]

GORDON L. HEATH

AFTER MONTHS OF UNCERTAINTY and apprehension over the Turkish attitude towards its 2.5 million Armenian subjects, in the spring of 1915 Henry Morgenthau began to receive disturbing reports of Turkish violence towards minorities.[2] As American ambassador to the Ottoman Turkish Empire, Morgenthau was the natural recipient of intelligence reports on an extensive variety of subjects, and a rapidly growing file of evidence made it clear that the Turkish government was taking advantage of opportunities provided by wartime conditions to engage in widespread and systematic massacres of Armenians. Morgenthau's appeals on their behalf fell on deaf ears among Ottoman government officials in Constantinople, and the massacres and dislocations of Armenians continued unabated.[3] However, his reports sent back to his superiors in the United States played

---

1. Funding was provided by the Southern Baptist Historical Library and Archives for researching the Baptist periodicals in this chapter.

2. Morgenthau, *Ambassador*.

3. The Turkish government also ignored a joint British, French, and Russian warning (24 May 1915) to cease the massacres. See Hovannisian, *Armenia on the Road*, 52.

a critical role in providing eyewitness accounts to the American public and government—and to the world—of the horrendous actions committed against a Christian minority by Germany's wartime ally.

It was an all-too-familiar scenario. Years earlier the American public had read of Turkish atrocities, for the Ottoman massacres of Armenians in the 1890s were extensively recorded in American newspapers. There were also public rallies in support of the Armenians, appeals to Congress to act to assist the suffering minority, and the establishment of organizations to provide aid to the suffering Armenians.[4] Yet, as the spring turned into summer in 1915, it became clear that the newly reported massacres of Armenians were on a vastly different scale from earlier ones.

US newspapers were once again quick to report on the massacres, and they provided extensive coverage. In 1915 alone, the *New York Times* printed 145 articles on the genocide.[5] Other major daily papers followed suit. The religious press also began to report on the slaughter of Armenians. In April 1915, the Methodist Episcopal Church (South) *Christian Advocate* reported "the massacres of Armenians by Mohammedans is being continued on an even greater scale."[6] In May 1915, the Baptist *Christian Index* expressed worry over the fact that "There have been during the past ten days a number of new and more or less startling developments in the war situation over the world . . . There have been unverified reports of new Turkish atrocities in Armenia."[7]

THE GENOCIDE

The concerns of Morgenthau and the newspaper editors were well-founded, for what was unfolding was the beginning of the first modern genocide.[8] Once a mighty Empire that twice advanced into the heart of Central Europe and besieged Vienna, the Ottoman Turkish Empire had devolved

---

4. Kirakossian, *Armenian Massacres*; Balakian, *Burning Tigris*.

5. Balakian, *Burning Tigris*, xix. For a summary of daily newspaper reactions, see Kloian, *Armenian Genocide*.

6. "Massacre by Kurds," *Christian Advocate*, 29 April 1915, 2.

7. "Current Events," *Christian Index*, 27 May 1915, 5.

8. The term "genocide" was invented in the 1940s by Raphael Lemkin to describe the Turkish handling of Armenians and the Nazi treatment of the Jews. As for what was the first genocide of the century, Ben Kiernan asserts that the German treatment of the Herero and Nama peoples of South West Africa in 1904 was the first genocide of the century. See Kiernan, "Twentieth Century Genocides," 29. See also Olusoga and Erichsen, *Kaiser's Holocaust*.

into the "sick man" of Europe by the end of the nineteenth century. Niall Ferguson notes, "the worst time to live under imperial rule is when that rule is crumbling,"[9] and that was the case for the Christian Armenians under Muslim Turkish rule. The Hamidian Massacres (1894–96) that led to 100,000 to 300,000 deaths were only a prelude to subsequent horrors. During the First World War, the Turkish government aggressively pursued a policy of genocide against the Armenians within its borders and estimates of the disaster usually range between 1,000,000 and 1,500,000 deaths (there were further mass killings to the south among Syriac and Iraqi Orthodox Christians adding another 500,000 deaths to the total).[10]

The Armenian Genocide started in April 1915. The methods of eliminating the Armenians were arrests, executions, and deportations. Deportation merely "served as a cloak for massacre."[11] Usually males were arrested first, and then taken away and executed en masse. Women, children, and the elderly were then rounded up under the pretext of being "relocated." Among the horrors of the "caravans to oblivion"[12] was the mass "sexual violence and gender-specific persecution of victims [usually female],"[13] the Islamization of children taken from Armenian parents,[14] the theft of property and land (never to be returned), the desecration and destruction of churches and holy places, and the extension of genocide to the Assyrian Christians in the Middle East (Syria).[15] The large-scale deportations of the

9. Ferguson, *War of the World*, 176.

10. Turkish authorities admit 800,000 deaths occurred (not counting tens of thousands of conscripts executed by the military), but not through genocide. See Dadrian, *Armenian Genocide*, 225. Other estimates are higher. For instance, of the 1,500,000 to 2,000,000 pre-war Armenians, 250,000 escaped to Russia. "Of the remaining 1,600,000 about 1,000,000 were killed, half of whom were women and children. Of the surviving 600,000 about 200,000 were forcibly Islamised; and the wretched remnant of 400,000 was found, starving and in rags, by the Allies . . . at the end of the war." Walker, *Armenia: The Survival*, 230. Leo Kuper claims 1,000,000 died ("Turkish Genocide of Armenians," 52). Lorne Shirinian claims between 1,200,000 and 1,800,000 died (*Quest for Closure*, 33). To be added to these figures are approximately 250,000 Assyro-Chaldeans of the Church of the East lost in battle or massacred. See Guant, *Massacres*, 300.

11. Kuper, "Turkish Genocide of Armenians," 49.

12. Graber, *Caravans to Oblivion*.

13. Derderian, "Common Fate," 1.

14. Marashlian, "Finishing the Genocide," 121.

15. David Guant's summary and analysis is a sober description of the massacres of Christians in eastern Turkey and further east and south into modern day Syria, Iraq, and Iran during the First World War, including communities such as the Syriac Orthodox, the Assyrian Church, the Chaldean Church, the Syriac Catholic Church, Armenian

Armenians continued into 1916, but the slaughter continued after the war while the Allies deliberated over peace terms, and even into the 1920s.

THE RESPONSE OF CHURCHES

This chapter is concerned with the responses of the American churches to the reports of massacres, and is particularly focused on what role those reports played in the churches' support for the war effort. Accounts of German atrocities galvanized American public opinion against Germany and for America's declaration of war in 1917. But what role, if any, did the genocide play in rallying support for a war against Germany's Turkish ally? There is no question that American Christians of all stripes were aghast and appalled at what they were hearing about the mistreatment of the Armenians, but how did that moral outrage translate into calls for military action against the Turks?[16] Attention here is on the relationship between calls for war and the massacres. Denominational periodicals are of particular interest, for they provided readers with editorial opinion, articles of interest, letters to the editor, sermons, official statements and reports, and summaries of church-related events. They played a critical role in the construction of patriotic wartime sentiment,[17] as well as offering a forum for making appeals for support for the destitute Armenians. Since the focus is on the massacres and their role in shaping wartime convictions, attention will be limited to the war years and not extend into the postwar years, even though massacres of Armenians continued long after ink had dried on the Treaty of Versailles (1919).

There has been significant research on America's political response to the Armenian genocide.[18] However, scant attention has been paid to the churches and the genocide, and what has been completed has almost exclusively focused on US missionaries and the work of Near East Relief (NER).

Apostolic Church, and Armenian Catholic Church (as well a small number of Protestant missionaries and converts). See Guant, *Massacres*. See also Khosroeva, "Assyrian Genocide."

16. North of the border in Canada the war was waged, in part, to put an end to Turkish atrocities. See Heath, "Thor and Allah."

17. For the nation-building role of the religious press, see Heath, "Forming Sound Public Opinion."

18. Peterson, *"Starving Armenians"*; Winter, *America and the Armenian Genocide*; Davis, *Slaughterhouse Province*; Balakian, *Burning Tigris*; Payaslian, "United States Response"; Moranian, "Legacy of Paradox"; Kloian, *Armenian Genocide*; Kirakossian, *Armenian Massacres*.

To be sure, the role of the missionaries in this drama was significant. Suzanne E. Moranian demonstrates how since the American missionaries were eyewitnesses to the disaster they were the "most critical figures in the relationship between the United States and the Armenians during the genocide era" and were "unmatched in exerting influence and expertise in the Turkish field and on the American home front, as well as in American policy, intellectual, and cultural circles."[19] Peter Balakian agrees, but provides a more specific, decidedly more critical analysis. He argues that the American Board of Commissioners for Foreign Missions (ABCFM), the largest Protestant missionary organization in the Ottoman Empire, did not support US military action for fear of jeopardizing its interests in Turkey, and that its chairman, James L. Barton, head of the ABCFM, engaged in a vigorous public relations campaign to keep America out of a war with Turkey. Barton, he claims, "embraced what Theodore Roosevelt called the pure hypocrisy of keeping the United States out of the war with Turkey, in part, to protect missionary interests in the Ottoman Empire, especially their vast real estate holdings, which were then worth about $123 million."[20]

There is no doubt that the massacres motivated an incredible outpouring of church support for relief operations. But what of calls for war with Turkey? Balakian is correct when he claims that there was reticence among ABCFM officials in calling for war with Turkey. Looking at the discourse of church officials in other sources such as periodicals, tracts, and sermons, it is obvious that there was also no groundswell of official church support for a declaration of war in 1915—or after for that matter—in order to punish Turkey and protect Armenians. However, the same sources also indicate that when America did enter the war, the battle against Germany was often conflated with that against Turkey. The "accursed partnership of Turk and Teuton"[21] had wreaked havoc on the world, and the war against the Teuton was, for all intents and purposes, a war against the Turk. Stated differently, though war was only officially declared against the Germans there is ample evidence of what could best be called a proxy war between America and Turkey. With that in mind, the following will, first, reconsider Balakian's criticism and argue that there was much more than just a selfish concern

---

19. Moranian, "Armenian Genocide," 185. For a helpful chapter on Near East Relief, see Peterson, *"Starving Armenians,"* chapter 3.

20. Balakian, *Burning Tigris*, 306.

21. Francis L. Patton, "Until Victory Comes," *Watchman-Examiner*, 8 August 1918, 1005.

of property that motivated considerations of missionary officials. Second, it will outline the conflation of the war against Germany with the Allies' war against Turkey. For some, America was contributing to ending the suffering of Armenians by waging war against the Kaiser in Europe as well as by being allied with nations that were battling the Turks in the Middle East.

COMMENTARY ON GENOCIDE

Once war was declared against Germany, commentary on the conflict was ubiquitous in the pulpit and in the religious press, and that commentary played a key role in providing news, nurturing patriotism, explaining war aims, and discerning God's providence in the midst of the titanic struggle. While the clash with Germany dominated wartime discourse, interspersed among such remarks was reporting on Turkish atrocities. Coverage of the atrocities can be broken into three general categories: details on the nature and extent of the genocide, depictions of Armenians and Turks, and descriptions of relief efforts and appeals for financial aid.

Denominational periodicals provided vivid details on the nature and extent of the atrocities committed against Armenians and Syrian Christians, as well as other minorities under Ottoman rule.[22] Initially there was some uncertainty surrounding the extent of the roundups and massacres.[23] However, by the final months of 1915 it was clear that an unmitigated disaster had befallen the Christians.[24] Titles such as "The Murder of a Race,"

---

22. In regards to non-Christian minorities, see "A Massacre of Jews in Palestine," *Baptist World*, 24 May 1917, 20.

23. "Massacres by Kurds," *Christian Advocate*, 15 April 1915, 2; "Current Events," *Christian Index*, 27 May 1915, 5; "Current Events," *Christian Index*, August 1915, 5; "Eastern Christians Being Persecuted," *Christian Century*, 26 August 1915, 10; *United Presbyterian*, 26 August 1916, 6; "A Cry for Help from Persia," *Presbyterian Banner*, 1 April 1915, 7.

24. "Armenian Massacres Confirmed," *Christian Advocate*, 7 October 1915, 15; "The Armenian Atrocities," *Baptist World*, 7 October 1915, 17; "American Missionaries in Turkey," *Watchman-Examiner*, 9 September 1915, 1160; "Armenians Massacred," *Watchman-Examiner*, 23 September 1915, 1225; "The Assassination of a Race," *Watchman-Examiner*, 28 October 1915, 1384; "Armenian Atrocities," *Watchman-Examiner*, 11 November 1915, 1450; John Sergus, "The 'Holy War' in Persia," *Christian Century*, 30 September 1915, 4–5; "Turks Slaughter Armenians," *The Continent*, 9 September 1915, 1198; "Gruesome Word from Armenia," *The Continent*, 23 September 1915, 1264; "When Have Men Done a Fouler Deed?" *The Continent*, 7 October 1915, 1340; "Greatest of All Martyrdoms," *The Continent*, 14 October 1915, 1361; "Is Extermination Incredible?" *The Continent*, 21 October 1915, 1393; Edward Arthur Wicher, "Dark Days in Persia and Syria," *The Continent*, 25 November 1915, 1586; "The Armenian Horrors," *United*

"Turks Slay Nestorians," "The Assassination of Armenia," "One of History's Blackest Crimes," "Blotting Out the Armenians," or "Crucified Armenia" provided readers with grim details of events unfolding in Asia Minor.[25] It was argued that what were occurring were "wholesale massacres of Armenians"[26] by a power that was taking advantage of the war to "wreck its vengeance on a helpless people."[27] "Never before in the history of the world has there been such an appalling amount of suffering due to hunger, destitution and disease"[28] lamented one author, with Armenians joining the sorry list of other peoples (such as Poles, Rumanians, and Serbians) who, in the words of another, had been "almost wiped out from the map of Europe."[29] Vivid descriptions of the suffering were provided, with authors trying to report adequately but sensitively to the "most brutal, the most ruthless, the most inexcusable, and the most widespread massacres of Christians in the last one thousand years" that were "deluging Armenia with the blood of men, women, and children."[30] Reports on the suffering of Armenians continued throughout the war and into the postwar years.[31]

Presbyterian, 30 September 1915, 8; "The Woes of Armenia," *United Presbyterian*, 14 October 1915, 4; "Armenian Massacres," *Presbyterian Banner*, 30 September 1915, 5; "Turkish Extermination of Armenians," *Presbyterian Banner*, 14 October 1915, 6; "An Orgy of Unbridled Hate," *Missionary Herald*, November 1915, 497; "One Instance," *Missionary Herald*, November 1915, 497; "Forward, for Christ," *Christian Herald*, 3 November 1915, 1091–92; "The World's Bitterest Winter," *Christian Herald*, 29 December 1915, 1340.

25. "The Murder of a Race," *Christian Advocate*, 7 October 1915, 1336; "Turks Slay Nestorians," *Watchman-Examiner*, 7 October 1915, 1294–95; "The Assassination of Armenia," *Missionary Review of the World*, November 1915, 837–48; "One of History's Blackest Crimes," *Missionary Voice*, February 1916, 52; "Blotting Out the Armenians," *Alabama Baptist*, 10 November 1915, 8; "Crucified Armenia," *Spirit of Missions*, May 1916, 323.

26. "The Balkans," *Catholic World*, January 1916, 561–65.

27. "Blotting Out the Armenians," *Alabama Baptist*, 10 November 1915, 8.

28. "The Suffering of Non-Combatants," *Missionary Review of the World*, October 1916, 727–28.

29. F. Aurelio Palmieri, "Catholic Lithuania," *Catholic World*, August 1918, 591.

30. "The Assassination of Armenia," *Missionary Review of the World*, November 1915, 837–48.

31. James L. Barton, "The Armenian Race Undergoing Assassination," *Christian Intelligencer*, 5 January 1916, 2; Viscount Bryce, "Armenian Relief," *Christian Intelligencer*, 7 March 1917, 155; "The Blood of the Martyrs," *Christian Intelligencer*, 13 June 1917, 370; Samuel T. Dutton, "Turkey and the Armenians," *Advocate of Peace*, April 1916, 106–7; Paul Shimmon, "A War Correspondent on Syrian Refugees," *Spirit of Missions*, June 1916, 407–8; "Besieged on a Mountaintop," *Missionary Voice*, March 1916, 122–23; "Editorial," *Home and Foreign Fields*, April 1918, 1; Wm. T. Ellis, "Seeing Armenia,"

As for depictions of the protagonists, Armenians were portrayed as a "helpless," "peaceful," and "agricultural" people unjustly and brutally assailed by "bloodthirsty" Turks.[32] The 1600-year Christian identity of Armenia provided a natural affinity to American Christians, and the Armenian faithfulness in the face of martyrdom was commended.[33] As for constructions of images of the Turks, accounts of Armenian atrocities went beyond describing the events to both confirm and amplify an image of the "Terrible Turk" that was common in the West.[34] Turks had a "fiendish policy"[35] towards minorities, and were a people who "wreck and ruin everything they touch."[36] Atrocities, it was argued, gratified the "mad desires of the 'Terrible Turk.'"[37] Their mistreatment of Christians for generations was noted, and their demise was openly called for: "For centuries the civilized nations of the world have agreed that Turkey was a blot upon the map of enlightened

---

Christian Outlook, 28 February 1918, 272–73; Israel Zangwill, "Armenia Outsuffers Israel," *Christian Advocate*, 1 March 1917, 205; "Lost Victories," *Christian Advocate*, 26 February 1920, 277; "A Million Armenians Die," *Christian Century*, 8 June 1916, 10; "A Million Armenian Murders," *The Continent*, 25 May 1916, 691; "What One Man Saw in Armenia," *The Continent*, 21 September 1916, 1229; "More Armenian Atrocities?" *The Continent*, 28 February 1918, 206; "Armenians May Become Extinct," *The Continent*, 11 April 1918, 395; Fred P. Haggard, "Getting under the Armenian and Syrian Problem," *United Presbyterian*, 3 May 1917, 2; Richard Hill, "Viewing Armenia's Woe from Ararat," *Lutheran Companion*, 3 November 1917, 543, 548; "Relief Funds," *Lutheran Witness*, 8 February 1916, 39.

32. "The Murder of a Race," *Christian Advocate*, 7 October 1915, 1336; "The Assassination of a Race," *Watchman-Examiner*, 20 October 1915, 1384.

33. "The Assassination of Armenia," *Missionary Review of the World*, November 1915, 837–48; "The Rescue of Armenia," *Missionary Review of the World*, November 1917, 808–9; H. H. Riggs, "Are The Armenians Worth Saving?" *Presbyterian Banner*, 19 December 1918, 8–9.

34. Moranian points out that negative portrayals of the Turks in American reporting can be traced back to the commentary surrounding earlier massacres in 1895–96. Moranian, "Armenian Genocide," 210. Apparently, for some, the conduct of Turkey was not surprising at all. See "Again the Unspeakable Turk," *Christian Advocate*, 12 August 1915, 2.

35. "The Rescue of Armenia," *Missionary Review of the World*, November 1917, 808–9.

36. Stephen Trowbridge, "Stories of Liberated Armenians," *Missionary Review of the World*, July 1919, 510–18.

37. P. C. Shilling, "Historical Sidelights on the War," *Baptist World*, 30 December 1915, 9.

Europe, a disgrace to civilization, and *ought to be* driven back into Asia from whence she came."[38]

On 10 July 1915, Congress passed a joint resolution asking the President to designate a special day to bring the attention of the nation to the plight of Armenians.[39] Description of relief efforts and appeals for financial aid were frequent in the religious press, and continued into the postwar years. The most important Christian organization created to respond to the crisis was the Armenian Relief Committee, formed in September 1915 (the title evolved from Armenian and Syrian Relief Committee to American Committee for Relief in the Near East, and finally to Near East Relief).[40] James L. Barton was selected as the chairman. Other prominent and influential church figures were chosen to the board, two of whom were close friends of President Wilson.[41] NER rapidly became the organizer of a vast network of people and groups for the purpose of raising support for suffering Armenians and Syrians, a herculean effort that "broke new ground in the history of American philanthropy."[42] Its publication *New Near East* provided vivid and compelling accounts of Armenian suffering and NER's efforts to relieve such misery. Providing actual assistance on the ground in Turkey were American missionaries with their almost century-long experience of Turkish culture.[43] Their sacrifices under extreme duress in order to save Armenian lives were heroic.[44] Barton stated that the churches and

---

38. B. F. Stogsdill, "Turkey: Its History and Prophecy," *Word and Way*, 9 September 1915, 6–8 (italics in original).

39. That became a regular event in following years, and Presidents Harding and Coolidge followed the precedent.

40. For a history of Near East Relief written by its chairman, see Barton, *Story of Near East Relief*. Other organizations were founded for fact-finding missions, political and denominational lobbying, or raising funds for NER. For instance, see "General Committee on the Armenian Situation, Executive Committee Correspondence, 14–29 January 1916" (MS G2826e, Presbyterian Historical Society, Philadelphia).

41. These were Cleveland H. Dodge and Charles R. Crane. See Barton, *Story of Near East Relief*, 7.

42. Moranian, "Armenian Genocide," 185.

43. Salt, "Trouble Wherever They Went."

44. In 1917, Barton sent a circular to American missionaries who had been in Turkey and had firsthand experience with the atrocities, encouraging them to record their experience. He hoped that their statements would counter the claims of some that accounts of atrocities were exaggerated. Barton later presented those statements to the US Presidential commission on the war. For a summary of those statements, see Barton, "Turkish Atrocities."

national committees were the most important organizations that cooperated with the NER to bring awareness to the plight of Armenians.⁴⁵ Offerings were collected at mass meetings, such as football games or a Billy Sunday revival meeting.⁴⁶ Less dramatic and more common was the collection of funds in local churches across the nation by ladies groups, men's organizations, children, or youth groups. Ministers often acted as collection agents, encouraging giving of money and goods to NER.⁴⁷ Religious societies such as International Christian Endeavor Society, Epworth League, and Episcopal Young People's Movement helped raise awareness and funds, as did Sunday Schools.⁴⁸ Sunday School children were asked to donate money for children in Bible lands, raising almost $1,000,000 in the first year.⁴⁹ Sunday School support continued throughout the 1920s. The amount of money and goods eventually raised by the NER was staggering: $116 million was spent over the years to aid over one million refugees, not to mention vast amounts of material goods donated to feed and clothe suffering Armenians and others in the Middle East.⁵⁰

Helping fund-raising efforts was the coverage of the genocide in the religious press. A cursory survey of the denominational press confirms that space was given to detail relief efforts and appeals for donations.⁵¹ Reflect-

---

45. Barton, *Story of Near East Relief*, 385.

46. "Give Millions Today to Save Armenians," *New York Times*, 22 October 1916, 2.

47. Ministers and churches were encouraged by the denomination to raise funds. For instance, see *Minutes of the Fifty-Eighth General Assembly of the United Presbyterian Church of North America, 1916*, 228; *Minutes of the Fifty-Seventh General Assembly of the Presbyterian Church in the United States, 1917*, 24; *Minutes of the General Assembly of the Presbyterian Church in the United States of America, 1917*, 154.

48. Barton, *Story of Near East Relief*, 386–87.

49. Ibid., 386.

50. Moranian, "Armenian Genocide," 194–96. See also James L. Barton, "Ten Million Dollars for Relief," *Missionary Review of the World*, July 1918, 491–96.

51. "Signs of Life in Turkey," *Missionary Review of the World*, October 1916, 730–31; "Help Persecuted Armenians," *Christian Century*, 5 November 1915, 10; John B. Calvert, "Armenia's and Syria's Emergency, America's Opportunity," *Watchman-Examiner*, 5 October 1916, 1289; "Our Sunday Schools and Armenian Relief," *Watchman-Examiner*, 6 December 1917, 1568; *Baptist Record*, 7 November 1918, 1; "Facing the Problems of Peace," *Baptist Record*, 14 November 1918, 4; "One Bright Spot in the Armenian Horror," *Missionary Voice*, May 1916, 196; "A Million Staving People: $5,000,000 for Relief," *Missionary Voice*, August 1916, 338–39; "Bethlehem and Calvary," *Missionary Voice*, December 1916, 529–30; "Help! Save a Life!" *Missionary Voice*, February 1919, 39; "Relief Supplies for the Syrians," *Christian Advocate*, 21 September 1916, 17; "The Christmas Ship for Syria," *Christian Advocate*, 28 December 1916, 5; "The Most Forlorn of Nations,"

ing back on his efforts to raise funds for relief, James Barton wrote that the nation's newspapers had been "of invaluable assistance" in bringing to the attention of the American people the travails of the Armenians, from the earliest days and onwards." He went on to say that the religious publications (over 300 of them) were an "ally in all the work of relief" and that the "entire religious press, including the Jewish and the Roman Catholic, was sympathetic and co-operative, backing the work of the Committee editorially and with specially prepared articles."[52]

A PROXY WAR WITH TURKEY

In the early months of the atrocities there were calls for action among church leaders, but those appeals were for diplomatic pressure or for prayer.[53] As the months progressed, and reports of Armenian distress grew increasingly more shrill and graphic, why did churches not call for military action against Turkey, especially after the US declaration of war against Germany?

Christian Advocate, 20 September 1917, 946; James L. Barton, "Ten Million Dollars for Relief," *Missionary Review of the World*, July 1918, 491–96; "A Day for Armenian Relief," *Christian Century*, 14 September 1916, 10; "Armenian Committee Reports," *The Continent*, 7 October 1915, 1327; "Missionaries Leaving Turkey," *The Continent*, 18 November 1915, 1547; "Women Rescue Armenian Girls," *The Continent*, 2 December 1915, 1612; "Relief in Asia Minor," *The Continent*, 10 February 1916, 179; "What Are We Doing for Syrians Here?" *The Continent*, 2 March 1916, 277; "To Save a People," *The Continent*, 25 May 1916, 689; "Armenian Relief Must Continue," *Christian Intelligencer*, 21 March 1917, 186; "You Will Not Let Me Starve This Easter Time, Will You?" *Christian Intelligencer*, 6 February 1918, 121; Graham C. Hunter, "Relief Work among Armenian Refugees," *United Presbyterian*, 28 November 1918, 10–11; Thomas H. Miller, "Armenian Relief Campaign," *United Presbyterian*, 19 December 1918, 14–15; "Editorial Notes and Comment," *Presbyterian of the South*, 13 June 1917, 1; "Armenian Need," *Presbyterian of the South*, 30 January 1918, 16; "The Greatest Tragedy of the Great War," *Presbyterian of the South*, 1 January 1919, 1; "Armenian and Syrian Relief," *Presbyterian Banner*, 10 May 1917, 5; "An Urgent Appeal," *Presbyterian Banner*, 8 November 1917, 5; "Armenian and Syrian Relief," *Presbyterian Banner*, 5 December 1918, 4; "Thirty Million Dollar Campaign January 12th, 1918," *Lutheran Companion*, 14 December 1918, 644; "The Cry of the Children," *Christian Herald*, 28 February 1917, 234; "Saving a Race," *Missionary Herald*, April 1917, 160; "A Turkey Bulletin," *Missionary Herald*, July 1918, 322–24.

52. Barton, *Story of Near East Relief*, 383–84.

53. "The Plight of Armenians," *Missionary Review of the World*, October 1915, 723–24; "The Plight of Armenians," *Missionary Review of the World*, November 1915, 805–6; "The Assassination of Armenia," *Missionary Review of the World*, November 1915, 837–48; "The Murder of a Race," *Christian Advocate*, 7 October 1915, 1336. There were also calls for continued neutrality. See "America First," *Baptist Standard*, 14 October 1915, 9. There was even a statement that the Allied and Central Powers were equally guilty of crimes. See "Lest We Forget," *Baptist Standard*, 27 April 1916, 1.

expect an American declaration of war with Turkey in 1915, or 1916, seems unrealistic considering the uncertain US domestic situation, and, as Samantha Power notes, domestic considerations have always been the determining factor in the American government's response to genocide.[54] There was still widespread isolationist sentiment in America in 1915, and no popular support for a war with Germany let alone distant Turkey. It was two more years before Americans en masse would support sending troops into the war in Europe, and it took direct German aggression towards Americans by way of unrestricted submarine warfare and meddling with Mexican–American relations to do it. Perhaps if significant numbers of American missionaries had been slaughtered there would have been more calls for punishing Turkey, but that did not occur. American missionaries were, for the most part, left alone by the Turkish authorities to carry out their extensive relief work among the destitute.

Certainly Barton and the Board of the ABCFM were wary of antagonizing relations with the Turks. Barton recorded that he was concerned for over 500 American citizens and a number of institutions with a "generation of interest and sacrifice,"[55] but that concern went beyond unease over potential lost property. His fear was also rooted in a pragmatic concern that a US declaration of war would only make things worse for those suffering under Ottoman violence. The Turkish authorities would then expel (or imprison) Americans in Ottoman territory, and that would mean that those they had been helping would be "at the mercy of a hostile government."[56]

A number of articles in the religious press directly addressed the issue of war with Turkey.[57] Pragmatic concerns reflected apprehension over the loss of generations of missionary work and property, but they also reflected the complexity of events on the ground. Anger at Turkey for the atrocities

---

54. Power, *"Problem from Hell."*

55. Barton, *Story of Near East Relief*, 3.

56. Ibid., 5. See also George B. Eager, "Bible Lands and the War," *Baptist World*, 26 April 1917, 11.

57. "Mission Fears about Turkey," *The Continent*, 15 February 1917, 187. "Reasons against War with Turkey," *Presbyterian Banner*, 27 December 1917, 6; Arlo A. Brown, "American Property in Jerusalem," *Christian Advocate*, 29 March 1917, 301–2; "Reasons against War with Turkey," *Presbyterian Banner*, 27 December 1917, 6; "Signs of Life in Turkey," *Missionary Review of the World*, October 1916, 730–31; "American Interests in Turkey Violated," *Missionary Herald*, November 1915, 498; "American Interests in Turkey," *Missionary Herald*, November 1915, 538; "Turkey and the United States," *Missionary Herald*, March 1917, 106; "How About Relief Work in Turkey," *Missionary Herald*, May 1917, 212.

was palpable, but the harsh and unpleasant reality was that the lesser of two evils at the moment appeared to be the postponement of a declaration of war. Restraint may not have appealed to a sense of righteous indignation, but for some it seemed the best of possible options, an example of *realpolitik* at work.[58] For instance, the *Christian Century* repeated Barton's claim that an American declaration of war would lead to the loss of missionary property, and would be a "calamity" because it would "increase the miseries of the defenseless people . . . by taking away their last protection."[59] *The Continent* provided two reasons for delaying a declaration of war.[60] First, America did not yet have sufficient military assets to make any declaration of war meaningful (it was all that America could do to field an army against Germany). Second, a declaration of war would only make things worse for those suffering: "That with such a declaration of war the last possible protection or aid for suffering people in the Turkish Empire will be withdrawn. Relief in food and clothing and protection is now wholly in American hands. Without that protection Armenians and other native peoples are at the mercy of a bloody foe. Instantly war is declared such service is at an end except in such roundabout ways as are proving ineffective in other lands." Consequently, the article concluded that no mission worker in Turkey would actually want a declaration of war at the present time.

While evidence is lacking for any statements calling for a formal declaration of war on Turkey, there is ample evidence of what could best be called a proxy war between America and Turkey. The two countries were not directly engaged in armed conflict, but it was clear who-was-backing-whom in the multiple conflicts and fronts. By 1917 America was at war with Germany (an ally of Turkey) in Europe. Britain and France were at war with both Germany and Turkey, and examples abound of American popular support for the Allies against Turkey. In much of the wartime rhetoric, the war with Germany had become conflated with the struggle against Turkey and thus it was believed that there was no need for a declaration of war against the Ottomans. In fact, waging war against Germany was deemed to be a way of ultimately defeating Turkey, for without German support, Turkish resistance would quickly collapse.

---

58. This was a departure from the missionaries' usual moralistic approach to international affairs. See Salt, "Trouble Wherever They Went."

59. Herbert L. Willett, Jr., "The Holy Land in the War," *Christian Century*, 20 December 1917, 14–15.

60. "Reasons for Delay with Turkey," *The Continent*, 18 July 1918, 812.

example of this conflation can be seen in the wartime rhetoric.

The enemy most often the target of wartime rhetoric was Germany, but it is striking how often Germany and Turkey were equally targeted. In a stirring dedication sermon John E. Gunn stated: "[W]e are determined never to yield one tittle of our American rights, privileges or liberties to any man or to any people, and most certainly not to that aggregation of Turks and Teutons now marshaled under the banner of frightfulness and piracy. . . . We are waging the most just war ever engaged."[61] The poem entitled "Armenia—1917" linked the Teuton and Turk, and Kaiser and Crescent, in the disaster unfolding in Asia.[62] Elsewhere the "accursed partnership of Turk and Teuton" was portrayed as the cause of the global catastrophe,[63] or, as one author declared, "Thor and Allah were linked in a hideous, unholy confederacy."[64]

One could easily be mistaken thinking that America actually had declared war on Turkey, for in some rhetoric it seemed to be the case. An early indication of that conflation can be seen in the publication "No False Peace," a call to action in February 1917 by prominent religious leaders. By that stage of the European conflict there was a growing sentiment among Americans that a declaration of war against Germany was imminent. The publication urged political action, and provided the requisite moral backing by noting a number of German atrocities such as their brutal advance through Belgium, the devastation of Serbia and Poland, and the sinking of the *Lusitania*. What is significant for this research is the inclusion of the "massacre of Armenians" near the top of the list. While the declaration may or may not have been a call for war against Turkey, at the very least it conflated a war against Germany with a response to the Turkish mistreatment of Armenians. Once war was declared, the conflation of conflicts became more apparent. J. Lovell Murray (Education Secretary, Student Volunteer Movement) said, "We are waging in Europe and Western Asia and Africa a war for the rights and welfare of mankind."[65] Along similar lines, one Baptist preacher proclaimed: "[W]e believe we are justified in entering the

61. Gunn, "Address at Dedication," 128.

62. Francis Bourne Upham, "Armenia—1917," *Christian Advocate*, 20 December 1917, 1361.

63. Francis L. Patton, "Until Victory Comes," *Watchman-Examiner*, 8 August 1918, 1005.

64. J. Lovell Murray, "Islam and the War," *Watchman-Examiner*, 28 November 1918, 1465.

65. Murray, *Call of a World Task*, 24.

list against Germany and her allies because we fight not only in self defense but in defense also of weak and helpless peoples . . . the United States could not have justified her cowardly indifference before the world, nor before her own children, had we not come to the aid of France which had been our friend in time of need, and to the rescue of poor Belgium, Serbia, Poland, Roumania, and Armenia."[66] "To all intents and purposes," another author noted, the Allies fought under "one supreme command" against the Central Powers.[67] In an address at the raising of a flag service in New York, the preacher listed the geographical spread of the war, the nations involved, the deaths and massacres perpetrated by Germany and Turkey, and concluded with a statement "We are in that war" with no distinction or nuance as to who was actually officially at war with whom.[68] Americans even shared in a common victory with the Allies over the Central Powers, including Turkey:

> America, with the Allies, won everything that America went to war for, and won it to a complete and glorious finish. . . . Autocracy in Germany, Austria, Turkey and Russia has been torn up by the roots. The Kaiser, whipped clear down to the ground, has abdicated, and his dynasty is at an end. The Hapsburg dynasty, for centuries the main support of Popery in Central Europe is at an end, and the Allies are occupying Constantinople, with the Turks completely at their mercy. . . . Five hundred million human beings have been released from oppression as a result of the war. And all this has been accomplished at a very small cost to America.[69]

America entered the war against Germany with the idealistic notion of ending German despotism and advancing democracy, and in some rhetoric America was also at war against the despotism of Turkey.[70] Turkish atrocities were deemed to be part of the larger pattern of the Central Powers' barbaric despotism. German complicity in the Armenian massacres

---

66. H. D. Wilson, "The Christian and the War," *Alabama Baptist*, 23 October 1918, 6.

67. Allan P. Ames, "What Shall We Do with Victory?" *Watchman-Examiner*, 17 October 1918, 1310–11.

68. Coyle, "Address at Raising of Service Flag," 187.

69. J. B. Gambrell, "Thanksgiving and Consecration," *Baptist Standard*, 28 November 1918, 5. See also Robison, "Patriotic Address at St. Leo's Flag Raising"; C. E. Hoffsten, "Weighed in the Balance," *Lutheran Companion*, 23 November 1918, 599.

70. Keefe, "Unfurling of Service Flag." See also "The Present Urgent Duty," *Spirit of Missions*, July 1917, 445; "As of Old," *Spirit of Missions*, June 1917, 373; "The Declaration Up to date—1779–1917," *Christian Advocate*, 28 June 1917.

n in comments such as that the Armenians "fell prostrate under
‑ing army of Hun and Turk."⁷¹ In fact, Turkish authorities were
…ᴜᴄɪᴇᴅ to be under the direct control of the German High Command,⁷²
and German officers stationed in the Ottoman Empire were accused of
knowing about atrocities (and even participating in rounding up some civilians) yet doing nothing to stop them.⁷³ Such a fusion of the despotism of
Hun and Turk was cause for one peace-loving Quaker to justify supporting the war: "[C]all to mind the little children of Armenia, the wronged
women of Belgium, the enslaved men of Servia [sic], and know that these
things can never again come to pass if your sons, your younger brothers,
be equal to the challenge which a free world dare not refuse to meet."⁷⁴ The
fusion of German and Turkish despotism was also used to rally support
for the war effort. The promotion of the Third Liberty Loan in 1918, for
instance, highlighted both German and Turkish atrocities in order to spur
giving to the war effort.⁷⁵ At a public address dedicating a new building in
a military camp, Charles W. Currier listed atrocities in Belgium, Poland,
and Armenia, and then asked, "Shall we permit all this to continue?"⁷⁶ Few
were shocked with Turkish despotism and barbarism, for memories of the
1890s remained, but some like Harry Emerson Fosdick were utterly astonished and saddened that a Christian country like Germany was complicit
in such barbarous behavior: "How could the Germans, bone of our bone,
and blood of our blood, calling upon God, perpetuate cruelties like that [in
Europe and Asia]?"⁷⁷

By 1917, it was obvious that moral persuasion alone could not bring
an end to Turkish mistreatment of minorities and that force—by the armies

71. Harry C. Rogers, "No Place for Neutral Church," *The Continent*, 26 September 1918, 1066.

72. William E. Borah, "The War of Ideals and the Way Out," *Advocate of Peace*, April 1918, 111–14; "Turkey Obeys Germany," *United Presbyterian*, 3 May 1917, 7; "Christmas," *Presbyterian of the South*, 5 December 1917, 1–2.

73. "A Million Armenian Murders," *The Continent*, 25 May 1916, 691.

74. Stephen S. Wise, "What Are We Fighting For? A Reply to the People's Council of America," *Advocate of Peace*, January 1918, 14–19. See also "Some Particular Advice for Friends and A Statement of Loyalty for Others," *Advocate of Peace*, May 1918, 146–47.

75. Abrams, *Preachers Present Arms*, 84–85.

76. Currier, "Address Delivered at Dedication of a New Building," 118. See also Abrams, *Preachers Present Arms*, 101; "The Assassination of Armenia," *Missionary Review of the World*, November 1915, 837–48.

77. Harry Emerson Fosdick, "Judas, Not Iscariot," *Biblical World*, September 1919, 451–58.

of America's allies—was necessary. Not only would the fall of Turkey help the American Expeditionary Force in France by opening up new strategic options for attacks on Germany,[78] but the advance of Russia and Britain would alleviate the suffering of Armenians and other minorities, provide provisions and protection for relief efforts, and open the door for further missionary work.[79] In other words, the "strong hand" of a Christian power was necessary to put an end to misery and open up possibilities:

> Not the least interesting effects of the British and Russian victories will be their probable influence upon the Kurds... [who] have been given almost free reign for their lawless savagery. Now the British are at their back door, and without doubt, it is only a question of time when they will be tamed by the strong hand of a Christian power. This promises that there will be no future ruthless massacres of the Christian population. Better still, this wild, but manly race, numbering several millions, will be open, as never before, to Christian influence. Altogether, we have reason to give thanks for the onward march of events in the cradle of the human race.[80]

The capture of Jerusalem by British General Allenby in December 1917 was a pleasant Christmas surprise for Christians, and its capture conjured up romantic crusading images of a by-gone era. It was good news for several reasons: not only did it return the Holy City to Christian control after centuries of Muslim rule but it also meant the end of suffering for those under Turkish oppression.[81] In the words of one commentator, the "unspeakable

---

78. "Current Events," *Christian Index*, 7 November 1918, 5.

79. "Persia Enlarging Influence," *The Continent*, 8 July 1915, 902; "Russians Advance in Turkey," *The Continent*, 23 March 1916, 358; "To Save a People," *The Continent*, 25 May 1916, 689; "Crucified Armenia," *Spirit of Missions*, May 1916, 323; "The Second Anniversary of the War," *Baptist World*, 31 August 1916, 5; "Current Events," *Christian Index*, 2 December 1915, 5; Franklin E. Hoskins, "What British Victory Means to Syria," *The Continent*, 26 April 1917, 513.

80. "The Mesopotamian Campaign and Missions," *Missionary Review of the World*, May 1917, 325–27.

81. George B. Eager, "Bible Lands and the War," *Baptist World*, 19 April 1917, 11; George B. Eager, "Bible Lands and the War," *Baptist World*, 10 May 1917, 15; George B. Eager, "More about the Fall of Jerusalem and Its Effects," *Baptist World*, 27 December 1917, 7; Arlo Ayres Brown, "The Last Crusade," *Christian Advocate*, 6 December 1917, 1300; "Jerusalem Delivered," *Christian Advocate*, 27 December 1917, 1388; "The Significance of Jerusalem's Fall," *Christian Intelligencer*, 23 January 1918, 80; "British Near Jerusalem," *United Presbyterian*, 6 December 1917, 8; "Jerusalem Captured by the British," *United Presbyterian*, 27 December 1917, 8; "Jerusalem Captured!" *Presbyterian Banner*, 20 December 1917, 5; "Jerusalem," *Presbyterian Banner*, 27 December 1917, 7; "He

t last been driven out from the streets and courts of the City of
We may hope that the dream and ambition of the Crusaders and
ι leaders all through these centuries has been realized."⁸²

Many Americans longed for Turkey's dismemberment and expulsion from Europe and especially the ancient city of Constantinople, reversing centuries of Muslim advance into the Balkans. This sentiment can be seen in the none-too-subtle words of one letter to the editor: "I should like to suggest . . . when Jerusalem is captured by the British . . . all the churches celebrate the victory . . . [and it is wished] that this war shall not end till the Turkish empire, hoary with iniquity, laden with unspeakable infamies, drunk with the blood of millions of saints—both execrable beast and false prophet—shall be wiped from the earth."⁸³ Postwar aims were for Turkish control to be reduced to areas of Turkish majority, with no control over minority populations.⁸⁴ Its government also had to be replaced, for it "as an institution must pass away in fact or in spirit if mankind is to be free."⁸⁵ Finally, it was hoped that the postwar settlement would protect and provide for the Armenians as they tried to recover from the disaster.⁸⁶ The Armistice of Mudros (30 October 1918) ended hostilities between Britain and the Ottoman Turks. Upon hearing of Turkey's defeat, one commentator's response summed up much of the animosity felt towards the Turks: "In the

---

Hath Redeemed Jerusalem," *Missionary Herald*, January 1918, 4; Anthony Arnoux, "Will The Turk Yield Jerusalem?" *Christian Herald*, 4 April 1917, 383–84; Anthony Arnoux, "Armies before Jerusalem," *Christian Herald*, 12 December 1917, 1319; "Observations on the Religious Horizon," *Lutheran Companion*, 16 November 1918, 587.

82. "The Recovery of Jerusalem," *United Presbyterian*, 20 December 1917, 4.

83. James Wallace, "When Jerusalem Falls," *The Continent*, 6 December 1917, 1507. See also "The War in the East," *Christian Century*, 7 November 1918, 5; Robert W. Perks, "England—The War—America," *Christian Advocate*, 5 October 1916, 1309–10; "The Three Armistices," *Catholic World*, December 1918, 414–21; "Should We Have Accepted the Austrian Proposal?" *Advocate of Peace*, October 1918, 261–63; "The Simplicity of Our Present Terms," *Advocate of Peace*, July 1917, 196–97; Frederic Hodgins, "The Future of the Near East," *Lutheran Companion*, 19 October 1918, 531, 533.

84. "Will the Butcher Turk Escape?" *Christian Century*, 10 October 1918, 4. See also "Labor and the New World after the War (Is. 32:17)," *Christian Century*, 29 August 1918, 16.

85. "No Explanation," *The Continent*, 30 November 1916, 1546.

86. "The Three Armistices," *Catholic World*, December 1918, 414–21; "Problems of Reconstruction in Europe," *Advocate of Peace*, December 1918, 339–41; "Brief Peace Notes," *Advocate of Peace*, December 1917, 341; "The Simplicity of Our Present Terms," *Advocate of Peace*, July 1917, 196–97; Manyard Owen Williams, "Armenia Enters the World-War," *Christian Herald*, 23 January 1918, 98.

final settlement with Turkey the Christian sentiment of the world demands that Turkey shall cease to exist as European power, and that the Armenian peoples shall be forever delivered from the yoke of the bloody Turk. It is well to be merciful, but it is neither wise nor Christian to be merciful to a crocodile."[87]

CONCLUSION

The Armenian Genocide motivated an extraordinary outpouring of church support for relief organizations. But why was there no groundswell of church backing for military action to punish Turkey and protect Armenians? Pragmatic reasons were given for not going to war against Turkey, the most significant being that it was thought that war between the two nations would lead to the expulsion of missionaries, thus ending the only significant relief efforts for the Armenians. Not wanting to add to the suffering of the afflicted, the churches presented arguments advocating against war. However, what made that difficult decision easier to bear was the sense that America was—in a way—already at war with Turkey. The heated wartime rhetoric often conflated America's war with Germany with events transpiring in Turkey. The "accursed partnership of Turk and Teuton"[88] had led to the global conflagration, and America's war against the Teuton was considered, for all intents and purposes, a war against Germany's partner Turkey. Stated differently, there is ample evidence of what could best be called a proxy war between America and Turkey. As a result, while there was no official declaration of war, the rhetoric of the day acted to salve the consciences of those who wanted to protect missionaries providing aid to Armenians but also punish the Turks for their atrocities. For some, America was indeed at war with Turkey.

---

87. H. H. Marlin, "Turkey Is Granted an Armistice," *United Presbyterian*, 7 November 1918, 7.

88. Francis L. Patton, "Until Victory Comes," *Watchman-Examiner*, 8 August 1918, 1005.

BIBLIOGRAPHY

Primary Sources

PERIODICALS/NEWSPAPERS

Advocate of Peace
Alabama Baptist
Baptist Record
Baptist Standard
Baptist World
Biblical Word
Catholic World
Christian Advocate
Christian Century
Christian Herald
Christian Index
Christian Intelligencer
Christian Outlook
The Continent
Home and Foreign Fields
Lutheran Companion
Lutheran Witness
Missionary Herald
Missionary Review of the World
Missionary Voice
New Near East
New York Times
Presbyterian Banner
Presbyterian of the South
Spirit of Missions
United Presbyterian
Watchman-Examiner
Word and Way

DENOMINATIONAL DOCUMENTS

Minutes of the Fifty-Eighth General Assembly of the United Presbyterian Church of North America, 1916.
Minutes of the Fifty-Seventh General Assembly of the Presbyterian Church in the United States, 1917.
Minutes of the General Assembly of the Presbyterian Church in the United States of America, 1917.
"General Committee on the Armenian Situation, Executive Committee Correspondence, 14–29 January 1916" (MS G2826e, Presbyterian Historical Society, Philadelphia).

Other

Barton, James L. *Story of Near East Relief (1915-1930): An Interpretation*. New York: MacMillan, 1930.

Coyle, John G. "Address at Raising of Service Flag, St. Augustine's Church, Bronx, N.Y. City." In *War Addresses from Catholic Pulpit and Platform*, 186-90. New York: Joseph F. Wagner, nd.

Currier, Charles W. "Address Delivered at Dedication of a New Building at Camp Humphreys, VA." In *War Addresses from Catholic Pulpit and Platform*, 114-20. New York: Joseph F. Wagner, nd.

Gunn, John E. "Address at Dedication of Knights of Columbus Hall, Camp Shelby." In *War Addresses from Catholic Pulpit and Platform*, 127-31. New York: Joseph F. Wagner, nd.

Keefe, William A. "Unfurling of Service Flag at St. Francis Xavier's Church, Waterbury, Conn." In *War Addresses from Catholic Pulpit and Platform*, 234-38. New York: Joseph F. Wagner, nd.

Murray, J. Lovell. *The Call of a World Task in Wartime*. New York: Student Volunteer Movement, 1918.

"No False Peace: A Warning by American Religious Leaders." *American Rights League Bulletin*, No. 23. February 1917.

Robison, William F. "Patriotic Address at St. Leo's Flag Raising, St. Louis, Mo." In *War Addresses from Catholic Pulpit and Platform*, 269-77. New York: Joseph F. Wagner, nd.

Secondary Sources

Abrams, Ray H. *Preachers Present Arms*. New York: Round Table, 1933.

Balakian, Peter. *The Burning Tigris: The Armenian Genocide and America's Response*. New York: HarperCollins, 2003.

Barton, James L., ed. *"Turkish Atrocities," Statements of American Missionaries on the Destruction of Christian Communities in Ottoman Turkey, 1915-1917*. Ann Arbor, MI: Gomidas Institute, 1998.

Dadrian, Vahakn N. *The History of the Armenian Genocide: Ethnic Conflict from the Balkans to Anatolia to the Caucasus*. New York: Berghahn, 1995.

Davis, Leslie A. *The Slaughterhouse Province: An American Diplomat's Report on the Armenian Genocide, 1915-1917*. New Rochelle, NY: Aristide D. Caratzas, 1989.

Derderian, Katharine. "Common Fate, Different Experience: Gender-Specific Aspects of the Armenian Genocide, 1915-1917." *Holocaust and Genocide Studies* 19 (2005) 1-25.

Ferguson, Niall. *The War of the World: Twentieth-Century Conflict and the Descent of the West*. New York: Penguin, 2006.

Graber, G. S. *Caravans to Oblivion: The Armenian Genocide, 1915*. New York: John Wiley & Sons, 1996.

Guant, David. *Massacres, Resistance, Protectors: Muslim-Christian Relations in Eastern Anatolia during World War I*. Piscataway, NJ: Gorgias, 2006.

Heath, Gordon L. "'Forming Sound Public Opinion': The Late Victorian Canadian Protestant Press and Nation-Building." *Journal of the Canadian Church Historical Society* 48 (2006) 109–59.

———. "'Thor and Allah in a hideous, unholy confederacy': The Armenian Genocide in the Canadian Protestant Press." In *The Globalization of Christianity: Implications for Christian Ministry and Theology*, edited by Steve Studebaker and Gordon L. Heath, 105–28. Eugene, OR: Pickwick, 2014.

Hovannisian, Richard G. *Armenia on the Road to Independence, 1918*. Berkeley: University of California Press, 1967.

Khosroeva, Anahit. "The Assyrian Genocide in the Ottoman Empire and Adjacent Territories."

In *The Armenian Genocide: Cultural and Ethical Legacies*, edited by Richard G.

Hovannisian, 267–74. New Brunswick, NJ: Transaction, 2007.

Kiernan, Ben. "Twentieth Century Genocides: Underlying Ideological Themes from Armenia to East Timor." In *The Specter of Genocide: Mass Murder in Historical Perspective*, edited by Robert Gellately and Ben Kiernan, 29–52. Cambridge: Cambridge University Press, 2003.

Kirakossian, Arman J. *The Armenian Massacres 1894–1896: U.S. Media Testimony*. Detroit: Wayne State University Press, 2004.

Kloian, Richard, ed. *The Armenian Genocide: News Accounts from the American Press*. Berkeley: Anto, 1985.

Kuper, Leo. "The Turkish Genocide of Armenians, 1915–1917." In *The Armenian Genocide in Perspective*, edited by Richard G. Hovannisian, 43–59. New Brunswick, NJ: Transaction, 1986.

Marashlian, Levon. "Finishing the Genocide: Cleansing Turkey of Armenian Survivors, 1920–1923." In *Remembrance and Denial: The Case of the Armenian Genocide*, edited by Richard G. Hovannisian, 113–45. Detroit: Wayne State University Press, 1998.

Moranian, Suzanne E. "The Armenian Genocide and American Missionary Efforts." In *America and the Armenian Genocide of 1915*, edited by Jay Winter, 185–213. Cambridge: Cambridge University Press, 2003.

———. "A Legacy of Paradox: U.S. Foreign Policy and the Armenian Genocide." In *The Armenian Genocide: Cultural and Ethical Legacies*, edited by Richard G. Hovannisian, 309–24. New Brunswick, NJ: Transaction, 2008.

Morgenthau, Henry. *Ambassador Morgenthau's Story*. Garden City, NY: Doubleday, Page, 1919.

Olusoga, David, and Casper W. Erichsen. *The Kaiser's Holocaust: Germany's Forgotten Genocide and the Colonial Roots of Nazism*. London: Faber & Faber, 2010.

Payaslian, Simon. "The United States Response to the Armenian Genocide." In *Looking Backward, Moving Forward: Confronting the Armenian Genocide*, edited by Richard G. Hovannisian, 51–80. New Brunswick, NJ: Transaction, 2003.

Peterson, Merrill D. *"Starving Armenians": America and the Armenian Genocide, 1915–1930 and After*. Charlottesville: University of Virginia Press, 2004.

Power, Samantha. *"A Problem from Hell": America and the Age of Genocide*. New York: Harper, 2007.

Salt, Jeremy. "Trouble Wherever They Went: American Missionaries in Anatolia and Ottoman Syria in the Nineteenth Century." *The Muslim World* 92 (Fall 2002) 287–313.

Shirinian, Lorne. *Quest for Closure: The Armenian Genocide and the Search for Justice in Canada*. Kingston: Blue Heron, 1999.

Walker, C. J. *Armenia: The Survival of a Nation*. London: Croom Helm, 1980.

Winter, Jay, ed. *America and the Armenian Genocide of 1915*. Cambridge: Cambridge University Press, 2003.

Index of Subjects

Alcatraz, 97
Allied Powers, 6, 29, 34, 61, 77, 137, 144, 164, 183, 184, 186, 193, 195, 197
American Bible Society, 177
American Board of Commissioners for Foreign Missions (ABCFM), 185, 192
American Committee for Relief in the Near East. *See* Near East Relief.
American Expeditionary Force (AEF), 1, 2, 6, 169–71, 173, 174, 197
American Rights League, 23, 26, 28, 29
Amish, 88, 89, 92, 96, 100
Anglo-Saxons, 6, 7, 39
Armageddon, 150
Armistice, 32, 33, 34, 48, 100, 121, 169, 170, 172, 177, 178
Armistice of Mudros, 198
Armenia, 12, 16, 181–99
    Armenian Genocide, 12, 182–90, 192, 199
    Armenian Catholic Church, 184
Armenian Relief Committee. *See* Near East Relief.
Armenian and Syrian Relief Committee. *See* Near East Relief.
Atrocities of War, 1, 76, 90, 124, 182, 184, 186, 188–89, 191, 192, 194–96, 199
Autocracy, 7, 26, 158, 195
Azusa Street Revival, 71, 76

Baptists, 4, 15, 154, 165, 181, 182, 186, 194
Battle Hymn of the Republic, 25–29
Belgium, 6, 26, 33, 36, 37, 58, 76, 83, 90, 194–96
Bluffton College, 94
Book of Mormon, 138
Boy Scouts, 25
Bulgaria, 1
Britain, 1–3, 6, 7, 13, 23, 26, 32, 33, 35–38, 58, 59, 61, 68, 90, 120, 131, 136, 137, 139, 151, 156, 170, 174–77, 181, 193, 197, 198

Camp McArthur, 96
Canada, 4, 6, 7, 26, 36, 101, 151–53, 156, 158, 160, 161, 163, 174, 184
Catholic Church of America, 49
Central Powers, 1, 2, 34, 35, 169, 191, 195
Chaplaincy, 5, 11, 29, 34, 41–50, 64, 144, 167–179
    Chaplains Aid, 42–45
    Military Honors, 171
Christendom, 5, 11, 150, 157
Church of God, 77, 78
Church of God in Christ, 81, 82, 85
Church of Latter Day Saints (LDS), 129–147
    Conference Meetings, 135, 136, 140–43, 145
    Mormon Battalion, 131
    Relief Society, 132, 133, 137, 138, 143

Index of Subjects

Clergy, 3, 5–8, 11, 15–17, 23, 25, 28, 41, 45, 47, 134, 150, 151, 156, 157, 159–63, 165, 169, 173, 174
Civil Religion, 5, 9, 17
Committee of Six, 44
Congregationalism, 15, 16, 22, 88, 154, 161
Constantinople, 181, 195, 198
Conscientious Objection, 3, 4, 10, 71, 74, 78, 80–84, 86, 87, 92, 93, 95, 97, 98, 101, 108, 110, 119–22, 153, 158, 160, 162
Court-martialing, 96, 97, 121

Democracy, 7, 12, 17, 23, 26, 37, 38, 40, 73, 87, 115, 195
Dublin Easter Uprising, 36

Earlham College, 122
Ecumenism, 18, 24, 26, 40, 44, 47, 48, 102, 113
Entente Alliance, 1, 37
Epworth League, 190
Episcopal Church, 34, 35, 40, 44, 45, 47, 165, 168, 170, 182, 190
Episcopal Young People's Movement, 190
Evangelicalism, 8, 15–30, 91, 110
Evangelistic Events, 15, 16, 18, 22, 24, 27, 55, 56, 71, 89, 110, 190

Farm Furlough Act, 96
Federal Council of Churches of Christ in America, 5, 44, 168, 169
'The Finished Mystery,' 155–60, 163
Fellowship of Reconciliation (FOR), 5, 113
France, 1, 2, 19, 25, 26, 33, 34, 36, 41, 46, 47, 58, 59, 68, 76, 90, 109, 120, 121, 134, 136, 170–78, 181, 193, 195, 197
Fort Leavenworth, 97, 153
Fort Oglethorpe, 96
Fundamentalism, 16, 18, 29, 69, 89, 91

General Ministerial Association of Vancouver, 161

German and Austrian-Hungarian League, 36
German Central Verein, 35
Germany
    Allies, 12, 16, 36, 76, 159, 182, 184–86, 193–197, 199
    Empire, 16, 76, 83, 100, 112, 144, 161, 182
    Kaiser, 6, 16, 23, 63, 83, 137, 186, 194, 195
    Military Activity, 1, 6, 23, 35, 58, 59, 76, 90, 116, 172, 178, 184, 192, 194, 196
    National Socialist Party (Nazi), 182
    Patriotism, 59
    Submarine Warfare, 15, 23, 175–77, 192
Goshen College, 91

Holy War, 3, 5, 6, 8, 13, 16, 29, 61, 144
Hamidian Massacres, 183
Huns, 5, 7, 142, 196
Hutterites, 11, 93, 97, 101, 153

Imperialism, 7, 16, 58, 75, 76, 83, 100, 112, 144, 161, 183
Influenza Epidemic, 2, 178, 179
International Christian Endeavor Society, 190
International Workers of the World, 153
Ireland, 4, 32–37, 39, 41, 176
Islam, 16, 183, 197, 198
Italy, 1, 26, 33, 136, 137, 140

Jewish People, 5, 18, 57, 72, 159, 179, 191
Jewish War Commission, 44
Jewish Welfare Board, 41, 168, 172, 174
Jerusalem, 197, 198

Ku Klux Klan, 33
Knights of Columbus, 6, 40, 42, 43, 45, 172, 174
Kurdish Peoples, 182, 186, 197

League of Nations, 2, 12, 125, 147
Liberty Bonds. See War Bonds.
Liberty Loans, 45, 98, 196

Index of Subjects

Loyal Citizens Vigilance Committee, 99
Lusitania, 16, 23, 76, 194
Lutheran Church, 9, 20, 21, 29, 53–69, 165, 168
    National Lutheran Commission for Soldiers' and Sailors' Welfare, 64, 65
    National Lutheran Council, 65, 68

Marine Expeditionary Force, 176
Mennonite Central Committee, 102
Mennonites, 4, 10, 87–104, 120
    General Conference Mennonites, 88, 90–94, 98, 101, 103
    Mennonite Brethren, 89–92, 98, 103
Methodists, 15, 165
    Methodist Episcopal Church, 182
    Southern Methodists, 179
Militarism, 3, 76, 111–13, 132, 137, 139, 151
Missionary work, 15, 56, 68, 102, 136, 144, 156, 159, 184–87, 189, 190, 192, 193, 197, 199
Moody Bible Institute, 27, 28

National Catholic War Council, 41–45, 48, 49
National Catholic Welfare Council/Conference, 49
National Council of Catholic Women/Men, 49
Naval Appropriation Act (1914), 176
National Catholic War Council (NCWC), 5, 41–45, 48, 49
Near East Relief (NER), 184, 189, 190
Nestorian Christianity, 187
Neutrality, 32, 34–37, 58, 59, 76, 90, 114, 117, 124, 136, 145, 175, 191
Nicaragua, 176
'No False Peace' Declaration, 8, 15, 16, 18, 22, 23, 25, 26, 28, 194
Non-combatant Military Roles, 85, 90, 92–95, 101, 121, 122

Oberlin College, 16
Ottoman Empire, 1, 12, 16, 181–99
Orthodox Church, 57, 58, 183

Pacificism, 3, 4, 9, 10, 15, 17, 19, 25, 35, 42, 57, 71, 73–76, 79, 81–85, 87, 89, 91, 93–95, 98 101, 103, 107, 109–111, 113, 115, 119, 120–125, 141, 143, 150, 151, 153, 160–162
Paris, 90
Paris Peace Talks, 178
Pax Americana, 2
Pentecostalism, 71–85
    Assemblies of God, 71, 73, 74, 79, 80, 82–85
    Pentecostal Holiness Church, 80, 81
Peoples Pulpit Association, 155
Permanent International Court of Arbitration, 112
Pietism, 9, 18, 20, 21, 56, 89
Poland, 33, 36, 37, 68, 194–96
Polygamy, 130, 132, 146
Presbyterians, 15, 172, 173, 186–92
Propaganda, 17, 78, 90, 112, 142, 152, 164
Protestantism, 3, 5, 8, 12, 15, 18, 21, 25, 26, 43, 53, 55–58, 60, 66, 67, 69, 89, 136, 161, 168, 177, 184, 185
    Conservativism, 8, 16, 17, 20–22, 26, 28, 161
    Fundamentalism. See Fundamentalism.
    Liberalism, 15–22, 24–29, 56, 57, 113, 161, 162
    Modernist, 6, 15, 18, 69, 110, 113

Quakerism, 4, 10, 107–26, 196
    American Friends Service Committee (AFSC), 108, 109, 118–22
    Hicksite Quakers, 109–14
    Peace Conferences, 111–15, 118, 125

Red Cross, 25, 61, 64, 90, 98, 99, 101, 119, 120, 174
Revivalism, 15, 16, 18, 24, 27, 55–57, 71, 89, 110, 190
Rhetoric of war, 5, 12, 36, 38, 39, 59, 93, 139, 141, 143–145, 193–195, 199
Roman Catholicism, 3–9, 12, 15, 18, 21, 25, 26, 32–50, 56–58, 72, 162, 168, 170, 177, 191

Index of Subjects

Romania, 195
Russia, 1, 26, 58, 59, 61, 68, 88–90, 136, 169, 181, 183, 195, 197

Salvation Army, 41, 174
Scandinavia, 54, 136
Second Great Awakening, 130
Sectarianism, 9, 17, 20, 21, 26, 73, 136, 156, 177
Sedition Act (1918), 63, 97
Serbia, 37, 90, 134, 136, 187, 194–96
Slavery, 26, 111, 116
Social Gospel, 4, 6, 16, 19, 22, 25, 136
Social Reconstruction, 32, 44, 48, 49, 120–22, 124
Socialism, 4, 100, 112, 153
Syrian Catholic Church, 183

Teutons, 12, 58, 185, 194, 199
Theocracy, 129, 154
Tri-Faith America, 5
Turks, 12, 184–88, 192, 194–96, 198, 199
Turkey. *See* Ottoman Empire.

Ukraine, 88, 89, 102
Unitarianism, 18, 27, 28
United States of America
    Adjutant General, 173
    Americanism, 16–30, 34, 67, 72, 75, 81, 82, 84 141
    Attorney General, 15, 97, 163
    Army Signal Corps, 172
    Chaplain Corps, 11, 68, 174–76, 179
    Congress, 7, 15, 29, 37, 38, 61, 92, 114, 140, 151, 153, 168, 173, 176, 182, 189
    Conscription, 10, 11, 77, 81, 93, 121, 137, 150, 151, 153, 158, 163, 183
    Declaration of War, 1, 4, 5, 7, 9, 32–38, 42, 45, 90, 98, 157, 176, 184, 185, 191–94, 199
    Department of Justice, 94, 162
    Domestic Violence/Vigilantism, 5, 11, 62, 63, 87, 96, 97, 99, 100, 107, 121, 152, 153, 162, 165
    Enlistment, 109, 116, 124, 140, 142, 144, 153

Espionage Act/Law, 94, 97, 98, 100, 152, 158, 160, 162
Federal Bureau of Investigation, 82
Immigration, 3, 49, 53–57, 66, 67, 72, 73, 88, 90, 136, 137, 153
Interventionism, 2, 8, 15, 16, 20, 21, 23, 24, 28
Isolationism, 2, 12, 53, 59, 88, 130, 132, 175, 192
Jingoism, 3, 17, 18
Nationalism, 10, 11, 19, 21, 41, 48, 72, 75, 77, 79, 84, 129, 138, 143, 145, 147, 160, 165
Nativism, 5, 9, 26, 33, 54, 62–64, 66, 153
Patriotism, 5, 10–12, 21, 22, 24, 26, 28, 34, 38–42, 49, 61–63, 71, 72, 77, 79, 85, 87, 95, 97–99, 115, 118, 121, 129, 131, 133, 138, 141, 143–46, 152–54, 156, 157, 159, 165, 184, 186
Secretary of War, 41, 42, 44, 92, 96
Selective Service Act, 78, 118, 119, 121, 162
War Department, 93, 95, 96, 119–21, 150, 169
War Draft, 90, 92, 93–95, 98, 119, 122, 123, 153, 159, 162, 163
War Bonds, 21, 61, 63, 64, 80, 82, 85, 90–92, 99, 100, 101, 143, 158, 159

Versailles, Treaty of, 147, 150, 184

Wars
    Germany—Denmark (1864), 58
    Korean, 175
    Napoleonic Wars, 58
    Russian Civil War, 169
    Spanish—American War (1898), 2, 5, 132, 172
    USA Civil War, 25, 26, 111, 116, 131, 133, 168, 172
    USA—Mexico War (1846), 131
    USA—Mexico Border War (1916–17), 42, 114, 169
    USA Revolutionary War, 30
    War on Terror, 30

Index of Subjects

World War II, 2, 74
Washington Committee on Army and Navy Chaplains, 168
Watch Tower Society, 149, 151, 154–60, 162–66
World Peace Foundation, 138

Yellow Creek Statement, 100
YMCA, 5, 19, 41–44, 142, 170, 172, 174
YWCA, 6, 41, 142

Zion, 11, 130, 147
Zimmerman Telegram, 15

Index of Persons

Abbott, Lyman, 16, 18, 22–27
Abrams, Ray H., 8, 17
Allgyer, Samuel, 99
Amburgh, William E. Van, 154, 155, 158, 162, 164
Allenby, Edmund, 197

Baker, Newton, 41, 92, 93, 96
Barnett, Joseph F., 81
Bartleman, Frank, 75–77, 80, 84
Barton, James L., 185, 190–93
Beecher, Henry Ward, 22, 25
Beecher, Lyman, 22
Bell, E. N., 79, 84
Bell, James Franklin, 162
Benedict XV, Pope, 33–35, 39, 40, 45
Bennet, Fred L. W., 139
Beidler, Harvey, 94
Bender, Harold S., 91
Bethel, Paul, 47
Bonaparte, Charles J., 15
Bontrager, Manassas, 100
Booth-Clibborn, Samuel H., 75, 77, 84
Booth-Clibborn, Arthur S., 75
Bourne, Randolph, 87
Brent, Charles H., 170
Brooks, Phillips, 25
Brown, William Adams, 44
Bryan, William Jennings, 20

Channing, William Ellery, 27

Churchill, Winston, 16, 125
Conrad, Orie, 96
Cooke, E. A., 161
Cooper, John Montgomery, 44
Cooprider, Walter/George, 100
Currier, Charles W., 38, 196
Cuthers, John, 138
Cutler, Harry, 44

Dean, James J., 39
Debs, Eugene, 100
DeCecca, Giovanni, 158, 159
Dewey, John, 71
Diener, Charles/Daniel, 99, 100
Doherty, Francis B., 170
Drury, Clifford M., 174, 175, 177
Du Bois, W. E. B., 22
Duffy, Francis Patrick, 34, 41, 46–48

Eerdman, Calvin Pardee, 173

Farley, John, 38, 43
Fisher, George H., 155, 157, 158, 164
Flannery, Edward, 39
Fleming, J. F., 176
Fosdick, Harry Emerson, 8, 9, 16, 18, 19, 196
Fox, George, 110, 112
Franz, John, 100
Frazier, John B., 179
Frodsham, Stanley, 75, 82–85

Index of Persons

Garland, Hamlin, 23
Gates, Susa Young, 139
George, Lloyd, 37
Gibbons, James, 37, 38, 40, 43–45
Gladden, Washington, 25
Glennon, John, 39
Goldberg, David, 179
Gray, James M., 27
Grubb, Silas, 90
Guilday, Peter, 44
Gunn, John E., 194

Hartzler, Jesse, 95
Hartzler, Ora, 96
Hayes, Patrick J., 44, 45
Hibben, John Grier, 16
Hillis, Newell Dwight, 16
Hofer, David/Joseph/Michael, 97, 101, 153
Holmes, John Haynes, 18, 19
Hoover, Herbert, 144, 146
Howarth, Samuel, 118
Howe, Julia Ward, 25–27, 28,
Huske, F. B., 178

Jones, Rufus, 120, 123, 125

Kauffman, Daniel, 98
Keefe, William A., 36
Kenkel, Philip, 35
Kerby, William, 44
King, Henry Churchill, 16
Kipling, Rudyard, 6, 7
Kratz, Maxwell, 91

Lenker, J. N., 58
Little, Frank, 162
Loucks, Aaron, 94
Lovejoy, Arthur O., 23
Lund, Anthon, 141
Luther, Martin, 57, 60

Machen, J. Gresham, 172
Macmillan, A. Hugh, 162, 164
Martin, Robert J., 164
Mason, Charles H., 81–83, 85
Massillon, Jean-Baptiste, 25

Mathews, Dean Shailer, 162
McCune, Elizabeth, 137
McDowell, Mary Stone, 107–9, 121
McKay, David O., 141
Millar, Wyatt, 108, 109, 111, 123, 124
Miller, Samuel, 100
Mitchell, Perry, 177
Moody, Paul A., 170,
Moody, Dwight L., 16, 19, 25, 170
Moody, William Revell, 16, 22, 26
More, Paul Elmer, 23
Morgenthau, Henry, 181, 182
Mosiman, Samuel, 101
Mott, John R., 44
Muldoon, Patrick, 44
Mundelein, George, 35
Murray, J. Lowell, 194

O'Brien, John Lord, 162
O'Connell, William, 40, 43
O'Dwyer, Edward Thomas, 36
O'Grady, John, 44
O'Rourke, A., 178
Orwell, George, 152

Pace, Edward, 44
Pannkoke, O. H., 60
Parham, Charles, 75
Patrick, Bower R., 176
Penrose, Charles, 135, 141–43
Perry, James DeWolf, 44
Pershing, John J., 1, 169, 170
Prager, Robert, 153
Preuss, Arthur, 35
Putnam, George, 23

Ralston, J. H., 27
Rauschenbusch, Walter, 4, 19
Repplier, Agnus, 23
Richie, A. I., 154
Roberts, B. H., 135, 142, 144, 145, 147
Robison, Fred H., 164
Roosevelt, Theodore, 22, 24, 25, 26, 34, 72, 73, 84, 138, 141, 176, 185
Russell, Charles Taize, 149–52, 154–56, 159, 160
Russell, William, 44

Index of Persons

Rutherford, Joseph F., 154–59, 162–64, 166
Ryan, John A., 44, 48

Sankey, Ira D., 19
Schellenberg, Abraham, 90
Schrag, John, 100
Schrembs, Joseph, 44
Schmauk, T. E., 58
Schroeder, Ferdinand, 95
Sharpless, Isaac, 112
Smiley, Albert, 111
Smissen, Carl Van Der, 90
Smith, C. Henry, 90, 95, 102
Smith, Joseph, 129, 133–36, 138, 140, 142, 143, 145, 146
Smoot, Reed, 132, 147
Speer, Robert E. 44
Spurgeon, Charles, 25
Stehman, Jacob, 99
Stowe, Harriet Beecher, 22
Sunday, Billy, 5, 8, 9, 16, 18, 19, 22–27, 29, 161, 162, 190

Taft, Howard, 138
Talmage, James E., 135

Tarkington, Booth, 23
Taylor, G. F., 80, 81, 84
Thatcher, Albert G., 115, 116
Tomlinson, A. J., 77, 78, 84

Voth, Albert, 97

Waring, George J., 46
Welch, J. W., 83
Wells, Emmeline B., 133, 138
Wertz, Victor, 100
Wesley, John, 25
Whimsett, Grover C., 177
White, Alice Paige, 118
Whitefield, George, 18
Wilde, Oscar, 165
Williams, Michael, 46, 48
Wilson, Woodrow, 1, 5–7, 20, 24, 28, 32, 34, 35, 37, 38, 40, 43, 50, 61, 83, 92, 97, 113, 140, 151, 152, 158, 162, 175, 189
Wipf, Joseph, 101
Wood, L. Hollingsworth, 114
Woodworth, Clayton J., 155–58, 164

Young, Brigham, 131, 133 f